AM I A MURDERER?

Calel Perechodnik

AM I A

MURDERER?

Testament of a
Jewish Ghetto Policeman

CALEL PERECHODNIK

edited and translated by
Frank Fox

■ WestviewPress
A Division of HarperCollinsPublishers

With heartfelt love to Anne

Copyright © 1996 by Westview Press, Inc., A Division of HarperCollins Publishers, Inc.

Published in 1996 in the United States of America by Westview Press, Inc., 5500 Central Avenue, Boulder, Colorado 80301-2877, and in the United Kingdom by Westview Press, 12 Hid's Copse Road, Cumnor Hill, Oxford OX2 9JJ

Library of Congress Cataloging-in-Publication Data
Perechodnik, Calel, 1916–1944.
   [Czy ja jestem mordercą? English]
   Am I a murderer? : testament of a Jewish ghetto policeman / Calel Perechodnik ; edited and translated by Frank Fox.
     p.   cm.
   ISBN 0-8133-2702-4
   1. Perechodnik, Calel, 1916–1944.   2. Holocaust, Jewish (1939–1945)—Poland—Otwock—Personal narratives.   3. World War, 1939–1945—Collaborationists—Poland—Otwock.   4. Jews—Poland—Otwock—Biography.   5. Otwock (Poland)—Biography.   I. Fox, Frank, 1923–   . II. Title.
DS135.P63P467613   1996
940.53'18'092—dc20
[B]   95-37124
                                                                                                   CIP

10   9   8   7   6   5   4   3   2   1

Contents

Illustrations

Foreword *by Frank Fox*

Every catastrophe in history is foreshadowed; there are always some signs in the sky warning people about the danger. Rarely does anyone believe them.

Sometimes it seems to me that it's a fairy tale—the assertion by the medical world that the heart is a chamber of delicate membranes that cannot stand suffering or emotion and that they burst, causing death. Today, I would advise those who construct fighter planes to build them out of heart membranes. They will . . . outlast the most enduring steel.

The greatest skill in this vile world is to be quiet when the heart is bleeding and the fists tighten.

—Calel Perechodnik

CALEL PERECHODNIK, a twenty-seven-year-old ghetto policeman in Otwock, a town near Warsaw, is witnessing and chronicling not only the end of a people but also the end of a world. Each morning he wakes to a recurring nightmare: An enemy possessed of unimagined hatred occupies his native Poland; only those Jews may live who are still needed to bury others. "In February 1941, seeing that the war was not coming to an end," and wanting to avoid the labor camps, he joins a force of around one hundred ghetto policemen. Other policemen deliver quotas of Jews, but he claims that he does not have a "sporting instinct" for rounding up fellow Jews and that his only duty is to deliver bread rations to Jewish officials and their families. Perechodnik hopes the uniform will provide a shield for himself, his wife, Anna, and their two-year-old daughter, Athalie. But on the fateful August 19, 1942, Perechodnik and other policemen help herd eight thousand Otwock Jews into the town square, where they are loaded into boxcars. The policemen are promised immunity for their own wives and children, but the German enemy deceives them. Perechodnik watches in horror as his wife and daughter are loaded into wagons headed for the Treblinka death camp.

There is nothing quite like this in the history of confessions. This is not Saint Augustine troubled by his own salvation or Jean-Jacques Rousseau remembering a childhood peccadillo. This is a twentieth-century man bereft of all beliefs, shorn of all human relationships, who begs to be understood even as he confounds us. He refers to his memoir as a "fetus," a second child born to his wife and to him. His style is by turns mordant and sentimental, accusatory and self-pitying, sardonic and sorrowful. His mind-numbing purpose is to discover that turn in history's road that took his wife and child to Treblinka. Contradictions abound. He expatiates on his father's petty absorption with money even as the parent struggles to obtain it for the family's survival. He anathematizes his faith even as he recites the blessings and prayers remembered since childhood. He blasts the perennial Jewish optimism even as he grasps at straws to stay alive.

With the death of the Otwock ghetto, Perechodnik and his mother find a hiding place in Warsaw. Father hides in a nearby village. For the Perechodnik family, as for a handful of other Jews, the remainder of their brief lives will be calculated by dividing the value of their few possessions into days left to live.

Who were these Jewish policemen, young men like Perechodnik, dressed in military-style long coats, leather belts, peaked hats, and high boots and armed with rubber truncheons? My friend, historian Simon Schochet, a survivor of a concentration camp who had the "bad fortune" to observe the Ghetto Police firsthand, described them in a letter to me as follows:

> They were young, in good health, well educated and fluent in Polish. . . . Although treated contemptuously by the Polish *intelligencja,* they worshipped Western culture and manners and exhibited the worst prejudices and snobbisms of the educated Polish classes. They showed disdain towards Orthodox Jews, felt shamed by their dress, manners and behavior, and blamed them for the ostracism suffered by assimilated Jews such as they. To the best of my knowledge and memory, I have never been told about a Jewish policeman of any ghetto who was a Yeshiva student. The young Orthodox men were not educated in Western fashions, nor were they sports-minded. Their backs were not straight. They were unfit to wear the tragi-comical uniforms of the ghetto police.

Schochet's remarks echo what Perechodnik himself writes in his memoir. Finding that "Polishness" has failed to protect his very life, he turns with vengeance against the "Jewishness" that stamps him irremediably as an outsider. Time and again he mentions his own Semitic appearance, which makes it impossible for him to escape to the Polish side. When he refers to his father's good "features," he cannot resist a comment on the old man's accented Polish speech. To highlight his own credentials, he quotes lines of classical poetry, uses French expressions and Latin proverbs. As for his beloved wife, she is "not well educated."

Schochet did not find any mitigating factors in the short life of Calel Perechodnik:

> The Jewish policemen . . . volunteered for the job and separated themselves from the Jewish people. They put on a uniform and wore it for years. They were tools of the killers. The Germans came to Otwock. They brought Ukrainians with them to destroy the Jewish community. They enlisted the Jewish policemen to help them in their plan and it was they who blew whistles continuously and led Jews to the waiting trains. Perechodnik was a collaborator in murder. And if he didn't kill people with his own hands, not all the Germans committed murder with their own hands either. Many just stood by and watched. . . . The Jewish policemen had all the food, comforts and women they wanted. Was he guilty of delivering his wife and daughter to the Germans? Certainly he was. What was the difference between Perechodnik and the other policemen? They did not confess. They did not atone. He did.

The Jewish policemen, described in many Holocaust reminiscences as brutal and rapacious (Warsaw ghetto chronicler Emanuel Ringelblum described their cruelty as "at times greater than that of the Germans, the Ukrainians and the Latvians"*) were an instrument of the Jewish Councils, themselves appointed by the Germans. Both the councils and their policemen (there was a detachment of women's police in the Łódź ghetto), in addition to maintaining certain basic services in ghettos, were used by the Germans in a macabre barter, trading sections of the Jewish populace—the poor, the very young, the elderly, and the ill—for the lives of the more useful and, often, the more affluent. The character of the Jewish police forces, like that of the councils and the ever-

---

*Quoted in Israel Gutman, *Resistance: The Warsaw Ghetto Uprising* (Boston: Houghton Mifflin, 1994), p. 143.

dwindling ghetto communities, varied from place to place, from the hermetically sealed Łódź ghetto, where no resistance was possible, to the Warsaw ghetto, where Jews fought the Germans and tried to assassinate the chief of the Jewish police. Itzhak (Antek) Zuckerman, the leader of the Jewish Fighting Organization (ŻOB), which led the Warsaw Ghetto uprising, maintained a network of informers among the Ghetto Police, who at times provided warnings of an impending deportation. His own escapes were made possible by the actions of Jewish policemen, and he noted that they too perished. Some committed suicide rather than assist the Germans. On September 21, 1942, Yom Kippur, the Germans assembled hundreds of Jewish policemen on the pretext that they would be awarded medals and shipped them and their families to Treblinka. "I didn't shed a tear," wrote Zuckerman.*

How do we judge Perechodnik's behavior in that age of unprecedented horror? How do we rank him on the scale of the human depravity that surrounded him? Was he not a victim, along with millions of other Jews? Does he not merit some sympathy or at least pity? Whatever we think of Perechodnik or other ghetto policemen, one cardinal fact cannot be ignored: Unlike the German invaders, no sadistic ideology, no voluntary commitment to brutality schooled them for that catastrophic moment in history. All of them would have lived a relatively normal life had not the war and the German policy of mass murder altered their existence beyond anyone's imagination. We may wish that Perechodnik had never joined the police force. We may wish that he had emulated the saintly Dr. Janusz Korczak, who insisted on accompanying his children to Treblinka. Perechodnik himself writes admiringly of a fellow policeman, Abram Willendorf, who removed his insignia, sat on the ground next to his wife, and awaited the cattle cars for Treblinka. But all the victims of the Holocaust were forced to consider choices unimagined in human experience. They all hoped against hope. And who, having read Perechodnik's account, could vouch for her or his own behavior under those circumstances?

---

*Itzhak Zuckerman, *Surplus of Memory: Chronicle of the Warsaw Ghetto Uprising* (Berkeley and Los Angeles: University of California Press, 1993), p. 245.

We live in an age of victimhood. The aging of Holocaust perpetrators and victims has blurred distinctions and muted authentic cries. One example will suffice. John Sack in his recent book *An Eye for an Eye: The Untold Story of Jewish Revenge Against the Germans in 1945* emphasizes that his sympathies were for all the victims. "I had great sympathies for the Jews . . . and yes, for the SS men in Poland, who didn't have the antidote of the Torah and the Talmud, or, in their vicious environment, of the New Testament. . . . A man without mercy isn't a Jew and I am a Jew."*

Rehabilitation of the guilty, impeachment of the innocent, and placement of Jewish policemen such as Perechodnik in the dock with those who invaded his country confuse cause and effect and serve those who wish to falsify history. Questions about the conduct of Jewish leaders are not new. In her 1963 work *Eichmann in Jerusalem: A Report on the Banality of Evil,*† Hannah Arendt used her formidable intellect to condemn the behavior of Jewish leaders. The response by scholar Gershom Scholem to that work is still pertinent. He wrote that among the members some were "swine and others were saints" and that "there were among them also many people in no way different from ourselves, who were compelled to make terrible decisions in circumstances that we cannot even begin to reproduce or reconstruct. I do not know whether they were right or wrong. Nor do I presume to judge. I was not there."‡

Calls for purer and braver victims have not ceased, testifying perhaps to the uneasy conscience of the living. In a paper presented in Warsaw in 1993 on the fiftieth anniversary of the Warsaw ghetto uprising, Lucjan Dobroszycki emphasized that the question was not why the Jews did not fight back, but how any resistance at all was possible. "Has anyone seen an army without arms," he wrote, "an army scattered over 200 isolated ghettos, an army of infants, old people, the sick, an army whose soldiers are denied the right even to surrender?"§

---

*John Sack, *An Eye for an Eye: The Untold Story of Jewish Revenge Against the Germans in 1945* (New York: Basic Books, 1993), pp. 171–172.
†Hannah Arendt, *Eichmann in Jerusalem: A Report on the Banality of Evil* (New York: Viking Press, 1965).
‡Quoted in Hannah Arendt, *The Jew as Pariah: Jewish Identity and Politics in the Modern Age* (New York: Grove Press, 1978), p. 243.
§Lucjan Dobroszycki, "Polish Historiography on the Annihilation of the Jews of Poland in World War II: A Critical Evaluation," *East European Jewish Affairs* 23, no. 2 (1993):47.

Perechodnik's memoir illustrates all too graphically the German strategy of humiliating Jews and leaves little doubt that it was a rehearsal for murder. His desperate cry reminds us that European Jews were abandoned by nations near and far and, most painfully, by other Jews. This was not lost on Adolf Hitler and his followers. When Perechodnik writes that Polish Jews faced only two options on the eve of World War II—total assimilation or emigration to Palestine—he expresses in extremis the hopeless situation of the Jewish masses in Europe.

A novel such as Aharon Appelfeld's *Badenheim, 1939,** which suggests that the signs of impending doom were plain to see, is, unintentionally to be sure, another example of holding the victims responsible. This has been called "backshadowing," a term used by writer Michael Andre Bernstein in his book *Foregone Conclusions: Against Apocalyptic History,*† in which he criticized the argument that the Jews of Europe should have known what was coming and not succumbed to slaughter. Such questions, of course, could only be asked after the fact. In the words of the Magister to Perechodnik: "Why are you Jews so passive? Why don't you do something?" Perechodnik does not bother to answer. He is simply surprised that such a question is asked. By that time the cataclysmic metal-gray wave had already swept over Jewish life in Europe. Indeed, that wave started to rise much earlier, but none could (or perhaps dared) imagine its depth.

Perechodnik loves the country he is unable to defend. Early on in his memoir he writes that he "knew Polish poetry better and liked it better than an educated Pole." He quotes from the Polish classics of Adam Mickiewicz, Juliusz Słowacki, and Jan Kochanowski. It is a terrible disillusionment to him that he has been denied his Polishness. In the debate on the arithmetic of suffering that resurfaced at the fiftieth anniversary of the liberation of Auschwitz, we might imagine Perechodnik using his

---

*Aharon Appelfeld, *Badenheim, 1939* (Boston: David R. Godine, 1980).
†Michael Andre Bernstein, *Foregone Conclusions: Against Apocalyptic History* (Berkeley and Los Angeles: University of California Press, 1994).

characteristic irony to say that the counting of 3 million Jewish dead as Polish would honor them with a status they did not always enjoy when alive.

Two Polish poets of that period, Julian Tuwim, who survived the war abroad, and Władysław Szlengel, who perished in Warsaw, expressed a very similar pain. Tuwim, whose skills in the Polish idiom were unmatched by any poet of his generation, wrote at war's end *We, Polish Jews*, and while noting the painful instances of anti-Semitism, proudly proclaimed his Polishness, a right as natural as breathing. "I am a Pole," he wrote, "because the birch and the willow are closer to me than the palm and the citrus, and Mickiewicz and Chopin dearer than Shakespeare and Beethoven."* Szlengel, who recited his poetry in a Warsaw ghetto cabaret, contrasts in his poem "Two Deaths" the death of a Pole killed by a bullet "for the Motherland" and that of a Jew, a "foolish death" in a garret or a cellar. In another poem, "A Page from the Diary of an *Aktion*," he proudly compares the sacrificial death of Janusz Korczak to the Polish heroic defense of Westerplatte.†

It is difficult to imagine how Perechodnik compiled such a record in the midst of the hell he inhabited. Even with his self-absorption, we sense a growing power as a writer, and the gallery of portraits that he leaves makes us wish that he had told us more, particularly about members of his family. Perechodnik knew that the Germans would destroy his work as surely as they were destroying Jewish life, and he was determined that it would survive him. He gave his memoir for safekeeping to his friend, the Magister. After the war, the latter's wife handed it over to Perechodnik's older brother, Pesach, who spent the war years in Russia. He in turn presented the original to the Yad Vashem Archives in Jerusalem; a copy was also deposited at the Jewish Historical Institute in Warsaw. It is not surprising that the memoir remained unpublished until recently. Perechodnik's condemnation of Jewish leaders and institutions, his expression of helpless fury in the face of betrayals by Polish neighbors, his blood-chilling cry of vengeance against the German people— these raise more alarm than interest.

---

*Julian Tuwim, *We, Polish Jews* (My Zydzi Polscy) (Jerusalem: Magnes Press, 1984), 28.
†Władysław Szlengel, *Co Czytałem Umarłym* (What I Read to the Dead), 2d ed. (Warsaw: State Publishing House, 1979), 105–106.

Comments in the Polish press, both at home and abroad since the book appeared in 1993, have confirmed this. In December 1993, a review of the book by journalist Michał Cichy in the respected *Gazeta Wyborcza*, started an avalanche of criticism and commentary that continued for several months. Cichy referred to Perechodnik as a "witness, victim and collaborator in the Holocaust" and described the memoir as a "primer of the most terrible truths, a book that the less 'stomach' one has for it, the more one should read it."* But Cichy's research, which indicated that units of the Polish underground killed ghetto survivors as they emerged from hiding during the Warsaw uprising, outraged many, and he was accused of besmirching the coming fiftieth anniversary of that revolt.

More recently, Gustav Herling-Grudzinski, a prominent Polish author residing in Naples, wrote in *Kultura*, a Polish-language magazine in Paris, that Perechodnik helped load his wife and beloved daughter into a cattle car in order to gain a "moment" of life for himself. "Is he a murderer?" the author asked rhetorically. "Not a murderer, but a zealous assistant to murder. If he could have understood that there was something worse than death, he would have gone to Treblinka with his wife and daughter."† As for Perechodnik's relatives, colleagues, and acquaintances, Herling-Grudzinski condemned them for having "torn asunder the chains that linked them with other people," For them, all that remained of life was "vegetating and peddling." They were "soulless, cruel and empty."

Paweł Szapiro edited the Polish version of *Am I a Murderer?* and stated in his Afterword that Perechodnik "took part to a significant degree in its [the Holocaust's] implementation" and that he was a "collaborator in the crime." To say that Perechodnik was a collaborator in extermination, a tormentor, or a perpetrator is a judgment we should hesitate to make. Most of the Jewish policemen were eventually killed, though not because of their deeds. They were killed because they were Jews.

For those who wonder how to distinguish between Perechodnik and his evil masters, a passage in the memoir is worth pondering. Perechodnik

---

*Michał Cichy, "Wspomnienia Umarłego" (A Memoir of the Dead), *Gazeta Wyborcza* (Electoral Gazetteer), December 15, 1993, p. 4.

†Gustav Herling-Grudzinski, "Dziennik Pisany Nocą" (Diary Written at Night), *Kultura* (Culture), no. 12/567 (1994):26–27.

writes that he will never be able to return to a normal life. He will not be able to remain as either Jew or Catholic, an honest man or a thief. He will be a nobody. He is haunted by what he has done and by what he has seen. He is full of remorse. We do not have a record of such contrition among perpetrators. After committing unspeakable atrocities, many of them settled down in their hometowns as policemen, judges, businessmen, or physicians. They accepted no blame and expressed no shame.

Szapiro chose the quote "Am I a murderer?" from Perechodnik's guilt-ridden work as a title for the memoir. (Perechodnik's own title in the manuscript at Yad Vashem is "A History of a Jewish Family During German Occupation.") The readers of this memoir may find Szapiro's title more appropriate as a description of Perechodnik's delirium than as a truthful depiction of his brief life. Perhaps the final word belongs to Primo Levi. He wrote that he did not wish to dwell on the notion that there was an "identification or imitation, or exchange of roles between the oppressor and the victim." He insisted that "to confuse them [the murderers] with their victims is a moral disease . . . a precious service rendered (intentionally or not) to the negators of truth." He concluded, "I do not know, and it does not interest me to know whether in my depths there lurks a murderer, but I do know that I was guiltless and that I am not a murderer."* These words would not have relieved Perechodnik's troubled conscience, but they should enable us to make a distinction between the cruel who choose to kill and the weak who wish to live.

We know more about Perechodnik's last hours from a letter written by Genia, a young woman who shared a hiding place with him, to his brother and just recently made available to me by Szapiro. (The letter is reproduced in this volume.) Genia wrote that Calel Perechodnik and his friend Sewek joined the Home Army (AK), the underground Polish army, but that Calel, struck down with typhus, was soon discharged. As Genia described his last moments, he took off his father's shoes and handed these as well as two shirts and a coat to her. He had only enough strength to kill himself. All of them carried cyanide pills, and she was sure that he took poison when his hiding place was discovered. Surely his friends would have wished him a speedy death.

---

*Primo Levi, *The Drowned and the Saved* (New York: Summit Books, 1988), pp. 48–49.

Perechodnik perished a year after the death of the poet of the Warsaw ghetto, Władysław Szlengel. The two were almost the same age. Living in their hermetically sealed ghettos, they could not have been aware of each other's existence, though each had to be aware of his ultimate fate. Szlengel's poem *Już Czas* ["It Is Time"] is proof that Perechodnik's description of the "bath" that awaited his wife and daughter at the Treblinka death camp was a fact known to others. They may also have shared an ineffable and terrifying vision of God as helpless as they, and condemned to death, as in the following:

> —*Now You won't escape Your end!*
> *For when we bring You to this place of slaughter*
> *A hundred dollar gold piece of the rounded sun*
> *Will not help You bribe the keeper of the "bath."*
> *And when the torturer whips You, bullies You,*
> *Rounds You up and rams You into the steaming chamber*
> *And shuts You with the airtightness of ages*
> *So that the hot steam chokes You, chokes You,*
> *You will scream and try to run—*
> *And when the agonies of suffering end,*
> *They'll drag You and throw You down a monstrous hole,*
> *And tear out Your stars—the jaw's golden teeth—*
> *Set You on fire,*
> *And You will be ash.*
>
>   —**Translated by F. Fox**

Acknowledgments

A number of friends and colleagues have helped generously in bringing out the English-language edition of Calel Perechodnik's memoir. Chief among these is Dr. Simon Schochet, whose unwavering support, intimate knowledge of the period, and sensitivity to nuances of language were of immeasurable help. Dr. Lucjan Dobroszycki, one of the foremost historians of Jewish life in Poland, used his good offices to obtain an agreement with the editor of the Polish edition, Dr. Paweł Szapiro, and the editors of the journal *Karta,* in whose pages I first read an excerpt of the memoir. Dr. Szapiro has also provided me with rare Perechodnik family photographs.

I am most grateful to Michael Hershon, who gave me expert advice on German wartime military terms and did so promptly from distant Australia. My son Julian spent many hours patiently assisting in the ongoing struggle with word processing. I wish to thank friends Dr. Jan Zaleski, Professor Alvin Z. Rubinstein, Jerzy R. Krzyżanowski, and Peter Obst and my editorial helpers, Susan McEachern, Jess Lionheart, Shena L. Redmond, and Jon Brooks, for their help and encouragement.

Needless to say, any errors in translation are my own.

Preface *by Calel Perechodnik*

It is May 7, 1943. I am Calel Perechodnik, an engineer of agronomy, a Jew of average intelligence, and I shall try to describe my family's history during the German occupation. This is not a literary work; I have neither the ability nor the ambition to attempt one. It is not a history of Polish Jewry. It is a memoir of a Jew and his family.

To be exact, this is a confession about my lifetime, a sincere and true confession. Alas, I don't believe in divine absolution, and as far as others are concerned, only my wife could—although she shouldn't—absolve me. However, she is no longer among the living. She was killed as a result of German barbarity,* and, to a considerable extent, on account of my recklessness. Please consider this memoir to be my deathbed confession.

I harbor no illusions. I know that sooner or later I will share the fate of all the Jews of Poland. A day will come when they will take me into a field, command me to dig a grave—for me alone—order me to remove my clothing and lie there on the bottom, and kill me quickly with a pistol shot to my head. The earth will be made even, and a farmer will plough it and sow rye or wheat. I have seen so many executions that I can just close my eyes and see my own death in detail.

I don't ask to be absolved. If I believed in God, in heaven or hell, in some reward or punishment after death, I wouldn't have written this at all. It would be enough for me to know that all Germans will roast in hell after they die. Regrettably, I don't know how to pray, and as for faith, I have none!

That's why I ask the whole democratic world—Englishmen, Americans, Russians, Jews of Palestine—to avenge our women and children burned alive in Treblinkas.[1] We Jewish men are not worthy of being avenged! We were killed through our fault and not on a field of glory.

My life may be considered fairly typical. I cannot claim to have an outstanding intellect or some accidental good fortune to make me stand out among others. Oh no! All the silly mistakes, all the errors committed by the Jews, I committed as well. All the misfortunes, all the tragedies that affected them, touched me in the same measure.

---

*Perechodnik uses the word *vandalism*, which is much stronger in Polish than in English.

This, then, is a history of one among many, one of millions of miserable people who were born—against their will and to their ultimate disaster—as Jews.

I was born in Warsaw, September 8, 1916, into a family of average Jews, a relatively well-to-do, so-called middle-class family. These were honest people, possessed of a strong family instinct, characterized on the part of the children by affection and attachment to their parents, and on the part of the parents by a sacrificial devotion to the material well-being of the children. I emphasize "material" because there were no spiritual bonds that tied me or my siblings to our parents. They did not try, or perhaps were not able, to understand us. To put it briefly, each of us was raised on his own: influenced by schooling, friends, books we read; conscious of our own material independence; and living in an atmosphere of free expression and thought in the years 1925–1935.[2]

My brother and I belonged to Bejtar,[3] a Zionist organization that propagated the idea of creating an independent Jewish state in Palestine. This did not interfere at all with my feelings as a good patriotic Pole. I adored Polish poetry, particularly that dating to the loss of independence—and especially of Mickiewicz. It really spoke to my heart because I connected it with the history of the Israelites. I assumed that Poles, so long oppressed by their enemies, would understand Jews, have compassion for us, and help in whatever way they could.

Even though I was not particularly religious, I believed then in God and in the historical mission of the Jewish people, the mission of spreading culture among the nations of the world. I was equally proud of Spinoza, Einstein, and other Jewish men of genius.

I did not pay too much attention to the problem of anti-Semitism. I believed quite deeply that anti-Semitism would automatically disappear with the progress of civilization and mankind's cultural achievements and that humanity's development would approach ever closer the immortal ideas of the French Revolution: liberty, equality, and fraternity.

Besides, I want it clearly understood that I personally did not come in contact with anti-Semitism. It's true that I could not study at Warsaw University, but because of that, I had an opportunity to go to France for graduate studies in agronomy.[4]

The period that I spent in Toulouse belongs to one of the most enjoyable experiences in my life. Such liberty, such respect for other people, such freedom to express one's convictions—all this was perhaps not possible in any other country.

In an atmosphere of freedom, among people of such an outlook, it was all the more amazing to read press reports about all sorts of anti-Semitic brawls at Warsaw University.[5] I didn't want to believe, and indeed could not imagine, that you could approach someone you knew, or someone you did not know, and give him a black eye or manhandle someone just because he happened to be born a Jew.

After I completed my studies with the result *très bien, avec felicitations du Jury,*[6] I wrote a thesis on the cultivation of hemp in Poland, a work of which no native Pole would have felt ashamed.

Before my final departure from France I visited the World's Fair in Paris and returned to Poland as a twenty-one-year-old, with an engineer's diploma. Although I still had a year's deferment for military service, a week after my return I presented myself before the board.[*] I was placed in category A,[†] but because Poland was such a mighty power, possessed of such a strong military and of so many educated and commissioned engineers-officers, I was obviously superfluous! Anyway—why beat about the bush?—they gave me a supernumerary status. They did it with me, my brother (also an engineer), and all of our Jewish friends who had a high school education or higher. They just did not want to have Jewish officers in the Polish army.[7]

I will admit frankly, this did not worry me too much. After all, I just wanted to fulfill loyally my obligations toward my country, one that provided me with the means to make a livelihood, protected my rights, and whose welfare was close to my heart. It goes without saying that no Pole will believe me, but people, please understand what I am saying! I saw my own well-being in the well-being of Poland.

What to do? I have to account for my attachment to Poland on a materialistic and selfish basis. If I wished to claim that I was sincerely and disinterestedly attached to Poland, that I knew Polish poetry better and liked it better than an educated Pole, that the Polish language was my mother tongue, one in which I first revealed to my beloved how I felt about her—no one would believe such words, and so I would rather not dwell on them.

In August 1938 I married Anna Nusfeld, a young girl who was completely dedicated to me and one whom I had loved for six years. My wife,

---

[*]This was the equivalent of the draft board in the United States.
[†]Category A meant he was eligible to serve, but not as an officer.

Calel Perechodnik, who died at 27

Anna Nusfeld Perechodnik, Calel's wife, with their daughter, Athalie

Calel with Athalie

Oszer Perechodnik, Calel's father, who died at age 55

Sonia Góralska Perechodnik, Calel's mother, who died at age 57

although not well educated, was a wise and outstandingly intelligent woman. Already before our marriage she was the co-owner of the Oasis movie house in Otwock. She was an orphan. Her parents died when she was still a child. She and her siblings were raised by an old grandmother. Actually, they raised themselves.

Later on, as still-young people, they built by themselves a beautiful movie house on a lot they had inherited from their grandfather. I can say

Władysław Błażewski, the Magister

with complete certainty that after twenty years of anguish and inhuman toil, they established themselves. They wanted to build another movie house in Otwock, but the mayor would not permit it. He'd rather there was no movie house in Otwock than for a Jew to be an owner of one. But never mind that.

Because I did not want to live on my wife's income, I opened a warehouse of building materials with my uncle Góralski. This business fully supported me and my wife. The income from the movie house was used for old mortgage debts, for fancy furniture in our home, and for our clothes. Altogether, at the age of twenty-two, I wasn't rich, but I was a very happy person. I had a loving wife, my work; I was settled and did not have to depend on anyone to support me.

One could ask why I did not go to Palestine. After all, as a Zionist I should have done that! I did not leave on account of my wife. She had suffered for twenty years, at times from cold and hunger. Her brothers had built the movie house with their own hands; she and her sister had carried bricks and mixed lime. God! How they had worked until the movie house had begun to prosper. Now, when they reached their goal, were settled, my wife did not have the strength or energy to throw all this away and start afresh in another country.

*The house of Oszer Perechodnik in Otwock, formerly 10 Kościelna Street,
now renamed Sikorski, 18*

Otwock Jews before execution by the Nazis

I did not take notice that the ground was on fire under our feet in Poland. I thought that I had a right to stay in Poland since I fulfilled all the obligations of citizen toward her. My wife and I decided that we would go to Palestine only after a certain period of time, that we would buy some land there, and that I would then work in my own profession, that of an agronomist.

War ✌

THE YEAR 1939 APPROACHED. The Germans armed themselves and got ready to fight the entire world. And what about the Poles? What did they do during that year of trial?

I have before me a calendar of the Samoobrona Narodu* [National Self-Defense] for 1939 (printed by Central Printing, Poznań, Square Nowomiejski, 7). I found this calendar in the home of a Polish woman who is now hiding me. Fortunately, she cannot read, and her husband, who died at the front, is not able to explain to her that "the Jew is the mortal enemy of the Church and Greater Poland," that "the evil of to-day's Poland has its chief abode in the Jewry," and that "we shall remove Jews from Poland, and the evil which now infests us will disappear from her." Such were the slogans of the Polish people.

And what was the position of the Polish government, the government referred to in today's *Nowy Kurjer Warszawski* [New Warsaw Courier][8] as Judeo-Polish? I will mention only the slogans: ban on ritual slaughter, economic boycott, limited access to university and government appointments, and other such matters.[9] This in spite of the fact that Jews officially subscribed to the National Loan,[10] and at the time the war broke out stood ready for the supreme sacrifice: to defend Poland and at the same time to defend their women, children, and homes.[11]

I will not talk about the events of that war. Suffice it to say, on September 7, 1939, I followed the command broadcast over the radio,[12] left my wife, and together with my brother, father, and uncle we made our way on foot eastward. Along the route, my brother wanted to join the army. They did not accept him, told us to continue further to the east, and said that this was where they were mobilizing.

This journey, which lasted more than eight days, will always remain in my memory. What an ideal brotherhood existed between Poles and Jews! How safely one could walk on the road at night! How generously and hospitably the Polish peasant received refugees! All were linked with brotherly ties, ties of love for the country, and hatred of the common enemy.[13]

---

*The Samoobrona Narodu was a right-wing organization that distributed calendars for propaganda purposes.

1

We pressed on until the moment the Bolsheviks entered the eastern territories. It made no sense to go farther. The Russians surprised us at Słonim, my mother's birthplace. We were well received by her large family. We remained in place and followed further developments.

What were the feelings of Jews at the time that the Bolsheviks entered Polish territory? This is a very touchy question, and I shall try to be completely honest and objective, writing the truth and only the truth.

The first feeling was that of immense happiness. This is nothing to be surprised at. From one side there was the German invader, proclaiming slogans of merciless destruction and murder of all Jews, from the other side, the Bolshevik, proclaiming slogans that for him all people were equal under the law. There was nothing to compare here. The Jews were happy, and I along with them. Although I had been against communism throughout my life, now I begged God that the Bolsheviks would occupy the area up to the Vistula. I was ready to lose the movie house, the business, my father's villa, in order to be able to live as a free man, without any racial restrictions.

Still, I did not jump for joy at the sight of Soviet tanks. I don't deny that there were Jews—old-time Communists—who disarmed Polish detachments, but can one blame this on all the Jews? I believe that the number of Jews who fell with arms in hand while defending Poland was larger than the number of Jews disarming Polish detachments.[14]

My brother and uncle remained in Słonim. This was the time when it was necessary to choose: to remain or to return. As for me, I returned to Otwock on October 22. (My father returned only in March of the following year.) Happily, I found my wife well, everyone safe and sound. And there a new life began.

As concerns the outcome of the war, I shared the expectations of all the Jews. Every Jew, without exception, from the start of the war until today, did not think that the Germans would win the war and remain in Poland forever. Everyone was absolutely convinced that Poland would rise again. Like the religious Jew who believes in the coming of the Messiah, so we believed in a German defeat.

If any Jews had said at the time that the Germans would remain here forever, then we would have had to logically conclude that for the German no Jew could exist *à la longue*.* One would have had to con-

---

*"In the long run" (French).

clude from this that one must save himself. To run away to Russia or, for a large sum of money—this was possible at the start of the war—go to Palestine or to America.[15]

A different psychosis, equally doomed in its consequences, was the belief that the war would not last too long—half a year at the most. Jews believed that, as did the Poles, and I think that the whole world believed it as well. This belief lasted up to the fall of France. Later, when England rejected Germany's peace proposals,* people again believed that the war would be over in a year. When a year went by, no one seemed to be disturbed. In another year, this time the next one, the war must come to an end. If one asked an intelligent Pole today when the war will end, he will reply that either in the fall or in the spring, perhaps after a year. Someday somebody will guess right.

For the time being, however, we are talking about October 1939. People are convinced, with the best of intentions, that shortly, to our great satisfaction, the Germans will be running away. In the meantime one has to make oneself secure, put goods in the care of Poles, transfer ownership of the businesses to them,[16] set aside some hard currency out of fear of devaluation, have some suits made, certainly place an order with the shoemaker for some high boots,[17] prepare provisions for half a year, and—wait.

Such thoughts dominated us all. Although Germans forbade the sale of property, Jewish property owners carried colossal sums of money to the Credit Society—in order to start a debt-free life after the war.

I myself settled the last mortgage payment for the movie house. I paid many thousands to the Credit Society for my absent father, and I was very pleased with myself. *O sancta simplicitas!*†

It goes without saying that the movie house ceased operating from the first day of the war, but when I returned, I was able to dispose of my building materials. I realized clearly that by liquidating my stock of supplies, I would never be able to resume that business, but I did not hesitate for a moment. First of all, I did not know a Pole to whom I could have transferred ownership. Secondly, I knew that after the war I would not be able to maintain at the same time the warehouse and the movie

---

*In July 1940, Hitler offered peace proposals to Britain that would have left the British in control of their empire and Europe under German domination.
†"O blessed simplicity" (Latin).

house because my two brothers-in-law who managed the movie house had been killed. The younger one, Mietek, as a soldier at the front. The older one, Wolf, buried a chest of dynamite and was informed on by a Polish woman, Miss Bukojemska, the mistress of the gendarme Michailis. Wolf was shot by Michailis in the game preserve forest with two other Jews: the writer Urke Nachalnik[18] and Gershon Randoniński. First they were severely beaten, had to dig their own graves, and were shot. They were the first three victims at Otwock.

Later on it turned out that they were lucky because at least they were buried in a Jewish cemetery. Thanks to the efforts of the Otwock town hall, and particularly our local doctor, Mierosławski, the Germans allowed the exhumation of remains. Families still had time to place monuments on graves. The fate of Jews in this war was to perish so that no one knew where their remains were scattered.

What was the attitude of the Germans to the Jews at the start of the war? It varied, depending on the location where the Jews lived. The worst conditions for Jews existed in the territories incorporated into the Third Reich. They were expelled in a barbarous manner from most of the smaller towns.

I know what happened in Nasielsk.[19] The Germans surrounded the town and announced that every Jew with his baggage had to report to the town square. There they took the baggage away from the Jews and chased them into the synagogue, where they were jammed together and forced to spend twenty-four hours. One woman who was late reporting to the square had to undress and was made to dance naked before the crowd in the synagogue. Then they chased the Jews out and packed them like cattle into freight cars. They transported them in these closed wagons for eight days, without food or water. What a Gehenna it must have been in these locked cars! How many children suffocated? How many died from hunger? . . . After eight days of such wanderings, the Germans kindly agreed to allow the Warsaw Jewish community to ransom those who had been expelled and only then released them from the wagons.

The same procedure was repeated everywhere. Town square, synagogue, pillage, freight cars, and aimless meandering of the train from town to town. I remind you that this was December 1939 and January 1940, a time of the severest frosts.

How many Jewish homes were robbed, how many people killed, this I will not mention. I have the impression that this was not done on an order from above, but that these were attacks provoked by the *Volksdeutsche*[20] and German officers desirous of robbery and bloodletting.[21]

Although there were no expulsions in the Generalgouvernement,* Jews lived with the constant fear that—and if—it would happen tomorrow. This fear, this uncertainty about tomorrow, poisoned every day, every thinking moment. With the passage of time, they took it into their heads that the Generalgouvernement was something different, that the Germans would not dare to deport them because of their fear of "world opinion."

In any case, there were no deportations in the Generalgouvernement. To be sure, they burned synagogues,[22] cut off the beards of Jews, robbed their homes and stores, and confiscated goods and properties. They cruelly mistreated Jewish women whom they seized for labor in the barracks. For example, on a freezing January day, they forced them to wash floors with their own underwear and then made them put these dirty, wet garments on their naked bodies and walk this way in the street.[23] There were many such incidents.

Some Germans mistreated Jews with their brand of "humor." There took place, for example, the following dialogue.

"*Jude*, what do you do for a living?"

"I am a merchant."

"That's nice. I am a boxer."

With this came the beating, with either a swollen eye, or one could count in one's hands the teeth that were knocked out.

Such harassments affected isolated individuals. The people at large protected themselves as best they could. One traded with less or more fear, and naturally one sold all one had so that there would be something to maintain life. In some small towns, the commanders were more humane, and life was not too bad. Some people even traded with the Germans and made some fair business deals with them.[24]

What were the relations between the Poles and the Jews at that time?

The brotherly phase of the period immediately preceding the war and the outbreak of the hostilities passed. Still, I cannot say that the relationship was one of enmity. When the Germans killed my brother-in-law Wolf, Dr. Mierosławski cried like a small child and even—as I have already noted—involved himself selflessly in the exhumation of the remains.

There were scattered incidents when the rabble would shout, "*Jude, Jude*" and point out Jews to the Germans.[25] But basically the relationship

---

*The Generalgouvernement was Polish territory occupied by but not incorporated into Germany. Most of the extermination camps were located there.

was correct enough. That which the Poles demanded—I am putting it unjustly—what they proposed, consisted of the following: signing over businesses to them, leasing them homes with furniture, or placing household goods in their care. Surely not all of them had intended to seize those goods, but, as it concerns Otwock, a month later no Jew realized a penny from 99 percent of businesses signed over to the Poles. Generally, the same was true of apartments, furniture, and all types of goods. They loudly commiserated with Jews, spun dreams of postwar plans, but every Pole wanted to acquire a Jewish business or possessions, admittedly in a legal manner, without the help of Germans.

For the most part, however, excepting sporadic events, the relationship was correct, although condescending.[26]

I remember an interesting conversation when I met with the janitor of my father's villa, one Janek Dębowski. This Jan obviously possessed a sound political orientation, beat a retreat from the army already on September 3, 1939, and came back home. Throughout September and October of that year he behaved contemptuously toward my mother, still the owner of the villa. I turned to him as soon as I arrived from Słonim and the following colloquy took place between us.

"What does Jan think—will the world become the same once more?"

"Of course it will!"

"Well, and what about Poland, Jan—will she ever be independent?"

"Of course she will!"

"And will Jan remember then how he treated my mother during the war?"

"Please, sir, I am a foolish man. Why didn't your mother say something to me? She knows that I am foolish."

And in fact he mended his ways, which by no means stopped him a year later from becoming a janitor for Ortskommandant Schlicht,[27] robbing Jews throughout the existence of the ghetto, and, during an *Aktion*,* snatching them in the Polish neighborhood and denouncing them to the gendarmes.

I will also add that in towns incorporated into the Third Reich where they expected deportations, Poles proposed to the Jews that they sell their belongings at laughable prices "because the Germans will take it from you anyway."

---

*Perechodnik uses the Polish word *Akcja*. The German word *Aktion* was used by both the Germans and their victims, and its terrifying portent was clearly understood.

At that time, I believed, I must confess, in all the customary political dogmas. I was very upset with the tragic death of my brother-in-law, but I envied him because he left behind a three-week-old son. My wife and I shared the Chinese cult of ancestry. It reinforced our desire of having descendants, which allows even the common person to say with pride, *"Non omnis moriar."** Moreover, I thought that nothing would happen to women and particularly to children, and, besides, the war was to end shortly. Suffice it to say that my wife became pregnant. We expected a baby in August 1940, and by then there wouldn't even be a trace of the Germans.

Because confiscations of furniture were becoming more and more frequent, I rented out my apartment to the court officer Stefan Alchimowicz.[28] I considered him and his wife as people outstandingly honest, noble-minded, and honorable, sincere Polish patriots. I rented out to them for free my completely furnished apartment, beautifully appointed and spruced up, partly with my bedding. I trusted their word, and I didn't want any document attesting to my rights. Moreover, I let them in on the secret that I had many valuable things in the attic that belonged to me and my family. I will admit that I was not disillusioned in them. This behavior is rather unexpected these days, but at the proper time they returned everything to me.

December and January passed. Germans forbade Jews the use of trains, decreed the wearing of armbands, established a Judenrat in a number of communities,[29] and registered Jews.

It is surprising how few Jews at that time traveled to different towns in order to start life anew as "native Poles." The majority of Jews behaved passively, so that the most decent people did not seek entrance to the Judenrat. Even though I could have been an official, I too made no effort because I did not want to serve the Germans.

As far as the movie house was concerned, the chairs were requisitioned, a competitor took our projector to his own movie house, and the building itself was occupied as a warehouse for grain by the Regional Farmers and Commerce Cooperative. In spite of the order for requisition, President Czarnecki and Director Henryk Erdman did not consent to seize the building without a contract with me, not willing, as they put it, to hurt a "Polish citizen."

---

*"I shall not wholly die," or "My work will be immortal" (Horace, Latin).

On August 19, 1940, my wife gave birth to a beautiful girl, whom I named Athalie. She was tiny and healthy. The whole family rejoiced, and all of us made plans for the future, thinking how we should raise her and how she would develop.

In July and August 1940, they began to deport Jews to forced labor camps in the Lublin area.[30] Of course, not all Jews found their way there. Judenrat sent them out on orders of the SS. The well-to-do had himself ransomed; the poor one went to work.[31] It was said by people who were there that horrible things happened in the camps. Not everyone believed them. I believed it when I saw a photograph of an acquaintance, a handsome and intelligent fellow. On the photograph made in camp I saw a face of an imbecile or a man from an insane asylum.[32] And for what the chief of the Arbeitsamt,[33] Hugo Dürr,[34] did with the Jews before he sent them out to work, let the devil remind him of this in hell, where he is very likely now.

Summer went by and November[35] arrived, when announcements appeared that starting in December 1940 ghettos would be established for Jews.[36] Jews would be able to take with them all their possessions, they were promised a Judenrat[37] as well as their own police force,[38] and there was mention of the possibility of leaving the ghetto and moving about the Polish neighborhood daily, with the exception of Sundays.

Practically all were taken in by such promises, and only a small percentage of Jews did not go to the ghetto. Even Jewish women—wives of Poles—went with their children to live in the ghettos. It was so easy to get in there, but there was no exit!

I also lived in the ghetto. I rented a room on Podmiejska Street from Glaska, the wife of our movie usher. Our furniture I had sold earlier. The more expensive things I continued to entrust to the court officer Alchimowicz, who lived in my father's villa. I prepared a supply of food for winter. For fuel, I chopped down a few pines near the movie house. That I, a citizen of Otwock, an engineer of agronomy, destroyed my own wood surprised and angered Czarnecki, the vice mayor of Otwock. He compared it to the removal of live and healthy teeth. I too was sad over my property, and it was a heartache to cut the trees down, but I had to do it. My father did not want to cut even one pine tree on his property, except for a few acacia trees, which grow back quickly.

If I relate such minor matters, it is only to bring out that the Jews were deeply convinced that they would shortly return to their homes, where they would again live as a free people.

The ghetto at first looked innocent enough. It was not fenced in, it was possible to leave it, the area was sufficiently large, and there was no shortage of apartments or food. Slowly, however, it was fenced in, and it was forbidden for Jews to leave the ghetto under penalty of death. At first this decree was only on paper. Jews were forced to sell their possessions, and this kind of barter spread farther. To be sure, by May or June one could only obtain two or at the most three cubic meters of potatoes for a complete suit, but somehow one could manage.[39]

In February 1941, seeing that the war was not coming to an end and in order to be free from the roundup for labor camps, I entered the ranks of the Ghetto Polizei.*

According to the prevailing opinion, a positive aspect of the ghetto was that Germans were not found inside. And so robberies and requisitions stopped. When they wanted something, they turned to the Judenrat, which obediently furnished them with everything. I removed my things from Alchimowicz, and *omnia mea mecum habebam*,[40] kept them in a small room. Thus, I passed summer and winter 1941 in comparative peace, taking care of and raising my little Alinka. Although my wife and I denied ourselves many things, there was nothing too dear for my daughter's diet. She was treated royally, we never left her alone in the house, and she therefore blossomed for us, developed and augured for us the best hope for the future.

The character of the Jews, I must confess, underwent certain changes during wartime. Life in the ghetto was peculiar enough; there was no lack of anything, and for money one could get everything. From Russia came ample food packages from relatives.[41] A rich person lived, dressed, ate, and drank, not afraid of being shipped to camp. One could always be ransomed for money. At the same time, the poor swelled up and died from hunger or disease as others looked on.[42] (It was then that an epidemic of typhus broke out.)[43] The majority walked by as if it were part of a daily occurrence.

Thus, an atmosphere was created in which everyone wanted, above all, to survive the war with his family, to survive as an individual, to be able to live as well as possible, and to sell as few of one's possessions as possible. There was some help for the poor, there were free kitchens,[44] orphanages,[45] but in point of fact it was not at all sufficient.[46]

Many Jews worked in German barracks and were treated relatively well there.[47] From this arose a general opinion that the Germans treat the Jewish worker well and have no quarrel with him, but hate only

---

*Perechodnik uses the German term for the Ghetto Police, although the name used officially by the Germans was *Ordnungsdienst*, "Order Service."

wealthy Jews. This was just one more illusion that cost the lives of hundreds of thousands of human beings.

June 22, 1941—the day the war broke out between Germany and Communist Russia. The history and consequences of that war are known to all, and I will not write about them. It is only important to note that German armies occupied the entire area of former Poland and advanced deep into Russia's interior. It meant that the Jews in the eastern areas of the Polish state came under German rule.

The Germans suddenly reminded themselves that Stalin is married to a Jewess, that people like Kaganowich[48] rule Russia, those like Rosenman[49] rule America, and other Jews, England. To put it briefly, "since there are Jews here and Jews there," there is no difference between a monarchic England and a Communist Russia. The war is conducted by the Allies only so that "international Jewry" should rule the world and exterminate all the goyim.

Germans asserted that in order to save 3 million Jews, the entire nation of "Russian dumkov,"* a nation of 170 million people, is marching to certain death with a song on their lips. The 400-million-strong British Empire, usually so egotistically disposed, fights against Greater Germany only because the latter do not want to recognize the right of Jews to rule the world. Because of this, it is necessary to announce a holy crusade of the Christian world against the danger of Jewish communism, Jewish capitalism, and Jewish poverty. Now that the whole world has gone crazy and wants of its own free will to place itself under the Jewish yoke, it is the sacred responsibility of the Germans to exterminate at least all the Jews of Europe. And to tell the truth, it will be a just punishment for the Moishes sitting in the ghettos of Central Europe since they baited and ordered their "Jewish President Roosevelt" to intervene with arms against the world. Because of this, it is necessary to exterminate the Jews to the last one so that not one will remain on earth. Then the world will be saved, reborn, and no one will make war anymore. Greater Germany will be rescued, European culture will be saved, Christian faith will flourish peacefully, humankind will improve, there will be no thievery, murder, or drunkenness. A new ideal world will arise. And thus a sentence of death was pronounced on women, old people, children, on the entire Jewish people.

---

*This is Perechodnik's version of the German *Dummkopf.*

What was the relationship between Poles and Jews in 1941?

Mutual relations on the whole worsened. First of all, Jews in the ghettos govern themselves. Poles cannot profit from them. Moreover, businesses and Jewish homes have come under Polish administration. It is clear that one can live without Jews. There are towns where there are no Jews, and Poles are doing well without them.

Secondly, Jews are ruining Polish apartments in the ghetto; the poor are cutting down trees at night.

Wouldn't it be better, every municipality asks itself, for the Jews to be expelled from town? There would remain furniture, apartments, clothing. Let them go.

And thus went petition after petition to the *Kreishauptmann*,[50] in which individual Polish mayors ask politely that they please remove Jews from the town because the town is, after all, a health resort. Others give as a reason that their town is an industrial one. Because of the Jewish presence, the cost of living is high, and there are typhus, black-marketeering, theft, and so forth. Could I possibly know what arguments were suggested by the mayor or the municipal councils? One ought to ask the mayor of Otwock, Gadomski, who excelled in such similar, oft-repeated petitions.[51]

One thing is certain: The Germans sensed very well that among the Poles not everyone is against the extermination of the Jews and, moreover, that among them are such who will aid in this as the price of inheriting the remainder of Jewish belongings.

And Jews? What are Jews doing at the moment when such heavy clouds are gathering over them? They are living most peacefully. They are not especially interested in politics; newspapers bore them—besides, who has time for this? Everyone must earn his daily bread, potatoes. And the war? It is known that it will end well, that the Germans sooner or later will lose it. When one Jew meets another and asks what is happening, he hears in reply that it will get better.

Alas, Jewish optimism is incurable. The Jewish police force, although it has absolute authority, takes into account the people at large. After all, nobody wants to be hanged after the war. But just in case, one threatens the other with postwar prosecution. For the moment all live in harmony, everyone concerned with his daily bread.[52]

Thus begins 1942, that accursed year in the history of the world, one that canceled the cultural achievements of all mankind. The year that released the wildest and the most sadistic human instincts. First came whispered news, news that the Jews believe—don't believe. After all, it is difficult to believe it; one has to see it with one's own eyes in order to have a clear idea how such things are possible and that, in the twenti-eth century.

They say, for example, that in Słonim they gathered in the town square fourteen thousand people—women, children, men—and all were machine-gunned.[53]

I ask you, people, is it possible to believe such a thing? To shoot with-out reason women, innocent children? Just like that? In full daylight? After all, the worst female criminal cannot be sentenced to death if she is pregnant—and here they apparently killed small children. Where are the people, fathers of families, who would have the courage to aim their ma-chine guns at helpless, small children? Where is the opinion of the cul-tured world? Where are scholars, writers, professors? How can the world remain silent? It is probably not true.

Following this news comes another one, even more monstrous: In Wilno, they killed sixty thousand people; in Baranowicze, twenty thou-sand. People stop thinking. To be sure, they believed it, but they can't visualize that one day someone can come and kill a two-year-old daughter, whose only guilt is that she was born of a Jewish mother and Jewish father.

Finally, we hit on an explanation. Those Jews were killed because they were Soviet citizens and—it is possible—because they fought the Germans. We are, after all, citizens of the Generalgouvernement; such a thing cannot happen to us. Moreover, there is a state of war there, whereas here we have a civilian administration.[54]

A worse tragedy to be comprehended by the provincial Jews of Otwock is that in January they took from Otwock two hundred healthy men—the sick were sorted out by doctors—and they were sent out to the Treblinka punitive camp.[55] There, apparently only fifteen from the whole group[56] are still alive. The rest were cruelly put to death on the spot.

Now the Jews of Otwock see the whole tragedy: Two hundred innocent people were taken and killed. It was fortunate that the Jewish police[57] did the choosing and sent out the poorest. Some are satisfied that they were ransomed; others—relatives of those who were sent out—swear vengeance against the Ghetto Polizei, naturally for after the war. The town is agitated.

At the same time not a day passes that several Jews are not killed for leaving the ghetto. They are killed on the spot, without a trial, buried in the fields. Now one rarely leaves the ghetto; fear strikes deeply in the hu-man heart. The Germans, for reasons best known to themselves, are offering the Jews a visual lesson that leaving the ghetto may be punished with instant death.

An intelligent and farsighted Jew has to ask himself the question, And what threatens those remaining in the ghetto? Perhaps also a death sentence? Unfortunately, such a question no one has posed to himself—no, not me either.

April 1942. Pitiful Passover celebrations(!) In various towns Jews ready themselves, in whatever manner, to observe the holidays solemnly.[58] The religious ones buy matzos; the poor prepare potatoes. Others set aside a supply of bread for eight days.[59] Then, like a thunderbolt out of a blue sky, strikes the news from Lublin.[60] For the time being, no one knows anything for certain, several versions circulate. Some say that Jews have been deported from town and that a small number of "useful" Jews—everyone added in his mind: rich ones—were rounded up for the Majdanek concentration camp.[61] Apparently terrible things happened: Many were killed, little children had their heads smashed against the pavement, and similar events took place.[62]

There was not one Jew who did not inquire about the course of the Lublin tragedy. What happened with the inhabitants of the ghetto? Were they transported for labor to the east? If so, what happened to the children and old people? And maybe they killed them? And if they did, why was it done and in what manner? Was the Lublin community at fault? Was this a sporadic occurrence? Or maybe a planned action?

Unfortunately, no one asked such questions loudly. In any case, when the eyes do not see, the heart does not ache, and anyway, we, the Jews of Otwock, are living through our own tragedy. The Germans have demanded four hundred men for labor. They say it is for Karczew, but could it be for Treblinka? This event, which from the present perspective has not yet become a tragedy, obscures before our eyes the tragedy in Lublin like a small moon can obscure a large sun.

From where does one take four hundred men for labor? Everyone says, "I can't go because I work for the police." "I am in the Judenrat." "I have a brother in the police." "I can't go because I run a business." "I won't go because I can afford to give one thousand złoty to the police."

No one remembers Lublin anymore. The policemen seize people day and night. They seize* them, release them; it is a brisk business.

---

*The Polish word łapać, here translated as "seize," may also mean "to take bribes."

Finally, four hundred men are sent to Karczew. *À present tout le monde est content*.[63]

The commandant of the Ghetto Polizei, Kronenberg, is satisfied because he personally talked to the *Kreishauptmann*.[64] He saved the ghetto from deportation, took the occasion to fill his pockets, and a few decent people that he did not like, he sent to camp.

The *Kreishauptmann* was also very satisfied. The Jews of Otwock quieted down and thought that they would not meet with any other misfortune. The Jews are also satisfied because, thanks to those who were sent out, the Germans will not deport them from Otwock because who will send the workers their provisions or do their laundry? The families of those who were sent out? That would be difficult; you women, mothers of small children, do the best you can. We can't help you.

Such were the thoughts that went through everyone's mind. Now I myself don't know whether to laugh or to cry on account of our naïveté. But then . . . I don't sit in judgment whether some prophet with a Jewish mentality could have foreseen the course of events. For that you would have to have in you the blood of the old Huns.

May passes quietly; June, too. People are really more calm because life here is like a spinning wheel: Everyone must work, earn his subsistence, pay taxes to the Judenrat or to the police. One has to buy furs and silk shirts for the commandant of the gendarmerie, Schlicht, and for the director of the Arbeitsamt, Dürr. We have to get bikes and top boots for the Polish policemen and prepare other expensive gifts for the gendarmes. You have to worry about the state of sanitation in town and design a new *Kennkarte*.[65] The last were especially burdensome. The Germans decided that by January 1, 1943, every Jew must have a new identity card. In connection with that one has to write to outlying towns for birth certificates and other necessary documents.

So much work—and indeed the day is too short for getting everything done. For politics, for some questions, for some thoughts about what will be, for that there is no time.

And what did I do during this time? Truthfully speaking, nothing. I didn't go out to seize people because I found it unbecoming, I was afraid what people would say. In any case, I did not have the "sporting instinct" for that. Together with a friend, Abram Willendorf, I collected the bread quota at the Jewish bakery, and we distributed it at the command post or for the functionaries of the Ghetto Polizei. I earned a modest livelihood. I sold a few of my things, naturally with great regret. And thus one day passed after another, week after week.

July 1942 arrived. What will the Germans do? Learned Germans confront a problem that cannot be solved by ordinary mortals and certainly
not by a people so highly educated and cultured as are the Germans, a nation of Nietzsche. They are confronted by a problem, a macabre problem
of murdering without exception all Jews in the Generalgouvernement and
according to which they have to fulfill certain conditions:

1. The Jews should not realize that they have been condemned to
   death.
2. The Jews may not be allowed to defend themselves.
3. To realize this goal, it is necessary to utilize the smallest number of
   Germans.
4. Jews themselves must be made to assist in this dirty work.
5. Other Jews must be made to clean up the abandoned ghettos.
6. Jewish corpses have to be hidden by Jews.
7. All personal possessions, gold, dollars, jewelry, must be handed over
   to the Germans.
8. Every Jewish town must be convinced that *es kommt nicht in
   betracht*.[66]
9. Every influential or well to-do Jew has to be convinced 100 percent
   that this does not concern him so that he will not run away but will
   wait until it is his turn.
10. Jews being deported should not realize that they are being taken to
    their deaths.
11. Jews at the point of death are not to be allowed to explode in fury;
    they must remain ignorant of their fate until the last moment.
12. The bodies of the 3 million must be utilized as a valuable raw mate-
    rial—for example, as natural fertilizer or as fat—and it is necessary
    not to leave any traces in the form of a cemetery.
13. It is necessary to render impossible any rescue in the Polish section
    of the city.[67]

This was certainly a very macabre, difficult problem because, after all,
it concerned the killing of 3 million people, all of them, to the last one.
According to the points stipulated above, it would seem unresolvable.
Nonetheless, Satan himself from hell would praise the Germans and
give them his highest decoration for a vigorous and precise achievement
of such a plan.

On July 22 Himmler himself appears in the Warsaw ghetto.[68] The
ghetto contains approximately seven hundred thousand people,[69] living

in houses, any of which could become a fortress.[70] Who knows, maybe the Jews have hidden arms? What concerns the Germans? A trifle. That is precisely what Himmler explains to the president of the Judenrat, Czerniaków.[71] The Warsaw ghetto is overcrowded. People are needed for labor in eastern territories. For that it is necessary to provide several tens of thousands of Jews, who will be loaded into freight cars and transported there. They will be allowed, as a matter of course, to take their moneys and knapsacks with their belongings. Those who will go voluntarily will receive free of charge three kilos of bread and one kilogram of marmalade. The arrivals will be assigned to different tasks. Certainly, it should be understood that the officials of the Judenrat, together with their families, the policemen also with their families, physicians with their families, Jews working in productive establishments[72] with their families, and altogether the well-to-do will not be considered in the count. All of them will receive a signed paper of legitimacy, with a swastika seal, so that they and their families and their homes will be inviolable, simply taboo. It only concerns the very poor, those in prisons and similar ones.

What did Himmler demand of Czerniaków? Trifles. Only that the Ghetto Polizei supply by themselves about ten thousand people to assemble in the square. There they will be segregated so that—God forbid—a useful Jew should not be sent out. Aha, and if Czerniaków would sign that the action is taken by the Jews on their own initiative, in order—I don't know—in order for what? Perhaps to improve housing and sanitary conditions in the ghetto.[73]

But the engineer Czerniaków, a highly intelligent and cultured man, it is not known if he had a foreboding, if he recognized the terrible truth that was hidden behind those fine words. Maybe he did believe but did not want to be the intermediary for the execution even of the paupers; suffice it to say that he rejected it and that same day killed himself. He was certain that his quiet and voluntary death would become the warning memento for the remaining Jews. All honor to You, Engineer Czerniaków! You have inscribed yourself with golden letters in the history of the Jews of Warsaw because you are the only one who has preserved the honor of that Jewry.[74]

And what was the position of the Judenrat, of the police, and of the rest of the population? This is a very painful problem. Every Jew thought about it: To repulse the Germans, not to carry out their orders, that is, after all, a rebellion. Then the army can enter the ghetto—and may God prevent it—and shoot the people. Condemned to death will be those accused of disobedience, particularly the officials of the Judenrat and the police. On the other hand, if the orders are carried out, the deportation will not affect us, the policemen, or us, the officials of the Judenrat, or us, the physicians or dentists, or us, craftsmen working in industrial shops; all of us and our families will not be affected by the deportation. It's difficult then; let God's will be done, most assuredly the German God, with whom it is always better to agree.

The Jewish police receive the order to provide the people for the square. The police, numbering two thousand, go about their task vigorously. Each one congratulates himself that he had the good sense to sign himself up for the police, secure in himself and his family. Everyone is certain that at such a time the "wardrobe will play for him,"[75] and sets about his task. And before anything else, they break open shops with food provisions, rob the goods so that they themselves don't go hungry.

When they had sent on transports those who were imprisoned, the people from assembly spots, the paupers from the street, the turn came for children in orphanages. It was a little unpleasant for the police to deport Dr. Korczak,[76] who stubbornly insisted that he wanted to be sent out with his children; but what was there to do if he wants this himself? If someone has pangs of conscience, he will deaden it with vodka. The day passes quickly.

Oh, Dr. Korczak! I bow my head before Your name! It is not your books that will immortalize you but your deed! You did not want to abandon at their last moment the poor Jośki, Mośki, and Srule.[77] You wanted to perish with them. All honor to your memory!

Hunger dominates the ghetto. No one is thinking about going out to smuggle something. The well-to-do are signing up for workshops. *Gazeta Żydowska* [Jewish Gazetteer][78] writes about making the town more productive,[79] there should not be freeloaders, everyone is ready to work for the Germans, of course, as the price of being freed from deportation.

The police take over entire rows of houses encompassing four city blocks and let it be known that they live there now with their families, that no one has the right to enter there. They take over the apartments of strangers after telling the people to get out, ordering them to leave all their possessions behind. They themselves hoard in these apartments extensive wealth. They drink, rob, and fulfill the orders of the Germans.

New workshops arise like mushrooms after a rain. Every workshop occupies a whole house. Some must come in, so others have to get out. On the way, families are separated, some lose their way and are loaded into wagons, husbands lose wives, sons their parents, mothers their children. Hunger rules the town; it is hell in the street and hell in people's souls.

For a week or two the Jewish police can handle it themselves; later Ukrainians enter and they conduct the *Aktion*. The slogan of the *Aktion* is speed and work. Jews! Work quickly, go from one place to another, get rich—lose it all—just don't think about anything. God forbid, don't think that you'll be finished in the same way.

Police! You may be sure that the Greater Germany will not forget about you. Physicians, Germans need you. Craftsmen, without you Germany cannot win the war. Well, then, speed, speed, and once more speed. Drink vodka and don't think. Is the human being a thinking person? Who said that? Is human life precious? After all, people are joining up voluntarily for three kilograms of bread and one kilogram of marmalade. But corpses are lying in the street; such is the end of those who disobey. And those who obey? Don't you know? Those who obey are riding to work, dragging with them their heavy rucksacks. Do they have to live in Warsaw? Is the life in the eastern territories not up to your standards?

Many tragedies take place on those sunny July days! If I don't write about them, it's because I leave that to those in Warsaw who have experienced it, and maybe they will live to the moment when they can convey their own suffering and that of others to their descendants.

A portion of Jews leaves Warsaw and succeeds in reaching other ghettos. After all, they'll be safe there. The guards let them through for money. On Umschlagplatz[80] they segregate the people, and for a bundle of money one can get ransomed. Be happy then, O wealthy ones! Stay in place! There is no need to run away.[81]

No one knows where the people are being sent. The trains leave at night. Where to? In what direction? It's not known.

How do Jews in other towns react to the news of deportations from Warsaw? How do the Jews of Otwock react?

For us it is not the faraway Lublin. This is Warsaw, where everyone has relatives and friends. Some even have passes and can travel to Warsaw. People come from there. There is a telephone connection. The telephones in the police stations,* in the Judenrat of the various towns, work without pause.[82] Instead of ringing just once in order to find what's going on and to draw proper conclusions, the Jews telephone daily for bulletins.

---

*There were police stations manned by Jews in the ghetto. Perechodnik refers to both Polish and Jewish stations as *Komisariat*. That word will be used only for the Polish ones.

They are interested in knowing what homes were emptied of inhabitants on a given day. What house numbers. What streets were blocked off. Some answer over the telephone that this day passed quietly; others say that it has been hot. Of course, one and the other are true. Warsaw is, after all, a big place. The Jewish dictionary is enriched with new expressions: We are going "into scrap," or "into chamois cloth" or "into soap." Everybody talks about it, but nobody takes stock of the threatening situation from the real, literal meaning of these words. And what conclusions should provincial Jews draw from the Warsaw *Aktion*?

It is certainly understood that the Germans do not let Jews draw the logical conclusions on their own. They suggest, instead, as if unwillingly, "appropriate" conclusions. Let Jews be happy that they are smart and have foresight. The *Kreishauptmann* in the Warsaw district, Dr. Ruprecht, sends a command to the Judenrat of Otwock, Falenica, Legionów, Wołomin, Jadowa, Radzymin, that they should furnish by August 2, 1942, a list of all their craftsmen, tailors, shoemakers, metalworkers, electricians, saddlers, who will be "together with their families and baggage deported to Warsaw in order to enroll them in a work process." It is clearly understood that they should provide a precise list of those who have their work tools.

The Warsaw ghetto is cheered by this order. Jews in the provinces are also cheered. It is not going well for the Germans; they lack people for work, particularly specialists. Nothing will probably happen to Jews working in shops, particularly since they will bring in families and baggage. Oh yes, the Germans know that if the families are deported, then the workers will not want to work. Factories will close and the German defeat will be at hand. The humorous shoemakers make fun of the remaining Jewish population.

"You see, you said that tailors and shoemakers are not people, and now we, with our work, will save the whole city."

The unskilled are also happy. They know that deportations will not happen until they take away the craftsmen. The deadline would be automatic—day or two after the shipping out of craftsmen, but never before that. Thus reasoned Jews. And apparently people argue that they are a wise nation.

But it is not a foolishness or naïveté that dictates such or another reasoning. It is the faith Jews have in the cultural achievements of the twentieth century; it is the misunderstanding of the mentality, the bloodthirstiness of the Huns, behaving in defiance of all human principles, of Christianity. All this blinds the Jews and stupefies them completely.

But it does not surprise me, for you have to have the very devil in you in order to see the course of events, and the Germans are acting with cunning. Lipszer,[83] the notorious leader of the gendarmes in the Warsaw region, appears at this time in Otwock. He demands of the commandant of the Ghetto Polizei, Kronenberg, expensive and valuable gifts for himself and for his friends. In exchange for that he announces solemnly that *"Otwock kommt nicht in betracht"*[84] and that if in the worst case such a command is issued, he will first notify Kronenberg, and something will be worked out. He does not say it, but he leaves a distinct impression that for money everything can be settled with him.

Judenrat are collecting petitions to others holding the office of *Kreishauptmann* to permit the opening of workshops. A frenzy of work overwhelms all the Jews in the Generalgouvernement. In Otwock, all are ready to work even without compensation for twelve, sixteen hours around the clock if only they would be allowed to stay in place. It is understood that such a condition cannot be voiced loudly.

The officials of the Arbeitsamt and Kreishauptamt are kindly letting themselves be bribed for enormous sums of money. After many ceremonies, uncertainties, rapid heartbeats, the much desired permit arrives. The names of the German dignitaries who signed this permit circulate from mouth to mouth. This one belongs to the SA,* this one to the SS,† and another is fifth in succession in the Nazi Party. Jews were probably not as happy when they received the Ten Commandments as when they received the permit to open workshops, especially since wagonloads of rags that are to be washed have now arrived at Otwock.

Look, you Jews, at what the Germans expect from you. Jewish women forget quickly that at home they used to hire washerwomen; they forget about their manicured hands. Everybody signs up for the laundry workshops. Great happiness reigns: There are workshops, there are rags, we will work, we'll remain in place. Warsaw is completely forgotten.

There is supposed to arrive shortly a wagon of planks for the carpentry shop. With their own hands Jews are preparing a place near the railway siding. They cut wood, fence in the area with barbed wire so that the boards will not be stolen. Everybody works with fervor and with best hope for the future.

---

*SA stood for Sturmabteilung, or "Storm Troopers."
†SS stood for Schutzstaffel, or "Guard Corps."

The place is ready. But there is a small difference: The Jews hope that the place is for the purpose of unloading the boards *from the wagons,* but the Germans know for sure that the place is for the purpose of taking all the Jews and loading them *onto the wagons.*

That is how the Jewish masses reacted to the events in Warsaw. What did the individual Jews think in Otwock?

The same as the Jews in the Warsaw ghetto. Above all, they took it as an axiom—such axioms are not provable—that the police force is secure, so there is no need to think about it. The commandant of the Ghetto Polizei draws up a list of policemen with their families—wives, children, parents—and sends this to the Arbeitsamt. Just in case everyone is asked to put down their occupation—a useful occupation; in the worst case one writes: a tailor's helper. Brothers are envious of their policemen brothers. The officials of the Judenrat are also secure. Workers in the shops? No, these are people chosen by destiny; thanks to them there will be a need for the Judenrat and the police. The wealthy? Who worries about the wealthy? From the beginning of the world the wealthy man has looked after himself.

Is it possible to think differently? Were there other ways out? To go to another town? This, after all, did not make much sense; there could be deportations from there, too. Besides, it is better to be in one's own town where one knows policemen and others. When it is too late, the Jews come to the conclusion that it would be better to get out of the Generalgouvernement, to Switzerland, for example. Now they are ready to sell to the Poles their possessions dirt-cheap and give a quarter of a million złoty for the right to go to Switzerland. But somehow no *macher** appears, and a journey abroad remains a pious wish. In any case, those who are 100 percent certain that they will remain after the selection prepare hiding places for themselves in case of an *Aktion.* Acording to vox populi, those able to go into hiding the first day will be able to emerge the next day and live on freely.

Many families at that time left Otwock secretly. Gossip had it that they went to Switzerland. But now I have the impression—even the certainty—that in a most ordinary way they rented out an apartment in a Polish neighborhood in Warsaw. That was how well-connected people did it, having the requisite Aryan looks and money.

---

*A *macher* (Yiddish) is one who facilitates, makes deals. Used pejoratively, it may mean a "trickster."

Now the Poles visit the ghetto more and more frequently. Their aim is to buy various things as cheaply as possible because—as they explain—"when they will deport you, you will leave it behind anyway."[85] My housekeeper, a woman who was brought up practically with my wife, also comes to us. However, it is not in order to assure us that we can count on her in time of need. Since we are made to feel that we are for her as living corpses, who is worthy of inheriting our things, especially bedding? Probably only she, who has known us for so many years and is fond of us. In her naïveté she even poses such a question to us. She leaves very surprised and angry because in order not to be bothered by her anymore, we gave her a black skirt.

Others kindly agree to hide Jewish things. Some, taking them, promise that in the worst of situations they will receive and hide the owners.

That the only and direct means of salvation for escape from the ghetto is the securing of a *Kennkarte*—or in the worst case, of a birth certificate—and a residence in a Polish neighborhood, of this no one is thinking. Of course, I am speaking about women and men of a suitable appearance. Also nobody has supplied himself for any price with a weapon to sell dearly one's life and the life of the nearest ones. Unfortunately, three years of slavery have done their work.

If it had to do with getting out of the ghetto and taking up residence in a Polish neighborhood, Jews—even if they had a grasp of the dreadful situation—did not do this for several reasons. On the one hand, the gendarmes impressed on them the certainty that leaving the ghetto was equivalent to a sentence of death, and on the other, they were dominated by a terrible fear of Poles. The Jews were afraid of being robbed in the Polish neighborhood and of being handed over to the gendarmes. And although one could hide from the gendarmes to avoid them—after all, there weren't so many of them in the street—how could one hide from the Poles who could easily recognize Jews? Thus reasoned the majority.

What did I do then? Nothing, and really worse than nothing. I was of the opinion that regardless of what was going on in the world, every individual ought to and needs to live normally, work, earn a livelihood, and so forth.

I was, after all, a policeman, one of the most prominent, employed by the so-called bread commission. I was also a personal friend of the Ghetto Polizei commandant Kronenberg, and I believed that I could feel completely secure about myself and my family.

At times I thought that it would be good if my daughter Aluśka, a beautiful two-year-old, blond with blue eyes, could be given to Poles to be brought up. I was ready to pay well for it and for a year in advance. For a year because, after all, the war would be over in a year. In the event of our death, I would be certain that our daughter would be adopted, if only on account of our real estate, of which she would be the only heiress.

The majority of the Jews at that time were of the opinion that the small children should share the lot of their parents and that it was not right to leave orphans in the world. I was of a different opinion. I thought that if my daughter was delivered to the right people, she would still be able to live a good life. The property would assure her of independence as well as of an opportunity for a proper upbringing. Aside from that, I thought that it is easier for parents to die when they know that they leave someone after them and that their family will not be completely extirpated. In my opinion it was up to me to find responsible people to whom I could entrust the fate and future of my child. This was well thought out and had a 100 percent chance of succeeding, but it was necessary to do it quickly. The rule *Periculum in mora*[86] should be dominant in our lives and not "Later, I have time," as I used to say from time immemorial.

I turned to the court officer Alchimowicz, for whom I had done so many favors and whom I considered an honorable and honest person, with a request that he relocate my child with his family in Lublin; of course for a payment, the amount for which I would agree to give in advance. He assured me that he would take care of it, that he would go to Lublin and very probably settle my daughter there. After this conversation I felt that my daughter was now safe.

I assumed that as of that moment Alchimowicz had a sincere intention to help me, but when he returned home and told his wife about it, she dissuaded him. To assume an obligation toward a Jew, and then to inform him that he should not expect much, when this concerns a human life—who today would treat such matters lightly?

As for me, I sat around and waited in the ghetto for a favorable resolution of this problem. As for putting an ad in the paper, that never crossed my mind; as for locating the baby in a home for foundlings, this was discussed, but the matter was dropped. My daughter, petted and pampered, was too precious for that. On the other hand, no one thought that the danger was that near and that an immediate "caesarean cut" might save a life.

As concerns the *Kennkarte*, I had no faith in that. My appearance is typical of an educated Jew. On the other hand, my wife's appearance, after certain alterations, tinting of hair, would be passable. So she asked me to procure for her a *Kennkarte.* She could not understand my indifference to the threat of a deportation. She repeated to me often that she could imagine what her brother went through the night before he was shot and that she wanted to save herself. I silently shrugged off her words, didn't even want to hear them, because they irritated me. It is possible that if I had had some ready hard currency, I could have arranged it—just to be left in peace. But first of all it was necessary to sell a suit, my English coat—that upset me. Besides, believing in all "assurances," I did not have a foreboding of danger.

The Aktion 〰

Saturday, August 15

I LEFT MY HOUSE before dinner. I lived on the outskirts of the ghetto, near the crossing barrier on Wawerska Street. Quite by chance, I met there a Polish acquaintance, the Magister,[87] talking to another Jew.

I must write a few words about this Magister. We met in November 1940 in Otwock, where he was (and still is) a civil servant.[88] I would visit him once a month, at times more frequently, and we talked mainly about politics. Once I invited him to the ghetto for potato pancakes. Another time he received me somewhat coolly, and I assumed he had personal problems. I don't remember whether this was in July or August 1941, but suffice it to say that I ceased visiting him after that.

I don't know what opinion he had of me. In any case, I considered him a person of engaging manners—honorable, honest, fiercely patriotic—in a word, a man on whom one can depend in an hour of need, one who can be counted on to help readily and selflessly. Since I knew him briefly, I had no evidence to prove all this, but I just felt it intuitively.

If I didn't fear insulting him, I would have told him that even though he was a native Pole, I sensed in him all the good aspects of Jewish character. That would probably be taken as proof of my Jewish chauvinism, something that in our times is seen as the greatest insult.

But let us return to our meeting. I greeted the Magister very cordially, and he joked a little about my elegant appearance, which seemed to have no connection with the war or the ghetto. Then, abandoning the lighthearted tone, he asked me seriously, "Why are you Jews so passive? Why don't you do something?"

This really surprised me because as far as I was concerned, there was nothing that could be done. We parted quickly.

Right after that I met my wife, Anka, walking with our child. I told her that I had met the Magister, and I asked her whether we shouldn't invite him to us to take some of our things for safekeeping. Anka basically agreed but wanted to delay it until Monday. I returned quickly to the crossing barrier, where the Magister had remained, and asked him to return the following Monday at five. He agreed right away and asked at the same time that I telephone him before that.

A trivial and meaningless condition, but how tragic would be its consequences.

Sunday, August 16

A day for washing and housecleaning. Our laundress washed everything, my wife cleaned in all the corners and changed the linen, while I took care of our child.

Monday, August 17

The mood worsened quickly in Otwock. A few influential and well-to-do Jews from the brushmakers' guild returned to the Warsaw ghetto. Apparently the *Aktion* was at an end there,[89] and now it would be Otwock's turn.

I returned home very upset. Our child was asleep. When I inadvertently awoke it, my wife yelled at me, and I replied sharply. In a word, we argued. I heard many unpleasant things. These would be prophetic statements, although I don't think that Anka knew how close she was to the truth. She said, What advantages had she derived from me? Of what use was it to her that I earned a livelihood and acquired so many useless things? She could sell these and we could live better; that she knows that when she is deported, she will leave it all behind; finally, that I did not procure for her a *Kennkarte* and that I generally did not protect her.

Hearing these words, I was, to be honest, indignant. I left the house in a fury and naturally did not telephone the Magister.

I can still hear Anka's prophetic words. They pound in my brain day and night and reach me like loud voices from another world.

You are guilty. You have caused our destruction! You are guilty. . . .

And maybe Anka, who loved me sincerely and was such a good wife, has forgiven me, perhaps prayed that I be allowed to live so that I, who alone remembers her, can honor her memory and erect a memorial stone for her. But can one be redeemed by a monument? Is it possible to be redeemed altogether for such sins? If I live, it is only so that the punishment will be greater and that before my death I will do penance for my deeds.

It is true that we Jews who are still alive envy those Jews who died in the first bombings, who died from typhus, who died earlier from whatever cause. At least they did not suffer. Somewhere it is written that there will come a time when the living will envy the dead.

Tuesday, August 18

It is a beautiful, sunny day. The town is quiet, when suddenly panic breaks out at one in the afternoon. Women are running and crying, trying to hide little children. I go quickly to the police station, where nearly all the policemen have assembled. I try to find out what has happened.

It seems that a Major Brand has arrived at Otwock, apparently the commandant of an *Umsiedlungsbatallion*,[90] and demanded to see the plan of the ghetto. Afterward, quite illegally in the opinion of the naive Jews, he appointed the commandant of the Ghetto Police, Kronenberg, to be as well the president of the Judenrat. Until this time, the Jewish Council was exclusively under the authority of the *Kreishauptmann*.[91] Brand also ordered that they demolish in twenty-four hours all brick houses in order to use the materials for a wall around the ghetto. Finally, he looked over a place set aside for a carpentry shop, gathered up the plans, and left the ghetto.

After this visit, the mood in town became extremely dejected. It was true that no one took seriously the order for walling up the town since it was impossible to fulfill. Nonetheless, everyone knew that deportations would take place. Only no one knew when and how it would be done.

Everyone drew different conclusions from the new situation. For me it was essential what the commandant of the Ghetto Polizei thought about it. Kronenberg, already the previous week, had received a letter from a former deputy of the Jewish police commandant in Otwock, one Rykner.[92]

I must explain what happened to him earlier. Rykner, because of certain infractions, was sent out in January 1942 with two hundred others to the punishment camp Treblinka I. About fifteen first-rank craftsmen from this group there remained alive. They worked and lived fairly well to such an extent that in May Rykner was able to come to Otwock, naturally with an SS man escorting him. He did not wish to discuss what was going on there, greeted his wife, and went away again. A couple of months later he came again, in a truck, took his wife and the children of those craftsmen to Kosów, a little town situated near Treblinka.[93]

This same Rykner wrote in the letter he sent to Kronenberg that the Jews of Otwock should be protected from the danger that threatened them. A couple of days later, on Friday, August 14, Rykner, uncertain if his letter had arrived, phoned Kronenberg. The pretext was the order for nails from Otwock for the Treblinka camp. When Kronenberg confirmed the arrival of the letter, this exchange followed.

"Do you know then what you must do?"

"I know!"

The human thinking process is inscrutable. Rykner wanted to warn the inhabitants so they could escape in time. Kronenberg, on the other hand, considered it to be in his interest that there should be no panic in town because only he would be held responsible for a mass escape.

I also don't know if Brand told Kronenberg that the deportations would take place the following day. I do know that Kronenberg knew about it because he conveyed this information to the policeman he was friendly with. He told his barber to come to him the following day at six in the morning, and he awaited him calmly. And he ordered the policemen to tell their wives to come to the workshops at the same time and stand by their tubs to show the Germans that they were ready for work. This was only for show because the laundry was not yet set up.

The officials of the Judenrat housed themselves and their families in the building that served as their headquarters. The tailors went to their tailoring workshops, that is to say, to the space that was set aside for that purpose. Sewing machines were there, but there was no work because the Germans had not yet sent the material. Nobody gave it a thought. Brushmakers went to look over the brushmaking equipment while awaiting the transport of horsehair. The carpenters walked aimlessly around the planing machine, waiting for the arrival of the boards. The masses, as masses do, were probably waiting for a miracle.

It's interesting that every catastrophe in history is foreshadowed; there are always some signs in the sky warning people about the danger. Rarely does anyone believe them.

That's how it was with Otwock. Director Dürr of the Arbeitsamt, leaving for summer vacation, said that when he returned, there would be no Jews in Otwock. Frank, the German inspector in the Karczew camp, also drew the veil aside. He had already informed certain workers in May that they alone with their families would remain in Otwock. He ordered that the families be registered and that he be shown the list that was drawn up. No one took these words seriously, but now, in the face of danger, the families of those workers felt secure. Their names were furnished to none other than inspector Frank, the authentic relative of the governor general,* and he, on his own, guaranteed them immunity.

Nonetheless, on that sunny day of August 18, everyone sensed deportations. Very few knew the precise time—they kept it a secret—but I can say boldly that 75 percent of the Jews guessed it. Still they slept calmly, certain that it would not affect them.[94] The remaining 25 percent of Otwock's Jews either left the town at night, hid themselves in the cellars, or awaited the course of events resignedly.

---

*The infamous Hans Frank was the governor general of the Generalgouvernement.

Hail to you, O German genius. Only you could so daze the people, bring them to such a state of collective stupor, that they huddled like lambs, awaiting their executioners. They did not even hide, but on the contrary, they gathered in flocks so that the executioners would not have to work too hard. There is one more interesting symptom of the general stupefaction. All of them were so certain they would remain that they prepared well-stuffed knapsacks for themselves.

I am no longer capable of answering the question of what we thought about as we packed. The knapsacks were a bit too heavy to escape with to other ghettos. Anyway, anybody could tell along the way that a Jew was fleeing. Maybe these knapsacks were packed so that in the worst of situations they could take them along to the wagons. We must not forget that 90 percent of the Jews had no idea where they were going. But I don't believe in this explanation. I have another idea, absurd on the surface, but now a year after these events, I believe it strongly. The packing of the knapsacks served only the Germans. Everyone took the best things, into which they sewed their entire fortune. Gold, dollars, and banknotes. These knapksacks went straightaway to Treblinka where the Germans did not even have to separate things. After all, only the choicest articles were brought. As for those who left their knapsacks at home, they saved their executioners the trouble of packing them. This was a real theater of marionettes, but what a tragic theater! Nevertheless, the manner in which the Germans implied to all the Jews, without exception, that they were doing all this for themselves, for their own good, for securing their material well-being for the future, this will remain forever Satan's secret.

Let us return to that Tuesday, August 18. After returning from the police station, I telephoned the Magister right away and arranged to see him at five, at the same spot, at the border barrier. The Magister appeared punctually, and we went to my apartment. There, together with my wife, we reported to him on the situation. We told him that probably nothing threatened us. Nevertheless, we wanted his help in placing our daughter in a suitable household. I told him that I wanted to pay in advance for what would be the cost of raising the child for a year, which I estimated to be twenty-five thousand złoty worth of goods. I assumed that this was enough because even if something happened to me, the war would be over in a year.

The Magister wanted to give me an answer in a few days, but I insisted that he come the next day. In my naïveté I told him that we had to hurry. We gave him for safekeeping a suitcase with our things. He was to keep it in his family's apartment in Warsaw, where he resided.[95] In addition to that, I offered him my silver pencil, and for his sister, whom I did not know, a bottle of Chanel cologne. I would have gladly given him more expensive presents, but I knew that I could have offended him with that.

I remember as if it were right now the moment I gave him the suitcase through the fencing enclosing the ghetto. The Magister fastened it to the bike's baggage rack and drove off. When I saw his back as he drove off, I had a foreboding, a presentiment. I wanted to call him back. What for? I didn't know. Did I want to give him another suitcase? Was it to ask him to take my daughter with him? Even if he could not find a place for her, we could take her back in a couple of days. I felt a strong pain momentarily and an unexplainable anxiety. In the meantime the Magister's figure became more and more distant, and soon I lost sight of him.

When I returned home, my wife and I started to pack our knapsacks. Then I went to town to take care of our usual daily chores with my friend Willendorf. I remember we took the flour from the electric mill, brought it to the baker so that he would bake us bread for the next day.

What did my wife do during my absence? This I found out from an acquaintance, a policeman, only a month later. She herself did not tell me. It seems Anka went to a photographer to have a photo made for her Polish *Kennkarte*. She wanted it ready for Wednesday morning.

Today I know that in Otwock there was a group of several score Polish citizens who that day knew exactly what would happen the following morning. Because around five o'clock in the evening a written telephone message arrived at the Polish police station,[96] asking that they reserve fifty freight cars for seven in the evening on Wednesday, August 19. It was also ordered that at seven that morning there be a roll call of uniformed and criminal police to take part in the *Aktion* to deport Jews.

The news about the ordered freight wagons did not circulate in town. But Jews did find out that there would be a roll call of the police. Polish policemen calmed them, saying that it was a regular weekly roll call. They themselves took advantage of this information, if only to remove from Jewish tailors or shoemakers items that were ordered, whether they were finished or not.

In other towns policemen felt that it was their obligation to inform the local Jews about the impending deportation. The Otwock police did not consider it their obligation and did nothing. For three years of occupation they sucked Jewish blood, collected constantly a bribe from butchers, bakers, smugglers, from every Jew who traded or who had any goods hidden since before the war.

Let us not forget that all of Jewish life during the war was illegal. A policeman could pick on anything. What do you live on? Where do the potatoes in the ghetto come from? Where did you get the bread? Where are the fields planted with rye? And if there are, where did you get the seed for sowing? Where did you get the meat? Throughout the war Polish policemen, who officially did not have the right to be in the ghetto, lived off that ghetto and lived well.

I don't reproach them for this. I understand that on their wages they could not live during times of devaluation. Still, it will always be to their shame that they did not render Jews that last service, that they did not warn them about deportation. I accuse them, and hold that they are, in equal measure with the German henchmen, responsible for the deaths of Jews.

Yes, there were a few instances when the policemen warned close friends of expected deportations. They made them promise, however, on their word of honor, that they would not reveal this any further. I know, for example, that Officer Pietras warned the administration of the hospital Zofiówka. Thanks to that several people were saved; some others, not having the means or the energy to save themselves, committed suicide that same night.[97]

Just the same, for the sake of justice, I must exclude from the ranks of the police the commandant of the Otwock *Komisariat,* Marchlewicz.[98] I cannot accuse him of living off the ghetto during the war. He probably never crossed that boundary, not before the *Aktion* and not afterward. I am absolutely certain that in his home you will not find any Jewish possessions. He personally never detained a Jew and probably sympathized with them. I cannot approve the basis for his action according to some noble rule of *splendid isolation*. Would that all the police at least followed his example, but he too should have fulfilled his obligation, certainly a moral one, to warn the Jews. That he did not do.

All this we only learned sometime later.

The night came, a sleepless night for all the inhabitants, without exception, in the ghetto. People walked the streets in circles, not being able to decide what to do. Rumors flew that the Polish police had already surrounded the ghetto and had arrested several hundred people in their attempt to get away. These people were to be executed the next morning.

Tales fly from mouth to mouth, acquiring more and more fantastic character; people turn like ghosts in the warm August night. Only the bakers, with a kind of atavistic strength, a strength instilled through custom since childhood, are baking as if nothing threatened them. They are preparing for the town black and white bread and rolls for children.

Four o'clock at night, seeing a lot of movement in town, we woke our child and with my aunt, Czerna Góralska, and her nine year-old son, Mulik, we went to our parents' home. They lived near the police station. Naturally, we did not forget to take with us the knapsacks, so that we barely made it there. We did not find our parents in. They ran away during the night to the Polish neighborhood. Only my sister, Rachel, the wife of the policeman Janek Freund, was at home. Anka right away undressed our child since the baby still had to sleep. We didn't even think that there wouldn't be time to dress her again.

Wednesday, August 19

At dawn the people begin to wander out en masse; all are crowding around the police station of the Ghetto Polizei, the Judenrat, the laundry, and the workshops. Satan looks on all this, surveys the living marionettes, and laughs as he has never laughed before. He sees how the "smart" Jews are unwittingly helping the Germans, how they are saving them work.

I go into town to get some information and also to collect the daily quantity of rationed bread. It is seven in the morning—I am actually at the bazaar—when a truck full of Ukrainians drives through the Karczew border barrier.[99] The first shots are fired. I run quickly home, and just then, from Warsaw Street, come in turn a heavy truck and, following it, a limousine of SS officers. Shots are heard from all sides; the ghetto is already surrounded.

The first victim is Dr. Gliksmanova, who lives near the Warsaw crossing point. A pleasant, good-looking mother of two children. She went out on the street with the intention of showing the Ukrainian her certificate, that she was a dentist for the general population and for the Jewish police in particular. As she held out her certificate with a pleasant smile, she was shot in the head and fell lifeless.

O lucky woman! You died at the moment when you least expected it, unaware that together with you were sentenced to death your beautiful small children.

The Germans had very little work to do. First they went to the Jewish police station. There they directed the assembled crowd to form ranks. They said that everyone was going to the square, where they would be segregated. The families of policemen were to be freed. At this time, the policemen ran as if possessed, not knowing what they had to do—they blew whistles with all their strength and without pause. Everybody feared for himself and for his family.

The Ukrainians fire and fire again. There are no shots into the air. Every shot is aimed at someone's head from a distance of no more than two meters. People fall, brains spatter, blood flows. Crazed, the Jews do not understand why the Germans are shooting because they are not hiding, are ready to stand in rows, everyone has his paper and certificate in his pocket that he is not subject to deportation. The engineer Rotblit, the originator and founder of the workshops in Otwock and a personal friend of the *Kreishauptmann,* approaches the officers. With a proud smile he hands over his papers. The officer accepts them with one hand and with his other one shoots him in the head. Engineer Rotblit falls. And the German, instead of looking over the papers of his victim, would rather look through the pockets, take his money, and remove the gold crowns from his teeth.

In the meantime there forms at the police station a group of wives of all the policemen, their children, and their close and distant relations. Only one woman in all of Otwock has not lost her head. That is Tola, the wife of the commandant of the Ghetto Polizei, Kronenberg. She tells her mother-in-law to stand in line, and she seats herself as the telephone operator in the police station. Earlier, her husband gave Major Brand two gold watches—she remains in place. Others have not even noticed that she is not in line.

At this time I run home as quickly as possible. My wife is beside herself, agitated, and is dressing our child. She herself is dressed in two dresses, a skirt, a blazer, a jacket, and a coat. She wants to hide in the cellar. I am overwhelmed by a terrible fear. There could be severe consequences for the child if they were to find my wife in the cellar. Then they would not consider that she was the wife of a policeman, and they would kill her, the baby, and others who had already hidden in the cellar. What to do? Oh God!

Beside myself, I return to the police station. I run to Kronenberg and tell him that my wife has hidden in the cellar and that I don't know what to do. The commandant of the Ghetto Polizei knows what to do.

"Bring her to the square with the child; on my responsibility, she will be released."

I run as if I had wings. I don't pay attention to bullets, which are whistling all around me, and I jump into the apartment. Thank God, Anka is still in the room, but in what a moment! She is halfway in the cellar. On the floor I can see only her head and arms.

"Anka," I scream, "Kronenberg has said to go to the square. Nothing will harm you. You will be freed."

"And where is your sister?"

"Rachel is in the police station," I reply, "with the group of policemen's wives."

Anka leaves the cellar. We close the opening so that her aunt Czerna and her son, Mulik, or others who have hidden there will not be found. I take my child by the hand, and I lead my wife.

We join a group of policemen's wives. We are surprised that this group is not a homogeneous one and has grown with the addition of others. We are happy that there will be a proper selection in the square. Anka and the child stand in line, and I am moving alongside. From the side of the Judenrat comes a huge serpentine line of people, officials, with the president at the head, and their families. All are marching quietly because they know that they are going to be released soon. In line is the finest pulmonary surgeon in Otwock and in the entire area, the chief doctor of the ghetto, Dr. Augarten. He wants to approach the officers of the SS and to prove his identity. After all, it is not for nothing that he was for so many years a medical practitioner in Hanover. The officer only wags a finger. It may mean that he knows all this, but in the meantime the doctor must stand with others in line; he will be released in the square.

In the meantime the Ukrainians have surrounded the laundry,[100] where women of the professional class and their children have assembled. They are standing at the washtubs and hold rags in their hands. Think of this: rags that will one day be made into clothes for Germans. And, indeed, a Ukrainian with a rifle watches so that no unauthorized person enters the laundry. Work, ladies; stay calm.

At this moment the secretary of the Ghetto Polizei, Ehrlich,[101] comes running with his wife and wants to place her in the laundry. The Ukrainian bars the way, threatens him with the rifle, does not let the wife go into the laundry. Ehrlich, despairing, returns to his nearby apartment and in the last minute hides his wife in the cellar. If he had known that the wives of the policemen are not threatened, he would probably have brought her to the square. It all had to do with the fact that Ukrainians did not let him through to the police station, and he thus did not know what was going on.

Suddenly the Ukrainians who are surrounding the laundry command that the rags be set aside, that all form ranks and march to the square. People change into automatons, dumbfounded marionettes—and even motionless because all at once someone is killed. No one can think. The whistles of the Jewish policemen, the shots of the Ukrainians, the corpses of familiar people underfoot. Helmeted German officers, with silvery shields* on their chests, resemble some demigods, in contrast with the destitute, humble crowd of Jews, with baggage on their shoulders, small children in hand, and a terrible fear in their hearts.

The Ukrainians are chasing the people from all the streets. Although everyone obeys and marches in even rows, shots ring out constantly. The Ukrainians are shooting most readily at young people, at beautiful girls. If they meet the old, the crippled, the paralyzed—they leave them "in peace." I saw a young woman whose legs were paralyzed. With tears in her face she was asking for a bullet—in vain. The family had to drag her from the end of town to the square, and from there she went to the wagon. I also saw a young woman, a minute earlier bubbling over with life and health—I saw her in the moment a Ukrainian with a shovel quartered her living flesh. He had no more bullets, grabbed a shovel by the handle, and struck at the living flesh between her breasts until he just cut her in half.

Everyone is marching toward the square in the direction of the carpenters' shop, which they fenced in with barbed wire with their own hands. Everyone is told to sit down. The square is large. It will hold them all. Ach, you are here. The whole town is here. Take note of the news that all of you will be sent out. No one will be released; the policemen will also go. They are already guarding us; the scales fall from our eyes. From the general population of twelve thousand inhabitants of the ghetto there are eight thousand sitting in the square. The overwhelming majority of these came on their own. They have betrayed us all.

My wife looks at me with a mute expression. I shall never forget that look. Finally she asks, "Calek, did they find Czerna in our cellar?"

Oh, if I had the strength to lie, to say that, yes, they found our aunt in the cellar and killed her on the spot.

Silently I deny with a motion of the head.

"Calek, where is Kronenberg's wife? Didn't he tell you to bring me to the square?"

I am silent. What can I say?

"Calek, and those who have hidden themselves, they will live. Is that true?"

"No, no, no," I answer.

---

*These shields were worn by the German traffic police, a unit called Verkehr-NSS. This stood for National-Sozialistische Kraftfahrer Korps, a paramilitary formation that oversaw the training of motorized and armored units.

Do I know? Am I able in my state to understand anything at this moment? There is a buzzing in my head, as if a waterfall were running through it. I don't understand anything that is going on. I have lost the ability to think and act.

The Germans know that is not safe for them if people have nothing to do and perhaps are thinking. They order us policemen to supply water from the public fountain for the whole crowd. I walk like an automaton, hear voices that I don't understand. Ach, that's right; someone is offering me money so that I can bring him water more quickly. Foolish man, what good is the money to me now?

The sun scorches more and more. My daughter did not eat anything today, and it is time for her second nap. She sleeps in the woods always at this time. Daughter, daughter, today is the end of your second year. Ach, if I knew, I would have, two years ago, strangled you with my own hands. Daughter, because of you your mother perishes, and maybe you will perish because of the foolishness of your parents. Who can possibly understand what is the cause and what is the effect? In the meantime, my dearest daughter, you are looking at me through the barbed wire with such serious eyes. You're not crying, not making any grimaces. In one hour you have grown up; you have become an old woman. Apparently you know that you have been condemned, some instinct tells you that. You stretch out your hands to me, but I have no right to take you. If I do that, I will immediately get a bullet in my head. Well, so what if I get it? Ach, that fear, the panicky fear of slaves!

The Germans, in the meantime, bring themselves chairs; they sit around, drink beer, smoke cigarettes, eat, and laugh. From time to time they fire into the crowd so that no one will dare get up.[102] To further frighten all, they pull out a few people from the crowd and beat them with clubs until they die.

Jews look on this, and—O wonder—still don't understand the terror of the situation. Some remind others about money owed them. A lady friend asks me to go to her room for money that she left on the table. Another acquaintance asks me if I would give him twenty złoty for the road because he has no money with him. Cursed money! Will people always think that it will save them from all misfortunes?

What do they all want from me when I don't know and don't understand what is going on around me? There remains with me only the knowledge that I have brought my wife and daughter to their deaths.

From the rows of people comes out a Jewess by the name of Kamieniecka. She walks up boldly to the officers and shows them a

Polish *Kennkarte*. She receives a few blows, but they free her. She is followed by thousands of eyes, and she shortly disappears into the Polish neighborhood. She is saved.

But Anka is not looking at her. She is looking at me; she says nothing, doesn't even reproach me for not getting her a *Kennkarte*. God in heaven! Am I guilty? I turn away, am silent. What can I say? Explain myself or ask for forgiveness? Can one really say anything in the face of death?

Only the German Satan is enraged because a Jewish woman has cheated the Germans and has saved herself. Now maybe it is possible to seek another satisfaction. A young, comely, elegantly dressed woman approaches from the Polish neighborhood. We ourselves don't know if she is Polish or Jewish. The German officers ask her politely what she wishes. In reply they hear that she is Jewish and wants to go with her mother, who is in the square. They are surprised and ask her several times, *"Polen oder Jude?"*[103]

For the longest time they cannot understand. When they finally realize what this is all about, they don't even bow their heads before such a sacrifice. She is beaten with clubs and pushed into the line.

Throughout this time the policemen were certain that they would also be deported. They were not allowed through on the side of the *Komisariat,* but they could circulate freely in town. Some tried to hide, but the majority did not consider escape.

Together with Willendorf I went into the town to find a little food for our children, who had not eaten anything that day. We went round and round without speaking to each other. Even though I knew that I could now hide myself to avoid being deported, I did not consider this. How could I? There Anka waits for some food for Aluśka, and I will hide myself and not bring it? To remain alone and to allow them to go away seemed to me so absurd that I did not take this into account for a moment.

We finally found some tomatoes and candy and then returned to the square. We also took along a few small pillows* for the children to take along to the wagons. This activity drained our energies. We were completely resigned, incapable of any act, thought, and even speech.

It is noon. Lipszer, the head of the gendarmes in the Warsaw region, is arriving. Following him is the inspector of the Karczew camp, Frank, together with the commandant of the Arbeitsamt, Dürr. They stand and confer. All the policemen must present themselves at the square in front

---

*These pillows were placed on larger ones as decoration.

of the police station, and there they will hear about their fate and the
fate of their families. Hearing this, the wives entertain the best of hopes.
We leave them calmer, and we station ourselves in two rows before the
police station.

Lipszer addresses us. His voice falls on us slowly, harshly. The German
pronounces each word with care. Is he a man or God? No one is certain
of that. Then he stops, walks up to our rows, and with a raised voice
turns to one of the policemen: *"Bist du ein polizist, di hunt einer um-
leigum?"**[104]

The sons of old Szwajcer gave him an old police armband in the
square, and in this way they took him out of the crowd of the condemned. Now, before their eyes, their father is shot down. They look as
he falls right under their feet, they don't stir, they stand at attention.

Lipszer is checking another suspicious one in line. And in point of fact
someone managed to grab an old police armband. He has no hat, no
number, but he has an authentic identity card signed by the Germans;
once he was a policeman. His heart beats like a church bell. If Lipszer
looks at the number on the armband and compares it with the number
on the identity card . . . He does not look.

To the question of whether anyone else intends to deceive the
Germans, there emerges from the ranks the town councillor,[105] (Motel)
Solnicki. On his arm he has, instead of the police armband, an armband
of the Judenrat—too bad, he must die. But no. There is only a short *"Du
blajbst."*[106]

Lipszer returns to the verandah, and his words again flow slowly. God,
what is he saying?

"You policemen will remain in Otwock. You will clean up the whole
ghetto. You will take to the warehouse all possessions, merchandise, and
furniture, and you will hold the people who are hiding under arrest until
the gendarmes arrive. You are not permitted to take anything, no goods,
no money. When you remove the curtains, don't tear them. It is not permitted to damage furniture; gold and dollars you must give to me personally. When the entire ghetto is cleaned up, you will be sent out to the
labor camp in Karczew, where you will work for the remainder of the
war. You will be released after the war. If your wives were here, I would

---

*The German quotations with their misspellings (there are others in the memoir) show
that Perechodnik's knowledge of both German and Yiddish was limited.

free them, but if they are already in the square, they must go away. Five wives who have remained have the official right to remain."

God, is he mocking us, joking, or laughing at us? First he tells us to provide our wives to the square, and then he tells us that if they are with us, they will remain? My brother-in-law Janek Freund is standing and weeping. *Mencz, bist du ein mencz?*[107] I say to myself. Oh, great God, here we are, one hundred men, men for men, and before us are a few gendarmes with rifles. Boys! Let's attack them; we'll die together—I think to myself. But nothing comes of it, and now Kronenberg speaks up. He did not give up his wife, only told me and others to provide theirs. What is he saying?

"Mir danken Herr Leutnant."[108]

Boys, say it together, everybody loudly.

Lipszer wags his hand as if to reject the thanks and probably laughs to himself. He knows perfectly well that when the time comes, he will "do his work like a Negro slave."* Here everyone is condemned to death. But we don't know that. What won't a Jew do to live an hour longer? Some of the policemen are happy; they just happened to live quite far from the police station, and their wives were able to hide themselves. Bachelors are happy for obvious reasons. And those who are losing their wives? Who is thinking of others, anyway?

There is one person who is thinking. That's my friend Willendorf. He wants to demonstratively give up his policeman's armband, give thanks for his life, and perish together with his wife and son. Kronenberg will not allow such a gesture. He says that if he wants to, he can join his wife, but without any display that can harm the other policemen.

Right after this, a group of policemen is dismissed to the hospital Zofiówka in order to bury the corpses of the Jews who were killed.[109] My brother-in-law Janek Freund also goes with them, while I am able to escape from this group. I return to the square. Anka is sitting there waiting to be released. What can I tell her? What can I do?

When I get to her place, her stretched-out, pleading hands seem to cry to me, Calek, Calek, are we free? The child also looks at me, with arms instinctively held out. I am quiet; the policeman Abram Willendorf now makes clear the situation with his behavior. He says nothing to his wife; silently removes and throws aside his armband, hat, and number; and calmly sits on the ground.[110] We are going away together, such is the silent answer of Willendorf, an honorable man.

---

*This is part of a saying that a slave will perform his task but is expendable.

Abram Willendorf, what can I now tell about you? For a year we were inseparable friends. We always went out together, you, a Communist,[111] I, a Zionist. You have saved the honor of the Jews of Otwock, the honor of the policemen. You have sweetened the last moments of your wife's life. And I, I, the intellectual, what did I do? Did I throw away my armband? No, I did not have the courage.

I could say that my wife asked me not to do this, that I should stay alive and remember her from time to time. If I write this, it is only to show what a noble and sacrificing person Anka was. I know well that even without such a request, I would not have had the courage to volunteer for death. The example of the crowd took hold of me completely. I thought as did the others: Let it be one day later, even under force, even with shame. I couldn't do it a day earlier, by myself, voluntarily, with pride.

One hour passes, another one. The Jews are apathetic, they no longer think—and about what should they think?

Anka, my wife, what were you thinking then? Maybe that near you sits your sister with her children? Maybe that not one of your family will remain alive? And maybe you are looking at your daughter, such a beautiful angel, and you remind yourself with what pain you bore her and with what difficulties and self-denial you raised her? What was she guilty of? Are you perhaps trying to penetrate, to understand these Germans, to wonder why not one of them approaches, takes Aluśka by the hand in order to play with her? There was never a person who did not stop by her in the street in order to look at the little one. And maybe you are thinking of the movie house that you built with your own hands. Are you perhaps thinking how tall and beautiful is the grass in front of your villa? How pleasant the day under the pines that you did not let me cut? How quiet and safe it is there? How nice it would be to stretch out there, to sleep as you did for so many years in the sunny days of August?

And maybe you are looking at the Polish policeman who is guarding you with a rifle in hand. He came to the movies for so many years, always kissed your hand through the glass opening of the cashier's booth, paid you compliments, told you how beautiful you were with the lamp shining on you, in the flush of youth—and now he is ready to shoot you if you get up. And maybe you are looking at the Poles who are riding by in crowded electrical trams, looking at the Jews of Otwock for the last time. Some are probably very pleased and are joking, seeing how polite the Jews appear to be in the square, really like a flock of lambs; others lower their heads quietly or make a sign of the holy cross, whispering, *"Requiescant in pace."** Indeed, they already see corpses in front of them.

Maybe you are thinking that if I remain alive, I will live for a long time, will marry and forget about you. And maybe you have a hope that in the last moment they will free you. It is beyond your comprehension that I could take you and cram you into a cattle car. Perhaps you are praying. And maybe you have collapsed from shock. Maybe you recall the good times in the casinos, walks in Zakopane. You remember your young life and the life of your daughter, and you want to live, live, live.

What did you think about, Aneczka? Throughout our married life I knew your thoughts, but on the last day you did not say anything, did not respond to me at all.

Eventually, I hear her voice.

"Calek, try to get poison for me and the child."

My sister, Rachel, the wife of Janek Freund, is asking me for the same thing. Where can I get poison? I am like a robot who can carry out a command but does not know what is going on around him. Finally, I go to the police station to telephone the Podolski pharmacy. How different my words sound over the telephone.

"This is Perechodnik speaking. I would like poison for three people, and please send it to the fenced-in area near the *Komisariat*."

Are these my words or the words of some other person? And why should they send it? It's true that I am about two hundred meters from the pharmacy, but I can't get there. I wait. The pharmacy has not sent it. A Pole on a bicycle loiters near the fence. He agrees to go to the pharmacy, returns shortly, and says that they will not give it to him without a prescription. A prescription? Where can I find a doctor? I know. Dr. Maksymylian Augarten is in the square. So many times he saved people from death; let him once prescribe a medicine for death. I return to the square.

"Doctor, please let me have a prescription for poison."

Augarten takes out his fountain pen, notebook, writes in Latin, signs it, dates it August 19, 1942, and puts down the same ready formula: for Perechodnik. I take the note through the barbed wire and leave without a word. It's not necessary to pay now for making up a prescription.

---

*"May they rest in peace" (Latin).

I return to the fence, throw the prescription to the waiting Pole. He returns after several minutes, throws me ten tablets of Luminol, and doesn't ask for money. Was it some stranger who has paid for me, or is it that the pharmacy would not accept money?

I am once again in the square. What effect does Luminol have? How much should one take? Whom can one ask? Someone says that three tablets are enough to cause death. My sister, Rachel, does not hesitate. She takes three tablets, dissolves them in water and drinks it with one breath. She does not say good-bye to anyone and only gives me a few little trinkets for her husband. The brave girl falls asleep quickly. I walk away.

My wife prepares for herself the fatal potion, wants to drink it without even saying good-bye to me. In the last minute her sister spills the liquid on the ground. Apparently she believes that they will survive even where they're going.

What were you thinking, my sister-in-law? Were you satisfied that you did not let your husband continue being a policeman and that he would perish because of you? He could have saved himself.

And what were you thinking about, you engineer Skotnicka? You, grand dame, you are smiling, your lips whisper, *"Non omnis moriar."* You're right; you succeeded already in wartime in sending your children to Palestine. Your son is probably fighting in the ranks of the English army—there is someone to avenge you. Your daughter has already completed the *Technium* in Haifa. God willing, she will marry, will have children who will be named after you. The Germans will not exterminate your family branch.

Of what were you thinking, Frau Schüssler, you a pedigreed *Volksdeutsch*? Forty years have passed since you joined your lot with that of a Jew. You surrounded him with real love and loyalty and shared with him the good and the bad. To follow him, you left your native Germany, during the war you lived with him in the Otwock ghetto, and now, voluntarily . . . What did you think about? Do you perhaps regret your sacrifice? Are you proud of your great love, which commands you to accompany your husband up to . . . Treblinka? Comfort your husband with kind words, you who are filled with shame that you are descended from the nation of barbarians.

Of what were you thinking, Miss Zylber? Already yesterday you had the opportunity to go to Lublin, to friends. You could have saved yourself. After all, every Pole should have considered himself lucky if you would marry him, you good-looking, rich, honorable girl. Maybe you can repeat after Lilla Weneda that you never knew the joy of life until you had to die.[112]

And what were you thinking about, you officials of the Judenrat? You were ready to do everything for the Germans, but they had contempt for you. It didn't even concern you that they did not refer to you as *Judenratem* but as *Judenferatem*—a traitor to Jewish affairs. That's true; you're sorry that you did not remain policemen.

And of what were you thinking, you rabbis, Jewish sages? Were you proud at that moment that you belonged to the Chosen People, that you were falling as sacrifices in the holy name of God?

And what were you thinking about, you wealthy Jews? Did you at that moment examine if the gold was well sewn into the suit? You were certain that it would save you even now.

And what were you thinking about, tailors, shoemakers, Jewish workers? Yes, yes, Gedalewicz, you must take with you a German uniform; you will show them there how nicely you can sew uniforms. Who will harm you? Be as workers with the best of intentions. They will not send you out.

And what were you thinking, you children of Centos?[113] A little boy said to me that it was shameful to send out orphans.

And what were you thinking about, you Jewish masses? You were passive, resigned, silent. Jews thought about everything, but not that they are descendants of Judah Maccabee.[114] Where is your spirit that would have sounded with a thundering voice, "Let me perish, but together with my enemies!"

Before you are scarcely two hundred men with rifles, and you are eight thousand and have nothing to lose. Stand up, all of you together, shout one cry, and you will be free in a second. The Jewish nation is cursed, it is old, it has no strength to fight its opponents.

I return to my wife; I give her four fresh pills.

The train wagons arrive. God, render a miracle! We turn to the Germans and beg them practically on our knees to have pity on our wives. The German Satan jeers at us some more.

"Good, they will be freed," they say to us solemnly.

On wings of happiness I run to my wife.

"Anka, Anka!" I yell. "You are saved!"

We take our wives and children out of the crowd. These are scenes out of Dante. Our mothers and sisters must go to their deaths seeing that their daughters and daughters-in-law remain alive. The policemen-bachelors pick out their fiancées or sisters—mothers give them their own rings to make it easier for them to marry.

Willendorf, Willendorf, what did you do? Now the wives of the policemen are being saved along with their husbands, and you have to go with
your wife and son to the wagons only because you showed contempt for
your armband. Unfortunately, now you cannot be saved.

Rachel, Rachel, why did you have to hurry so? Ach, you sacrificial sisters, nurses from Zofiówka! You want to save Rachel, give her an injection. You know that you too will perish, and in spite of that your hand
will not tremble at the last injection. But where do you find milk for the
injection on this cursed day? But you don't give up; you make a different
injection. The dose of Luminol was, as it proved, insufficient. Rachel is
awake and is placed between the wives of the policemen. Hardly conscious, she holds in her hand her husband's police identification.

Anka, Anka, will a poet be found to write of the nobility of your soul?
Just a while back the specter of death appeared before your eyes, and
now with dawn's light barely illuminating freedom, you are ready for further sacrifices and devotions. You ask me in a pleading tone, "Calek, let's
take my sister's daughter, we'll list her as our daughter. Let her be saved
with us; we'll take care of her."

You're asking in vain, begging in vain. Indeed, love is blind since you,
noble one, have loved me, one unworthy of you. Oh, I know—I could
have explained to you that I refused that because I sensed that with two
children, they would certainly not let you go. No, I will not say that. Why
should I deceive my own conscience? On that day reason did not guide
us but a blind instinct that revealed to us the real human face, the nobility of some, the vileness of others.

At last a group of policemen's wives is assembled on the side. They tell
us to load the remaining people into cattle cars. O cursed Germans! How
wise you are! How quickly we become the obedient marionettes in your
hands! We work briskly; the demon of revolt no longer dominates us, not
even a feeling of pity for the remaining Jews.

"*Beǉgo, Beǉgo*,"* shout the Ukrainians. "There are not enough train
wagons. Load two hundred people to each car."

The policemen lead their own fathers and mothers to the cattle cars;
themselves close the door with a bolt—just as if they were nailing the

---

*There is no such word in Ukrainian. It is possible that Perechodnik is using a word similar
to the Polish *belkot*, which connotes "babble" or "gibberish." Or the Ukrainians may be
shouting *Bij jego*, which in Polish means "Hit him."

coffins with their own hands. One policeman hands his father poison, and seeing this, his brother, a handsome sixteen-year-old, shouts and weeps, "Zygmunt, Zygmunt, and for me?"

The tempo of work grows wild. The temples throb; there is an unbearable pain in the heart and a single thought that we will soon take our wives and children away and run from this accursed place.

It is dusk; all are loaded up. The Germans are going to the wives of the policemen and are starting to separate them—children will not be released.

"Calek, Calek, what am I to do?"

"Zygmunt, what am I to do?"

"Mojsze, what am I to do?"

Beside myself, I grab Aluśka, blood of my blood, bone of my bone, and I place her to the side. She stands alone, hungry, sleepy, surprised. Maybe she does not understand why the father, always so good to her, leaves her in the dark. She stands and does not cry; only her eyes shine, those eyes, those big eyes.

Suddenly we see that the Germans are pointing their guns at us. A command is heard.

"All policemen to the side of the square on the double march! In two lines!"

It seems to us that we are standing in one place, but no, our legs, in spite of our will, carry us to the other side of the square.

The German Satan reveals his true features. Now there is no longer any point in playing the comedy. For one hundred people the Germans are willing to fatigue themselves and do their own loading into the train wagons.[115] Our dear ones are going away into the dark night without farewells. From the distance I see only a cloud of dust and silhouettes that I cannot distinguish. All has been lost. Hurry now, policemen—you executioners of your own wives and brothers—render them their last turn; give them some bread through the windows of the wagons. Let no one say that the Germans begrudge Jews some bread.

A long whistle—Anka, you have started off on your last journey. God, have mercy on me!

Allow me, Anka, at least in my thoughts, to accompany you farther. For ten long years we were together. When I went away for my studies, I sent to you right away the necessary documents so that you could also come to me. You had a passport, but they didn't want to give you a visa. Alas! Maybe we could now be together in France. *Qui le sait?**

You are in the fourth cattle car from the locomotive, a car that is almost completely filled with women and children. In the whole car there are only two men—are these your protectors? You are sitting on the boards with your legs tucked under you, holding Aluśka in your arms. Is the child sleeping already at such a late hour? Is it maybe suffocating for lack of air on such a sultry August night? Has human excrement so poisoned the air that one cannot light a match?

You are sitting alone in the midst of this crowd of condemned. Are you maybe finding some comfort that this fate has not only touched you but also all those around you? No, you are not thinking of that. You are sitting, and there is one thing that you do not understand. How is it possible? Your Calinka, who loved you for ten years, was loyal to you, guessed at and fulfilled all your thoughts and wishes so willingly, now has betrayed you, allowed you to enter the cattle car and has himself remained behind.

Maybe he already went home, went to sleep on clean bedding, which you have just changed the other day, and you sit here with Aluśka in your arms, in the dark, in the crowd, without air.

I know you clench your fists, and a wave of hatred toward Aluśka sweeps over you. That is, after all, his child. Why do I have to have her here? You are getting up; you want to throw the little one out the window.

Anka, Anka, do it, throw out the child, and don't let your hand shake! Maybe the child will fall under the wheels of the speeding wagon, which will crush her to a pulp. And maybe, if there is really a God in the world, there are good angels who will spread an invisible carpet so that nothing will happen to her. Maybe your Aluśka will fall softly to the ground, will fall asleep far from the train rails, and in the morning some decent Christian, captivated with her angelic looks, will pick her off the ground, cuddle her, take her home, and raise as his own daughter.

Do it, Anka, do; don't hesitate for a second!

Unfortunately, you fall to the floor again, hug Aluśka to you, beg her to forgive you for such thoughts, for that wave of hatred toward her and her father that swept over you. Your body is shaken with a quiet, bereaved weeping. May it bring you forgetfulness!

---

*"Who knows?" (French).

You have just passed by Świder, Jósefów,[116] and suddenly you see movement at the window. These are your two protectors, the only men in the wagon; they have decided to escape. The weeping of the women, who are afraid to remain alone, does not help. Nor do the words of Solnicka.

"Why are you running away? You can get killed. When we arrive, we will work and live on."

No, these men cannot listen to these women who are strangers to them. They have to save themselves; they want to live to see their own wives and children. Jurek jumps first and after him, Berek Kejzman.

Anka, Anka, why don't you follow them? Once you played football with a boy's team, in Otwock you were the best biker, and now you are incapable of doing this? Is the baby holding you back or hatred toward me? Are you thinking, Am I supposed to jump, run away? But where will I go? Am I supposed to return to Calek?

For ten years, since you met me, I took the place, for you, the orphan, of father, mother, and brother. I cared for you. You didn't do anything by yourself without my knowledge and help—now you're not able to decide by yourself. You go on sitting, cuddling the child, and you envy Kejzman. His wife saved herself earlier; now he will see her, and they will go on living together.

Yes, there is no prophet who might appear before you, who will be able to tell you the future history of Kejzman and also of other Jews. Today I know their history. Not long ago I envied him. Envied him because he was in the same cattle car with you, that he lives with his own wife, that he is happy with his daughter. Now I know that if Kejzman knew his later fate, he would not have jumped out; he would have remained in the wagon. And you, helpless women, you wouldn't have envied him.

You are already in Falenica. The train stands at the station a long time. From all cars one can hear an animal cry.

"Water, water, water!"

Where is there a person who would at least bring a bottle of water for the parched lips, even if only for the children who are slowly dying from thirst and lack of air? A few brave boys from the Falenica ghetto bring under cover of night a few bottles of water. It has to last for eight thousand thirsty people.

Boys, boys, don't be afraid. Nothing will threaten you! Tomorrow at this time you will be loaded into cattle cars, and you will beg for a drop of water. Who will give it to you?

The train goes farther. It is already in Warsaw. The last time you were in Warsaw was in January 1940. You traveled to the bank to pay off the old debt on the movie house. Did you expect that you would visit the city again under such conditions?

Aluśko, Aluśko, are you still alive? Have you not yet suffocated? Anka, do you still have a little water? And maybe Aluśka is sipping* your tears?

I want to believe that the transport of the Jews of Otwock arrived at Treblinka right away, the next day, on Thursday. Some say that the transport from Falenica, which came on Friday, was exterminated before the Otwock transport. I remember that when someone told me that, I attacked him with my fists. What right did he have to tell me that? Am I to be told, by my friend, in addition to all that has happened, that my wife agonized forty-eight more hours in that cursed cattle car?

I close my eyes: The cries for water are ever fainter, people have no more strength, they lose consciousness. And the children? The children are probably no longer alive. I see the train is passing the Kosów station. Yes, in Kosów there are fifteen families from Otwock. Do they thank God that they saved themselves? What do they think now? Are they weeping over the inhabitants of Otwock?

The train leaves Kosów and detours to the special railroad siding of death that leads to Treblinka. Treblinka II is no penal camp. It is the place that celebrates the triumph of the evil soul of the German race. It is the cemetery of 3 million Jews, a cemetery where no one will find human bones. Clever Germans are converting them into fertilizer that the Polish farmer will receive as a bonus for the grain furnished to the Germans. Yes, yes, Jews—in the opinion of Germans—your work, your sweat, your creative energy did not fertilize the Polish soil enough. Your ashes will improve it.

The gate opens, the locomotive chugs, the train stops, the doors of the cars are opened, the Jews can come out.

Anka, Anka, in what condition did you come out of the cattle car? Were you holding little Aluśka by the hand? Or did you perhaps leave her in the wagon together with other corpses as well as human excrement? But maybe Aluśka was still breathing. Will anyone ever answer that question for me?

---

*The Polish word *spija* does not have a good English equivalent. Its heartbreaking meaning is that of a butterfly sipping nectar.

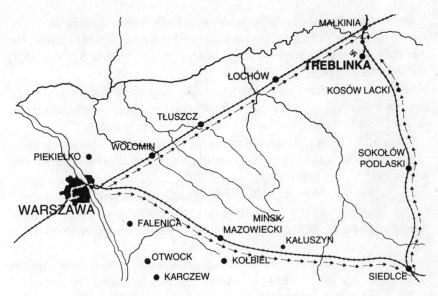

The rail route from Warsaw to the Treblinka extermination camp

The people are coming out of the wagons. They fill their lungs full of air, forgetting that they have come to a place of execution. They are happy with the outdoors, with the beautiful August day, and maybe—who knows—maybe they have hope. The Germans stand around them, well fed, in uniforms, helmets, and silvery shields on their chests, machine guns in their hands. These are gods. You must obey them!

A senior officer comes out and speaks to the crowd. What does he say? What information does he convey?

"People, don't be afraid; nothing bad will happen to you. You will go to the east, and you will work. Now, because you have lice, you will take baths. Later you will get food, and tomorrow you will travel on. Let the women and children go to one side; they will bathe first. Let each one remove her clothes, put them neatly to the side so that she will be able to find them. Shoes have to be tied in pairs. There are towels. Get ready quickly because time is urgent."[117]

The women separate themselves from their husbands, fathers, brothers. They must strip themselves before the crowd. Are they ashamed? Does it no longer matter to them? They put together their clothes—but oh God—from where come such heaps of clothes? Are these the clothes of other Jews? If so, how did these Jews go on to work? Aha, they probably gave them clothes made of paper.

The crowd of naked, silent women, mostly with children in hand, moves forward to a huge building, where they are supposed to bathe. On the building is printed with large letters *"ALLE JUDEN BADEN SICH UND FAHREN NACH OST."*[118]

Silently, old women with flabby breasts, young, tall women, slender like poplars, the rays of the sun reflecting on their bodies, enter. The sun sets in blood red color and with it, hope.[119]

Anko, Anko, let your beautiful eyes gaze for the last time at the heaven, at the sunset. Send me your last greeting—a benediction or a curse. The sun will relay your gaze to me.

All the women have entered the building, the doors close automatically, from the interior is heard an enormous cry—it is all over. The door is opened; people's bodies are thrown out. The building is readied to receive new people so that they may "bathe."

Men, what are you doing during that time? What does Abram Willendorf do when he sees his wife go into that building? Do you know that you will never see her again and that shortly you too will perish?

Men perish in the same way. A portion of the strongest and the healthiest is taken to Treblinka I, and after two months' work under inhuman conditions where they will be squeezed out like lemons, useless, they too are exterminated. After all, there is no shortage of fresh people. Are not fresh transports arriving each day? They work with the clothes, separate them, load into wagons; part of them work with the corpses. It doesn't matter what they do. Sooner or later they will also be killed.*

Evening comes.

What has happened suddenly to the Germans, these who are afraid of God? The guards fall to the ground; they hide themselves in air raid shelters. Bolshevik planes fly over Treblinka.[120]

---

*Perechodnik's account of the killings at Treblinka corresponds in the main to other contemporaneous reports. He did not know about the use of gas. Other writers mentioned electrical current and steam. The Warsaw ghetto poet Władysław Szlengel in his poem "Mała Stacja Treblinki" (Little Station Treblinka) concludes in the last verse: "There hangs from times past / (An ad, in any case) / The worn sign that says: / Here you cook with gas" [translation by F. Fox] (Władysław Szlengel, Co Czytałem Umarłego [Warsaw: State Publishing House, 1979], pp. 74–75). Cf. *The Black Book of the Polish Jewry* (New York: American Federation for Polish Jews, 1943); "L'Extermination des Juifs Polonais" (1943), memoir in the Hoover Institution Archives; and Z. Klukowski, "Niedola i zagłada Żydów w Szczebrzeszynie" (Misery and Extermination of Jews in Szczebrzeszyn) (1942) *Bul. ZIH*, nos. 19–20 n.d. These contemporaneous accounts assumed that electrical current was used. See Israel Guttman, *Resistance: The Warsaw Ghetto Uprising* (Boston: Houghton Mifflin, 1994), pp. 141 ff.

Well, then, brave Jews, take advantage of the time! Run, Konigsberg!
Run, Rybak! Now or never.

Where is Konigsberg? Where is Rybak? You ran away from Treblinka in
order to tell the world untrue things about Greater Germany! You will be
preaching *Greuelpropaganda?*[121] No, Germans don't worry about escapees. They will come with a transport of Jews from another town.

Where is Konigsberg? Are you still alive? Did he return to Treblinka?

Anka, Aluśka, Rachel, and you sisters and brothers of mine, how I
would like to say from the depths of my afflicted heart the prayer *El Mole
Rachamim*[122] for the repose of your souls. May God in the Highest grant
your souls a deserving rest. We the sons, brothers, husbands of yours still
living, we shall avenge you with blood. Amen.

*Ma femme bien aimée Annie, tu seras vengée! Ma petite fille Athalie, tu
seras vengée! Les cendres de trois millions hommes, femmes, enfants
brulés à Treblinka, vous serez vengés!*[123]

After the Aktion ✍

August 20

WE RETURN HOME from the square. Home? Does a Jew need a home now? I remember those of us who went. I, Zygmunt Wolfowicz, his brother, Tadek, as well as Rubin Grynhorn. We lived on the same street, we lost our families at the same time, and now we are returning home, instinctively clinging to one another.

Were we overcome with fear at the sight of the dead ghetto? No, we were just afraid to remain alone before such a severe and all-knowing judge, which is one's own conscience. That is what we were afraid of, even though none of us realized that.

We walked slowly. No one spoke a word. We could not think; we could not grasp the fact that our wives, children, and sisters were now in cattle cars and that shortly only their ashes would be left. We could not understand that we would never see them again, never hear their voices. We were not willing to accept the fact that we too were condemned to death. We could not cry. We felt nothing. We were panic stricken for one reason mainly: to enter our apartments alone.

We finally decide to enter Wolfowicz's apartment together. I remember this as if it were yesterday. An empty place yawns. On the wall we see only the smiling faces of the wife and child; of course, these are only photographs. We turn away our heads. We don't want to look. Silently we sit down to eat the evening meal—after all, nature has its own laws. We smear the bread thickly with butter and drink strongly sweetened cocoa.

God, is this an orgy? No, it is the last supper of the condemned.

We shall have such a meal daily; one of these will surely be the last one. Will it be today's? Not yet. After all, the Germans must have had a reason for letting us live. We arrange to meet tomorrow at four in the morning.

Later I turn to the other side of the road, to my parents' house. My aunt Czerna Góralska has been hiding under the flooring all day. She is also waiting for the death sentence. If the deportation is over, what is to be done with her? I don't know. Either way, I have to go and get her bread and water. It is after midnight. I pass empty and dark houses that were filled with life twenty-four hours ago.[124] Although I look down at my feet, I still stumble in the dark over corpses—I don't know and I don't want to know if these are friends or strangers. I cannot look at smashed heads and pools of blood. At last I am in my parents' house. I open the trapdoor from the basement, and my aunt is there. I give her the bread, a bucket of water, and I tell her resignedly, "Everyone in Otwock has been deported. Anka and Aluśka are probably no longer alive. They also took Rachel."

My aunt looks at me as if under a spell. With an indifferent tone of voice I have informed her of her death sentence, her son's, and at the same time I have told her of the death of people closest to us. My aunt knows that there is nothing to say, nothing to ask. Perhaps she is sorry that my wife perished and that she, thanks to me, has gained a temporary respite.

The trapdoor falls. I continue to stand. I can't move from the spot or turn my eyes away from her. I see Anka, standing on the stairs leading to the cellar; only her head and arms protrude. I hear my own words clearly.

"Anka, Kronenberg told you to report to the square. Nothing threatens you. You'll be freed."

Is this my voice? Am I a murderer, my wife's executioner? I, or that Kronenberg? And maybe the two of us are only marionettes of destiny, of the evil fate of Israel.

I cannot tear my eyes away from the trapdoor, thinking of those who are hiding. God, why didn't the Germans find them in the basement? Why didn't they kill them? Why didn't I at least lie to Anka that this is what had happened?

I leave slowly. I decide to go home. Ahead of me is the spectral wandering amid the corpses. I go with my eyes closed. I know the way by heart. I have trod it several times a day. Until today I have been greeted by the smiling face of Anka and her words directed to our daughter: "Look, Aluś, Daddy's coming. Daddy!"

I open the door—damn it!—the Ukrainians didn't even enter our apartment. Anka could have sat there securely. Ah! It would have been better if I had found the home plundered, burned, destroyed. It is a mockery to think of the state in which Anka left it! The toilet articles are all in their place; everything shines, waiting for people who would breathe a spark of life into those dead objects. But there will be no more life here.

It's two o'clock at night, so it is the next day: Thursday. I lie down on the couch. I am afraid to lie in bed because it is still warm. I leave the light on. Is there some association in my mind between this room and the closed cattle car in which two hundred people are going on their last journey? No, I am not comparing anything. I don't think about anything. I just fall asleep.

My friends wake me after two hours of sleepless dozing. Rise up, slave, take a shovel, bury the corpses. Be brisk and alert so there isn't any trace left of German barbarism. You have to bury one thousand bodies.

Fortunately, we don't have to dig pits because Jews were forced to prepare them ahead of time. They thought, it's true, that they were preparing air raid shelters; later on women threw trash into them and poured
in dirty water. Now it is enough to drag over the corpses, throw them
into the channel, fill it with sand to ground level, and it's finished. There
is no need to search the pockets. The Germans did that. They even took
from the corpses the gold crowns from their teeth.

There is no need to proceed with the Jewish ritual. The bodies are not
washed or wrapped in white sheets or placed in coffins; no one marks
the place of burial or recites prayers for the repose of dead souls. It's all
unnecessary. These are not people being buried, only Jews.

We work in silence. In one pit lies the corpse of an unknown woman;
we throw on her the body of my friend Mulik Noj and on top of him the
body of the thief Fiolek. Quickly, we throw sand over them.

The Poles stand beyond the fencing on Szkolna Street and look. Do
they look at us as gravediggers? Do they perhaps want to express compassion? Do they maybe want to jeer at us? Perhaps they wonder why we
do this, why we didn't run away from this cursed town. Who knows?
They look at the blood that marks the ground and are quiet. No one will
remove his hat or cross himself. But at least they say nothing. The dread
of this moment commands silence.

How did this day pass? How many corpses did I bury? What did I eat
that day? I don't remember anything. I only remember one thing: When
we passed by the apartments from which we heard the voices of those in
hiding, we ran from them as one does from lepers. We didn't want to carry
them off to the police station because we were afraid to answer their
questions about what was going on in town. It seemed to us that from
each house, from each street, from each corner, we were observed by gendarmes. This was not a fear; it was a psychosis. I wanted to escape the
thought that my neighbors were hiding and that I did not hide my wife.

I did not come across my brother-in-law Janek Freund that day or several days thereafter. Anyway, why would I have sought him? Would it be
to tell him about the last moments of his wife, Rachel? Maybe it would
be to tell him that even though he left her to herself and didn't even
come to the square to bid her good-bye, she did not curse him, that on
the contrary, she begged God that he should save himself. Rachel was
certain that Janek had escaped to the Polish neighborhood and that
there, with his Aryan looks, would live like a Pole. Why talk about all that?

The following night, also spent outside the house, passed. I only went
there to bring food to Aunt Góralska.

Friday came, the first one when it was unnecessary to give my wife money for shopping. Now a human being was quite free, without any responsibilities. That Friday went by like a bad dream.

Saturday, a solemn day of rest. Rejoice, Jews. Go and pray, and after dinner go for a promenade.

That Saturday things are different in Otwock. Perhaps Jews do pray, and afterward they go out of apartments, cellars, hiding places, and are looking for Jewish policemen to take them to the police station. They cling to them.

"Remember," they say, "that we reported ourselves. Don't forget to say that to the Germans."

We promise them because what can we do? At times we say that it makes no difference, that they will be killed anyway. Then Jews turn away their heads; they don't want to talk to us in the middle of the road. They don't believe because they don't want to believe us. And rightly, a person should be hopeful until the last minute. From afar this joint march looks as if a Jewish policeman is leading a group of his brothers to death, but in reality they are guarding him. They are afraid that he might run away and leave them alone on the dead streets. They remind us unceasingly that they reported themselves to us voluntarily.

"Don't forget, policemen; tell the Germans that."

Thus pass Saturday and Sunday. Every night I bring food for my aunt, and I find out from her that Janek is doing the same thing. I try not to talk to her about her future fate. I still don't know what became of my parents. I live as in a delirium.

Monday. I decide to act. I telephone the Magister, and I arrange to meet him at our old meeting place, near the fencing. When we meet, he doesn't express any sympathy and says only that in the face of terrible misfortune words have no value. In any case, I don't even hear what he says. I have to find out something else. I have to drink the cup of sorrow to the last drop. So I ask, "Did you find a place for Aluśka?"

"Yes," he replies. "My childless sister wanted to raise her. Actually, I shouldn't be telling you this."

I feel my legs giving out under me. The thought flies through my head: murderer, murderer. I almost lose consciousness momentarily; then we say good-bye. What more is there to say? Ah, there is something else.

"Will you please come tomorrow at five?" I ask. "I would like to give you a suitcase."

At this moment Satan is very likely laughing at me. Tomorrow? Again tomorrow? And who knows what will happen tomorrow? Will I always put everything off for later?

Tuesday, August 25

In the morning I leave my summer coat with Zygmunt Wolfowicz. When I return an hour later, it appears that the entire apartment has been wrecked and pillaged. The ghetto is still surrounded by Polish rabble. The Poles jump over the fence, break down doors with axes, and rob whatever they can. At times the looters come across murdered Jews, but what does it matter? They argue and fight among the not-yet-cold bodies; one tears out of the hands of the other a pillow or a suit of clothes. And the Jewish corpse? Like a corpse, it lies quietly, does not speak, does not bother anyone; it will not even appear to anyone in their sleep. After all, the Poles have a clear conscience. Surely they justify themselves in their own minds: "We didn't kill them, and in any case, if we don't take it, the Germans will."[125]

I am not sorry about the coat, and I am not sorry about the money that it cost. Still, without a coat I will not be able to show myself in the Polish neighborhood, where you have to appear decently dressed in order not to attract attention. The loss of a coat, in certain circumstances, may be the equivalent of a death sentence. But to have the energy to look for a coat in someone else's home, that kind of energy I don't have.

After meeting Grynhorn in the street, I go to his apartment, and we find there a Pole who has already packed a bag of the most valuable things. He is angry and surprised. What right does Grynhorn have to disturb him? But having no way out, he leaves the bag and runs away. Wolfowicz had no luck. The Germans took his family away; then the Poles took all of his property. Is he saying this? Is this from his own lips?

"You wait! I will live to see the end of you, bandits. Yes, I will see it as I will see the end of the Germans!"

He is yelling at those hyenas, jackals, waiting patiently all day in order to rob even the corpses. Finally Wolfowicz walks away, but the mob is dissatisfied. A Jew has abused them, told them "a falsehood" to their faces; it is necessary to find an earthly justice that would punish him.

Just then two German soldiers approach; one of them even understands Polish. The mob, indignant over the impudence, turns to them for justice. A Jew dares to say that he will live to see the end of the Germans, or their end, the end of such decent people.

"Hand over this Jew!"

I approach just then. Everyone is pointing their hands at me.

"That's the one who said it!"

The soldier takes out his pistol.

"Did you say it, or didn't you?"

My solemn oath that someone else said that doesn't help. The German does not believe me at all, his eyes glint with malice, he will shoot me momentarily. . . .

Just then some poor woman speaks out. This is not the one; the other one did not have glasses and was taller. Others contradict her. The soldier does not shoot. Maybe he believes, or maybe he doesn't want to scare away with a premature killing of a policeman other policemen whose services are still needed. He lets me live, and I, not having anything else to do here, walk away as quickly as I can. I don't know whether to thank God or that old woman who saved me or whether to curse those who knowingly wanted to have me killed.

The Magister appears at the appointed hour. I ask him to come again in two hours so that I can give him a suitcase. Our conversation does not last longer than ten minutes, but it is long enough for my aunt's room to be completely stripped by Poles.

I prepare two suitcases in my room. In one I pack expensive and decent things so that I can dress myself elegantly; in the other, practical items necessary for life in camp. For, indeed, later I must go to a camp.

Two hours pass and the Magister comes. Beyond the fence that divides the ghetto from the Polish neighborhood, I see Głaskowa, my former housekeeper, wife of the ticket seller from the movie house. I ask her to carry the suitcase and give it to the Magister. I promise her one hundred złoty for this. Głaskowa takes the suitcase and is about to deliver it when the Poles gathered at the fence realize that this is not an act of robbery, but goods taken by agreement with the rightful owner, a Jew. They attack her. Głaskowa escapes to the ghetto. I take the suitcase away, and I arrange to meet with the Magister tomorrow.

In the evening I carry to the police station a suitcase with things for camp. Then I go to Janek's apartment to ask his help with the second suitcase. I am afraid that my apartment will also be robbed.

I have not seen Janek since the day of the *Aktion*. I did not search for him particularly, he did not seek me, and so several days passed. I knew that he was alive because he brought food daily to my aunt, as I did. I found him in the apartment, carefully shaved, elegantly dressed, and clearly getting himself ready for a journey. He put into a briefcase a shirt, pajamas, a hand towel, and some toilet articles.

"What happened?" I asked, surprised at these preparations.

"Listen, Calek," he replied, "let me reveal a secret to you. Our commandant, Kronenberg, and his deputy, Ehrlich, and several other policemen and their wives hired a covered truck. They intend to drive to the Częstochowa ghetto. I want to ride with them."

"Janek, won't there be the same *Aktion* in Częstochowa?"

"You're foolish. Ninety percent of the people there work in shops; there are factories producing weapons for the Germans. There we will be safe."

"Janek, what shall I do? When Kronenberg leaves, the Germans will kill all the policemen."

"You know what," my brother-in-law sympathizes with me, "come with me. Maybe they will take you, too."

After this conversation I didn't have a shadow of a doubt what had to be done. Escape from the ghetto! I was now happy that the Magister hadn't taken my suitcase because in that case I wouldn't have had anything to wear. I put on my elegant suit, and since I didn't have a coat, I grabbed my light overcoat and ran to the police station.

I looked over the entire apartment before leaving. I knew that everything would be stolen, but I did not regret it. I repeated to myself that it was because I stayed and watched over my things and sat like a fool in Otwock that I lost my wife and child. I didn't want to be that foolish again. I had to save myself. After all, I did not abandon my wife like a coward only to be killed several days later.

I did not find anyone at the police station except those who were planning their escape. After a few minutes the policeman Sztajnhard appeared, guessed quickly what the plans of those assembled were, and began to whine like a little child that they should take him along.

My appearance came at an awkward moment for Deputy Commander Ehrlich, and he wanted to send me on a tour of duty. I refused emphatically and argued that I was assigned to the other side of town and that I had already been there the entire day. Leave me alone. Leaning against a tree, I waited for developments. The night was warm and humid. I remember how heavy the coat felt. People wandered around in the dark like ghosts.

After midnight I found out that Kronenberg had not agreed to take me along; he was enraged and refused to take Janek as well. My brother-in-law informed me of all this, gave me the key to his apartment, where my father's belongings were kept, and said to me, "Good-bye. I can't take you with me."

He went away and I remained alone. What to do? Sztajnhard continued to whine, begging to be taken. I felt a deep repugnance. I could never lower myself like that! I decided to approach Ehrlich personally and apologize to him. He did not accept it and with a mocking tone said that I could talk about this in front of everyone. So I asked him right away if they were ready to leave.

"Yes," Ehrlich confirmed without hesitating, "we are leaving momentarily."

"Without taking into consideration that I asked you," I continued, "you will not take me? You will drive over my corpse?"

"Yes," Ehrlich repeated, "we are leaving right away. Without you!"

"Are you saying to me," I said loudly now, "that for you the end justifies the means?"

Wham! In that moment I received a hard slap to my face. I ran away. There was such ringing in my head that I couldn't concentrate my thoughts. I had only one idée fixe: I had to run away from the ghetto that night because tomorrow I would be shot there.

My eyeglasses were broken and I had to go to my home on Podmiejska Street for another pair. On the way, I stopped at my father's apartment. I told my aunt Góralska that Janek had run away, that Kronenberg might run away at any moment, and that because I too had to escape, she could not count on me anymore.

I left my aunt and ran quickly on Podmiejska Street. A carriage drove by, and I saw in it the commandant of the Otwock gendarmes, Schlicht. I hid quickly in the shadows so he wouldn't see me. It didn't even cross my mind that this was an excellent time for revenge. I could have told Schlicht that if he went to the police station, he would find the whole group there loading in the car.

I couldn't find another pair of glasses at home, and I finally discovered that I had them on me in my jacket pocket. I left the house and wandered aimlessly, not knowing where to go, who would receive me, and who would want to help. I suddenly reminded myself what Franciszek Stańczak, an office manager from the gymnasium, had told my father. Already before the *Aktion* he had said that he would gladly help my father and hide him in the school building, which was empty in the summertime. I thought I would go there, spend the night, and in the morning send Franciszek to the Magister. I knocked at Stańczak's door once, twice. Finally, Franciszek opened it.

"What has happened, Mr. Perechodnik?"

Haltingly, I explained what had taken place and asked for his hospitality for one day. In exchange I offered him three hundred złoty. I put the money right on the table. Franciszek did not want to accept it. He said he was afraid and didn't want to do it. Finally, he agreed to keep me for one day, but he wanted both money and a pair of pants. Was he crazy? Where would I get a pair of pants for him?

I continued to ask, but nothing helped. He wanted both money and pants, and . . . knew very well why. Not having a way out, I gave Franciszek the key to my brother-in-law's apartment and told him to go there in the morning and take out of the suitcase a pair of pants. Only then did Franciszek agree. I also asked him if he would take a letter tomorrow to the Magister and also if he would find out whether Kronenberg had got away.

After this long haggling Franciszek led me to the gymnasium garret, and I fell asleep right away. This was the first night that I felt secure, just as in former days. The dawn woke me. I got up and through a small window I could see the dead ghetto. The first thing I saw was the entire Stańczak family dragging heavy suitcases from my brother-in-law's apartment. Resignedly, I just shrugged my shoulders. I understood the game over the pair of pants, but it was too late. He stole everything, the devil take him.

I was swept only momentarily by a flame of revolt when I saw my leather bag, which contained all the photographs of my wife and daughter.

The morning passed slowly. At ten, Franciszek appeared with breakfast for me.

"Unfortunately," he declared with a hypocritical smile, "your brother-in-law's apartment had been robbed before I arrived, but I know who took the things, and maybe I can get something back."

I listened to all this in silence and did not betray even with a single word that I had seen him and his entire family carrying my suitcases. I only asked if he had not "accidentally" taken my wife's bag with the photographs. It turned out that he had taken the photographs and would save them for me. He was also at the Magister's, who promised that he would come during the lunch break. There was nothing left for me to do but thank him for all his concerns.

Franciszek also told me that he had seen my brother-in-law Janek and that Kronenberg had not left. I didn't understand any of this. Why didn't he go to Częstochowa? Why did Janek allow the robbery at my apartment? I couldn't collect my thoughts. I had only one idea in my mind: Will the Magister come? And even if he does, is he in a position to help a Jew?

Thinking about all this, I took a walk around the school, where I had spent eight years. The benches were in the same places. I tried to remember who had sat where, what the teachers had looked like at the blackboards. It's hard for me to believe that I was once a person equal to others, that I had had the right to live, play tricks on teachers, play with my friends. . . . And now? Now I trembled at my own shadow, hid like an animal, and that at my own expense. I had attended the gymnasium for so many years, received a diploma that had cost eight thousand złoty. And today, for a twenty-four-hour stay in the garret, I had paid the equivalent of three hundred thousand złoty. I didn't know whether to laugh or cry.

I looked around some more and saw the names of my schoolmates cut out with scissors on the desks. It always amused me, remembering that *nomina stultorum scribuntur ubique loquorum.*[126] Now I see that nothing will remain of Jews, except for names carved somewhere.

The Magister came in the afternoon and went upstairs to see me. It turned out that he had already bought a ticket for me to Warsaw. He brought me a typical hat with a feather and advised me to leave for Lublin and join the partisans who were prowling about in that area. He asked if I had any more money and added that if I wanted to sell my things, he would send to wherever I was anything that I would need. Having said that, he left.

I was undecided. It's easy to advise a Jew to remove his glasses, go to Lublin, and join the partisans. How does one get there? And where does one find partisans?

The day was coming to a close, and I still didn't know what to do. Finally I decided to return to the ghetto and see what had happened.

Franciszek was very glad to be getting rid of me. I left him my new hat, which the Magister had brought me. The first person I met in the ghetto was my brother-in-law Janek. He told me that no one had run away to Częstochowa. Everybody was frightened of gendarme Schlicht, who had been driving around the ghetto that night in the carriage.

It also appeared that Kronenberg had understood my words as a promise to denounce the escape to the Germans. Then I found out that Janek also had not intended to escape. When he bid me good-bye and said that he was leaving, it meant that he was simply going to sleep, which he finally did. When he got up in the morning, he saw Franciszek from afar carrying my things. He didn't interfere because he thought this was happening at my request.

This is a real tower of Babel. People's thoughts and expressions get all mixed up, and from this there follows a whole chain of misfortunes. I didn't understand Janek, Ehrlich did not understand me, and my apartment on Podmiejska was robbed. My brother-in-law's apartment was robbed by Franciszek as well. It occurred to me that this was the equivalent of a sentence of death on my parents. What will they live on now?

It is likely that at that moment I stopped believing in God; I stopped believing in a historical justice. What could the little Jewish children have been guilty of that they died in such a vile way? Now I ask myself if I was not guilty of something and whether I did not pull down on myself that tower of Babel.

I was indeed guilty, although no one knows about it. I did not tell anyone, and no one in the world can betray me. If this diary is to be honest, I must write about it. On the day of the *Aktion,* my sister gave me for her husband, Janek, several trinkets, and among these were a gold watch and fifteen hundred złoty. I had intended to give him everything right away, but as it happened, I did not see him for several days.

When I finally met with Janek, he surprised me with the news of the planned escape to Częstochowa. I had no money on me other than what my sister had given me. All the currency Anka took with her to Treblinka. It should be understood that I didn't want to take from her even a few złoty. Like all policemen, I wanted to leave her everything. Of course, I could have easily secured that fifteen hundred złoty, even ten times that. It would have sufficed to bend down and search the pockets of the dead, which I was never willing to do, not then and not later.

When Janek surprised me with his plans to escape to Częstochowa, influenced by something inside me, I handed him various trinkets, including the gold watch. But I didn't tell him about the money. I wanted to save myself, and I simply appropriated it. Now I decided to return it without telling Janek that I was giving it to him. Truthfully speaking, money has been my undoing. If I hadn't had it, if I hadn't thought about escape to Częstochowa, then I wouldn't have gone to Franciszek. I have paid a hundredfold for my deed, not to mention that to this day I am tormented by pangs of conscience.

After all that I found out from Janek, I realized that I had to explain the entire misunderstanding to Kronenberg. Whether he believed me or not, it was enough to conclude this whole problem.

With this ended the first stage of my stay at the desolate ghetto following the *Aktion*. It lasted over a week. I lived in lethargy for those seven days, not understanding the misfortune that had befallen me. The only feeling that I recognized was a panicky fear of death. After a while I realized that I would never see my wife. By then we had received information about how executions were conducted at Treblinka.

I became completely apathetic. I did not watch over my apartment on Podmiejska, and it was completely robbed. I lived in the building of the Judenrat, in a room that another policeman, a lawyer by the name of

Sołowiejczyk, had vacated. I stopped thinking about saving myself, seeing that it was an impossibility.

A boat of destiny rocked me over the rough waves. Where to? In which direction? No one knows. I did not have the energy to take the rudder in my own hand. For that matter, no Jew could guide his own fate. A rapid current and a strong wind pushed all Jews into one direction: to Treblinka. At best, death awaited us at the hands of the gendarmes.

For days on end I lay senseless on my bed; at night I went on duty at the police station.

I will now try to describe what was happening at the other ghettos. The *Aktion* in Falenica[127] took place on Thursday, August 20. For a change, the Germans started it not at seven in the morning but at three at night, when it was still dark. That same day there was an *Aktion* in Rembertow, where they gathered up the Jewish population and chased them like cattle on foot to Falenica. Here all of them were loaded into cattle cars. Many women, children, and the weak men were shot on the way when they couldn't keep up. I often imagine how it must have been; then I always think that those killed by bullets then and there were the lucky ones.[128]

On the other hand, what did the Germans do with the Jewish police? Well, it's the way of the world. After finishing the *Aktion*, and after the policemen had loaded up the people into the cattle cars, they took the same policemen and loaded them up as well. The policemen had the sad honor of having the Germans do the loading with their own hands.

Only those remained alive who happened to be on a tour of duty at border barriers—I don't know what happened to them later. I only know that they weren't the only ones who survived. In Falenica there is to this day a sawmill belonging to Najwert.[129] It is managed in receivership by a German board. The Jewish laborers work there with the owner in charge. These workers were not taken—on the contrary, the group was enlarged with Jews selected at the *Umschlagplatz*.[130]

Look, Jews, how the Germans honor workers, Jewish craftsmen. Be calm, Najwert! Be calm, workers at the sawmill! Nothing bad will happen to you at the hands of the Germans. Work and be assured you will live.

That same day there was a repeat of the *Aktion* in our town. Almost all of the remaining Jews who were in hiding reported themselves, enough so that several hundred people were sent from Otwock on foot, under the escort of the Polish police; they were loaded on cars going to Falenica. Mothers went out with the Otwock transport, the children, the following day on the Falenica transport, the fathers two days later on the Mińsk transport. What was the difference? All the Jews were assigned a common rendezvous, though not in this world: *Treblinki, dort wo jeder Id hot sajn ort*.[131] These are the words of the newest Jewish song.

On Friday, August 21, there was an *Aktion* in Mińsk Mazowiecki.[132] Yes, in that Mińsk where there were so many workshops, where most of the Jews worked, where there was such a good *Kreishauptmann*. He was known among the Jews in all of Poland; for a petty several hundred złoty he would give a pass for two people to travel by train to the Generalgouvernement. Thanks to this pass many a Jew eluded the Warsaw *Aktion*.

I remember my conversation with Willendorf some three weeks before the Mińsk *Aktion*.

"Abram," I asked, "is there any opportunity for rescue for the ordinary Jews in the event of an *Aktion*?"

"Certainly, Calek," he answered unhesitatingly. "Those who have money should look into getting a pass in Mińsk. When the *Aktion* starts in Otwock, they'll be able to leave the ghetto and take the train to Mińsk. I believe that the Jewish population there will be safe because they have a good *Kreishauptmann*."[133]

How naively ring the arguments of Willendorf in my ears today! And yet that was how the majority of "wise" Jews spoke and thought. Those who provided themselves with passes and were able to escape to Mińsk were deported anyway, just a few days later. On the other hand, there were those who were not able to run away the day of the Otwock *Aktion* and tried to save themselves by showing the Germans their passes. The Germans honored them and did not chase those fortunate Jews, the holders of those passes, into transports; they just simply, and on the spot . . . shot them.

That same week there were many more roundups in different towns of the Generalgouvernement, and then they halted. My naive reader may ask whether this was an accident. Well, not really. With the Germans there are no accidents. Throughout the first week of the *Aktion*, the knowledge that neither the Judenrat nor the police nor the workshops were to be protected did not reach other towns. Their population calmly awaited the *Aktion*, thinking what the residents of Otwock thought before they were deported. That week news of the course of deportations made its way from town to town, together with the Ukrainians. It should be understood that this was a bit too late to draw conclusions. Later on, when it was known in the entire Generalgouvernement that entire towns

BEKANNTMACHUNG

BÜRGERMEISTER
Der Stadt OTWOCK

Ich bringe zur öffentlichen Kenntnis und genauer Beachtung die nachstehende Anordnung des Herrn Kreishauptmanns des Kreises Warschau-Land vom 9.d.M.:

1) Das Stadtgebiet südwärts der Bahnlinie, das von der Bahn, Narutowiczstr., von der Gemeindegrenze Karczew, von der Batorystr., der Matejkistr., der Androllstr., der Teil zwischen der Matejki- und Holzeitstrasse) und der Heizeitr. umgrenzt wird, muss spätestens bis zum 20. Oktober 1940 von Juden geräumt werden.

2) Das südlichste "Kiny", das von der Gemeindegrenze Karczew (der Gemeindegrenze Karczew, der Kulturabteilung und der Wojskastrasse (der Teil zwischen dem Kleinbahngleise und der Batorystrasse) umgrenzt wird, muss spätestens bis zum 1. November 1940 von Juden geräumt werden.

Die aus den vorgenannten Gebieten auszusiedelnden Juden dürfen nur in das zukünftige Ghetto-Gebiet (die Altstadt) umsiedeln.

Ich warne, dass diejenigen, welche dieser Anordnung in der festgesetzten Frist nicht nachkommen, streng bestraft werden.

Der BÜRGERMEISTER
gez. **JAN GADOMSKI**

Obwieszczenie

BURMISTRZ
miasta OTWOCKA

Podaję do wiadomości i ścisłego wykonania zarządzenie Pana Kreishauptmanna pow. Warszawskiego z dnia 9 b.m.:

1) Dzielnica miasta leżąca na południe od toru kolejowego, w granicach: Tor kolejowy, ul. Narutowicza, granica gminy Karczew, ul. Batorego, ul. Matejki, ul. Androllego (od Matejki do Heizeit) ul. Heizeit winna być z ludności żydowskiej oczyszczona do dn. 20 b.m. październik.

2) Dzielnica miasta "Kiny" w granicach: Gmina Karczew, Gmina Falenica, Tor kolejowy winna być oczyszczona od żydów w terminie zakreślonym do dnia 1 listopada r.b.

Zamieszkujący te wyżej wymienionych terenach żydzi winni się przenieść na teren Starego Miasta (przyszłe ghetto).

Ostrzegam że winni niezachowania powyższego zarządzenia w ścisłe określonym terminie, będą surowo karani.

(-) **JAN GADOMSKI**

Bekanntmachung

Hiermit gebe ich die Verordnung des Herrn Kreishauptmanns Warschau-Land vom 20 September 1940 zur Kenntnis und verlange genaue, gewissenhafte Ausführung der obigen Verordnung der genauen Durchführung.

1) Der Stadtteil von Otwock und zwar ein Teil von Śródborów und Sopliców Stór südlich von der Strasse Narutowicza, gelegen zwischen der Bahn, der Gemeindegrenze Karczew, von der Batorystr. und zwischen der Grenze der Gemeinde Karczew, muss in 8 Tagen von Juden geräumt werden.

Die, in diesem Stadtteil wohnenden Juden, müssen in obenbestimmten Termin ihre Wohnungen verlassen und zwar die Stadt Otwock (alte Stadt) umsiedeln.

Dieser Stadtteil befindet sich östlich-zwischen dem Eisenbahngleise, südlich-zwischen der Strasse Narutowicza (Vom der Krajowa), bis nach Śródborów zwischen der Heizeitr. und dem Kleinbahngleise und nördlich zwischen der Grenze mit Falenica (Świder).

Der nicht übereilende Termin des obigen 8 Wochen so bald Oktober u.l. nicht nach der obigen Verordnung richt erfüllt wird, streng bestraft.

Gesetzliche durch den Herrn Kreishauptmann
Dr. RUPPRECHT

BÜRGERMEISTER
(-) **Jan Gadomski**

OBWIESZCZENIE

Podaję do wiadomości oraz ścisłego i terminowego wykonania zarządzenia Pana Kreishauptmanna pow. Warszawskiego z dnia 20 września r. b.

1. Dzielnica miasta Otwocka, mianowicie część Śródborowa i Soplicowa, strona południowo-wschodnia od ulicy Narutowicza położona wewnątrz granic: od strony wschodniej – tor kolejowy, od strony południowej – granica gminy Karczew, zachodniej – ulica Batorego i granica gminy Karczew, winny być w ciągu 8-miu dni przez żydów oczyszczona.

Żydzi zamieszkujący tym terenie zajęci winni w wyżej oznaczonym terminie przenieść się na teren miasta Otwocka (stare miasto), położony w granicach: od strony wschodniej – tor kolei szerokotorowej, od strony południowej – ulice Batorowa i Granica od Świdra, od strony zachodniej – tor kolejki wąskotorowej i od strony północnej granica z gminą Falenica (Świder).

Nieprzekraczalny termin wykonania powyższego – 8 tygodnie i do dnia 10 października r.b.

Winni niewykonania niniejszego zarządzenia podlegać karze.

BURMISTRZ
(-) **Jan Gadomski**

Bekanntmachung

Hiermit gebe ich die Verordnung des Herrn Kreishauptmannes Warschau-Land vom 19. September 1940 zur Kenntnis und verlange genaue, durch Termin bestimmte Durchführung der obigen Verordnung.

1) Der Aufenthalt in Kreise Warschau-Land ist nur für den Juden erlaubt

a) welche mindestens sechs Monate im Kreise-Warschau-Land wohnhaft sind.

b) welche eine spezielle Bewilligung vom Herrn Kreishauptmann für den ständigen Aufenthalt im Kreise Warschau-Land besitzen.

2) Jede Bewilligung, die vom Herrn Kreishauptmann für einen zeitweiligen Aufenthalt in Otwock gegeben wurde, ist nun ungültig.

Dasselbe betrifft die Juden, die auf Grund der ärztlichen Zeugnisse den Aufenthalt zwecks Kuration erhielten.

3) Juden, welchen nach dem obigen (Punkt 1 und 2) der Aufenthalt im Kreise Warschau-Land verboten ist, müssen ihren Wohnsitz im Kreise Warschau-Land während zwei Wochen verlassen.

Diejenigen Juden, welche sich nach der obigen Verordnung nicht richten, stehen zur Verfügung des Herrn Kreishauptmann und werden mit dahin. G-Ständen bestraft und in ein Konzentrationslager verbracht.

4) Neue Anträge, die für die Bewilligung eines ständigen oder zeitweiligen Aufenthalt bitten, werden nicht in Betracht genommen, so wie auch die Anträge die den Ort und Wohnungswechsel betreffen.

Deshalb ist jedes Einsenden der Anträge zwecklos.

Für die Ablehnung wird eine Gebühr in Höhe von 10.000 Zloty erhoben.

5) Genehmigungen anderer Dienststellen, welche den Juden im Kreise Warschau-Land den Wohnort zuweisen, sind nur dann gültig, wenn die Erlaubnis des Herrn Kreishauptmann vorliegt.

Gesetzlichen durch Herrn Kreishauptmann

BÜRGERMEISTER
Dr. RUPPRECHT
(-) **Jan Gadomski**

Obwieszczenie

Podaję do wiadomości oraz ścisłego i terminowego wykonania zarządzenie Pana Kreishauptmanna pow. Warszawskiego z dn. 19 września r. b.

1) Pobyt w powiecie warszawskim jest dozwolony TYLKO dla żydów

a) którzy co najmniej od 6-ciu miesięcy zamieszkują w powiecie warszawskim.

b) którzy posiadają SPECJALNE pisemne zezwolenie Pana Kreishauptmanna na STAŁY pobyt w pow. warszawskim.

2) Wszelkie zezwolenia wydane przez Pana Kreishauptmanna na tymczasowy pobyt w Otwocku są nieważne. Dotyczy to również i tych żydów, którzy na podstawie świadectwa lekarskiego otrzymali zezwolenie na pobyt w celu kuracyjnym.

3) Żydzi, którym w-/dług powyższego (p. 1 i 2) pobyt w powiecie warszawskim jest wzbroniony, winni opuścić ten teren w przeciągu dwóch tygodni.

Winni niewykonania (ej) zarządzenia zostaną zaaresztowani i oddani do dyspozycji p. Kreishauptmanna, przyczym zostaną oni ukarani wysokimi grzywnami pieniężnymi i odesłani do obozów koncentracyjnych.

4) Nowe podania o zezwolenie na osiedlenie się w powiecie warszawskim nie będą tymczasowo nie będą uwzględniane, nie będą również uwzględniane one podania o zmianę miejsca zamieszkania w obrębie powiatu warszawskiego, dlatego też wnoszenie podań jest bezcelowe.

Wraz z odmowną decyzją pobierana będzie opłata do wysokości 10.000 zł.

5) Zarządzenia innych władz, wyznaczające żydom miejsce zamieszkania w obrębie powiatu warszawskiego, są ważne tylko wtedy, gdy zostają na nich zatwierdzone i za zezwoleniem Pana Kreishauptmanna.

podpisał Kreishauptmann
(-) Dr. RUPPRECHT

BURMISTRZ
(-) **Jan Gadomski**

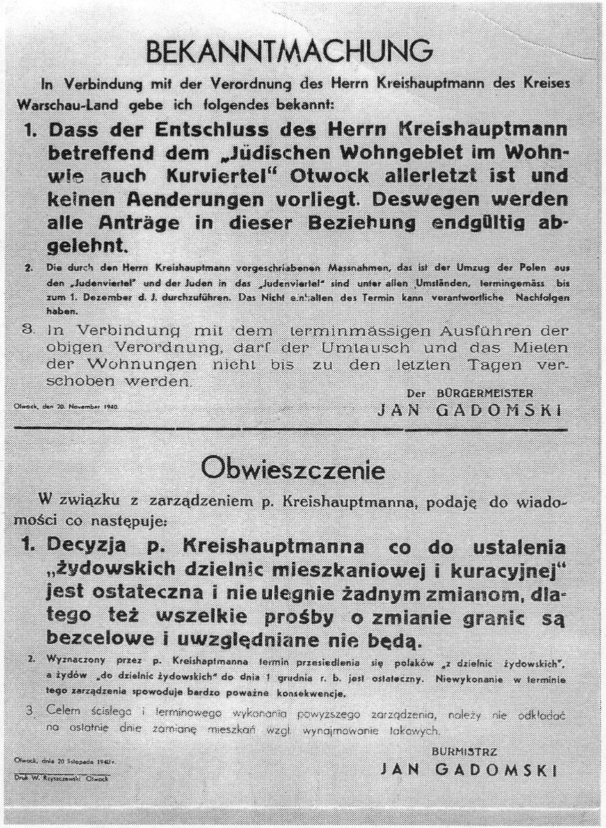

BEKANNTMACHUNG

In Verbindung mit der Verordnung des Herrn Kreishauptmann des Kreises Warschau-Land gebe ich folgendes bekannt:

1. **Dass der Entschluss des Herrn Kreishauptmann betreffend dem „Jüdischen Wohngebiet im Wohn- wie auch Kurviertel" Otwock allerletzt ist und keinen Aenderungen vorliegt. Deswegen werden alle Anträge in dieser Beziehung endgültig abgelehnt.**

2. Die durch den Herrn Kreishauptmann vorgeschriebenen Massnahmen, das ist der Umzug der Polen aus den „Judenviertel" und der Juden in das „Judenviertel" sind unter allen Umständen, termingemäss bis zum 1. Dezember d.J. durchzuführen. Das Nicht einhalten des Termin kann verantwortliche Nachfolgen haben.

3. In Verbindung mit dem terminmässigen Ausführen der obigen Verordnung, darf der Umtausch und das Mieten der Wohnungen nicht bis zu den letzten Tagen verschoben werden.

Der BÜRGERMEISTER
JAN GADOMSKI

Otwock, den 20. November 1940.

Obwieszczenie

W związku z zarządzeniem p. Kreishauptmanna, podaje do wiadomości co następuje:

1. **Decyzja p. Kreishauptmanna co do ustalenia „żydowskich dzielnic mieszkaniowej i kuracyjnej" jest ostateczna i nie ulegnie żadnym zmianom, dlatego też wszelkie prośby o zmianie granic są bezcelowe i uwzględniane nie będą.**

2. Wyznaczony przez p. Kreishauptmanna termin przesiedlenia się polaków „z dzielnic żydowskich", a żydów „do dzielnic żydowskich" do dnia 1 grudnia r.b. jest ostateczny. Niewykonanie w terminie tego zarządzenia spowoduje bardzo poważne konsekwencje.

3. Celem ścisłego i terminowego wykonania powyższego zarządzenia, należy nie odkładać na ostatnie dnie zamiane mieszkań wzgl wynajmowanie lokowych.

BURMISTRZ
JAN GADOMSKI

Otwock, dnia 20 listopada 1940.

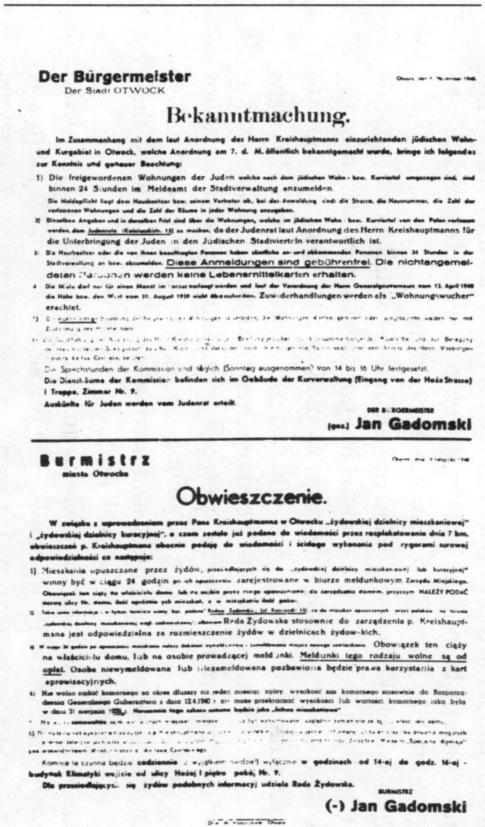

Der Bürgermeister
Der Stadt OTWOCK

B-kanntmachung.

In Zusammenhang mit dem laut Anordnung der Herrn Kreishauptmanns sinngetätigten jüdischen Wohn- und Kurgebiet in Otwock, welche Anordnung am 7. d. M. öffentlich bekanntgemacht wurde, bringe ich folgendes zur Kenntnis und genauer Beachtung:

1) Die freigewordenen Wohnungen der Juden werden nach den jüdischen Wohnbaren, baw. Kurviertel umgezogen und, auf Zeiten 3 Stunden im Halten mit der Stadtverwaltung anzumelden.

2) Die Mitteglied ist laut dem Ausweisung, seinen Vertreter ab, bei der Anmeldung nach die Dauer, die Neumannten, die Zahl der vollemen Wohnungen und die Zahl der Räume in jeder Wohnung anzugeben.

Jan Gadomski

[second notice heavily faded — portions illegible]

(-) Jan Gadomski

Proclamations in the name of the German authorities, signed by Mayor Jan Gadomski of Otwock: the first announcing the "cleansing" of certain areas of Jewish inhabitants and preparations for placing them in the ghetto; the second announcing that no appeals to resettling are possible had disappeared into Treblinka, the Germans temporarily stopped conducting the *Aktion*. They allowed new axioms to fix themselves in the Jewish brains—as, for example, that Częstochowa *kommt nicht in betracht* because everyone there works in arms factories. In a word, a fortunate town! The same thing applies to Kraków. After all, they are not going to murder Jews before the eyes of the governor and representatives of foreign countries. Oh no! That's quite impossible.

Equally secure is Kołbiel as well as Sobin. In these small localities, situated not far from Otwock, the ghettos are not even fenced in. Since the Jews live there together with Poles, they would first have to create a ghetto if they wanted to deport Jews. Yes, one can stay there securely. This conviction was strengthened by the fact that when the Otwock police station acquired a significant number of arrestees,[134] the Germans did not shoot them but sent them in trucks to Kołbiel. Jews were transported to Kołbiel from other still smaller localities and were allowed to take along their personal possessions. Lucky Kołbiel! And why not Wołomin?

After all, the Warsaw *Kreishauptmann* arrived in Otwock and handed a pass for Wołomin to Dr. Pemperow,[135] the physician whom the Germans installed in the Karczew camp. Apparently, there was a lack of surgeons in that ghetto. If the Germans wanted to deport Jews, the *Kreishauptmann* would not care about the state of health of the inhabitants. Is it not true?

What did the Germans really want to achieve? That's easy: a temporary quieting of the ghettos, which were left for later, in order to attract throngs of Jews hiding in various holes. These towns played the role of "flypaper."

I knew Jews who saved themselves in five towns. They were able to hide in time, even to jump out of cattle cars several times, and yet finally they made it to Treblinka. The behavior of the Germans is now clear to me, but then few rarely understood and realized that a sentence without appeal was pronounced on all.

Many wealthy Jews from Otwock saved themselves on the day of the *Aktion* by hiding in cellars. Many had relations or sons as policemen who provided them with food the first day. Later, however, they all began to ask themselves what to do next. That same question was asked by the policemen at Otwock. They wondered whether to remain in the ghetto and go to camp later or whether to run away. And if to run, then where and when?

During the five-week stay in Otwock we were never sure of the day or the hour. Everyone estimated his chances depending on level of energy, financial possibilities, and, particularly, whether he saved his family or not. I emphasize that conclusions were drawn dependent on level of energy, not intelligence. For the time had come when all of us proved to be the same fools.

How many close relatives were saved? Seventy-five percent of the wives were lost on the first day of the *Aktion*. Maybe 10 percent of those could have saved themselves. I think of such women as my wife, of good appearance, elegant in manners and dress, with financial means and Polish friends. Only such could pass for Poles in Polish neighborhoods. Others would have to perish.

The majority of those who lost their wives lost their energy and the will to live. They didn't have the courage to kill themselves. They existed rather than lived,* not caring about anything; they surrendered passively to their fate. There were others, not many, to be sure, who fairly quickly forgot the loss of their wives. With an unshaken faith they looked to the future, prepared themselves to go to camp, and in the meantime they "made money," ate, drank, and did not deny themselves anything. These were, on the whole, people from the lower social classes. It is worth noting that the Jewish police had in its ranks the same number of lecturers, physicians, and engineers as it did illiterates.

It is also necessary to tell about those whose wives were able to save themselves. The policemen from the circle of the merchants saved their wives during the *Aktion* because they knew that nobody would be paying attention to them close to the selection. One of these, cabinetmaker Kuc, a foolish enough man, did the best trick. On the day of the *Aktion* he kept watch over the border barrier at Wawerska Street, and there, as if it were the most natural thing in the world, he stationed his wife and son in the police booth. The Ukrainians walked by, the SS walked by, and even though they saw a woman with a child, they did not order her to fall into line. So tell me, is it necessary to be an educated man, or is it better to simply have an ounce of luck?

The policemen who sold their things in the first two weeks also sold other people's possessions, dug up money buried by others, and one nice day they just disappeared from the Otwock horizon. Some of them ran away to Kołbiel, some to Kosów. That was a town near Treblinka where the Rykner family, as well as other people from Otwock who worked in Treblinka I, lived.

---

*The Polish expression may be more closely translated as "The forces of life kept them going."

The well-to-do policemen, those from better circles, decided to run away with their families to Częstochowa or to Kraków. For a colossal price, literally hundreds of thousands of złoty, they got from German businesses trucks that took them to those towns. That's how Rynaldo escaped, one of the most talented police swindlers, but also one who saved hundreds of people from the *Aktion* in Warsaw. He was able to do this because he displayed a pass made out to the field gendarmes. Making use of it, he took Jews out of Warsaw under the pretext of different investigations. That's how he saved, for example, the daughter of Sławin, whom he represented to the gendarmes as one accused of *Rassenszande*.[136] Rynaldo was a genius of a certain genre, certainly a genius in time of war.

Like Rynaldo, the family of Ehrlich's brother and the families of Cwertner, Klajner, Holcman, and Rubin escaped. Some of them had, as I saw for myself, train passes to Kraków that were sold for a lot of money by the Warsaw *Kreishauptmann*. For the most part, though, they escaped using trucks. It happened that in the evening someone full of hope for a safe life in a new place got into a car, and in the morning— without money or his things—was content if he could get back to his hiding place in Otwock. The truck drivers stationed *Volksdeutsche* on the road to stop the vehicles, rob the Jews, and throw them straight out into the open field.

Probably, had my wife saved herself, I would have also run away to Częstochowa. And maybe I would have located myself in a Polish neighborhood. There was a small group of policemen who, together with their wives, chose the proper, and really the only, way to safety. They prepared papers for themselves, collected all their money, and took up residence in a Polish neighborhood. It's true they were educated people, of good Aryan appearance, and also possessed other possibilities.

Where are you, Drs. Feldhof, Kadyszyn, Tinder, Zajnkram? Are you still alive? I want to believe that you succeeded, that you will survive the war. But why, Tinder and Zajnkram, did you send your mothers-in-law to Częstochowa, together with other family members? Did you do it involuntarily, or did you want to get rid of an additional burden? . . . I know you; that was the result of indecisiveness, uncertainty, which will still turn out for the best. You did it in good faith. May God forgive you and help you.

At that time there was no policeman who could have escaped from the ghetto and found a hiding place* in the Polish neighborhood. The ma-

---

Zamelinował, from the word *melina*, was a slang word used by the underworld to connote hiding from police. It is of Hebrew origin.

jority of Poles didn't even want to hear about it, and those who were ready to receive—these were not known. About ten policemen, craftsmen, cabinetmakers, and tailors reported to the Rembertow gendarmerie to be sent out to work.[137] They argued that there was no safer place from the jaws of the lion. Because the number of needed workers was limited, they argued about who would go. And so from day to day the number of policemen dwindled. Their places were taken by other young men, mostly brothers or relatives of those who had run away. They got the armbands from them and started work. The commandant of the Jewish police, Kronenberg, did not interfere with anyone's escape and only requested that they leave behind the hat and armband. This was done, of course, without the knowledge of the gendarmerie. For the time being.

One day Kuca, the secretary of the gendarmerie commandant, Schlicht, informed our commandant, Kronenberg, that a Jewish policeman had come to her and proposed that he would reveal where the policemen's wives were hiding in exchange for a pass to Warsaw. Kuca, to whom Kronenberg had sent expensive gifts from the moneys of the Judenrat for three years, returned the favor and informed us of the betrayal in our ranks. Everybody asks himself the question, Who could have done this? I discover that the suspicion falls on me. I am furious because I never spoke with the Germans on my own initiative. Soon, however, the problem is cleared up. I find out that Christian Herzig betrayed his colleagues, beguiled by the mirage of the pass, which anyway was of no use to him. This offspring of one of the wealthiest and most influential Jewish families in Poland, an educated engineer, a bachelor, dared to do something like that. I remember that when they brought him before Kronenberg, he told him to remove his hat and asked, "Did you talk to Schlicht's secretary or not? Tell the truth because you are standing before God Almighty."

Herzig at first denied, but then he confessed. He wanted to run away, but those policemen present at the interview caught him. Kronenberg hit him first; others joined in. It wouldn't have taken much to lynch him. I didn't touch him, even though I thought he deserved the worst death. I am not the only one who thought so. In the evening, a field gendarme came to the police station, and on the orders of Kronenberg they took Herzig out and shot him on the spot. Before his death, he yelled, "Why do you kill me? After all, I am not a lousy Jew, only a Christian."[138]

In fact, he was a convert, as was his whole family. His cries did not help him; he lived like a traitor and died like a vile traitor.

One might have the impression from the whole complex story that we were not afraid of the gendarmerie, as if the gendarmerie had no idea what was going on in the ghetto. It wasn't like that at all. If one talks about deputizing other Jews for the policemen who ran away, that Kronenberg had to do. If he had not, it would have been obvious that the policemen were running away. Then he would have suffered a penalty. Because the Germans knew in general the number of policemen, no lists were maintained, and one could, with very little risk, accept new people.

Basically, there reigned among us a terrible fear of any uniformed German. Our slogan was *Der ferater szlaft nicht*.[139] We gave the gendarmes enormous sums of money and gold, which the policemen found on corpses or which they received from Jews facing death. Gold burned in the hands of most of the policemen. They were afraid not only of holding onto gold; they were even afraid of their own shadow.

There were sound reasons for this. Every few days, mostly two days a week, there arrived in Otwock the gendarmerie from Rembertow, with Lipszer in charge, and together with the Polish police they searched apartments. What was done with the Jews found there? Some were killed on the spot; others were imprisoned. They were guarded by Jewish policemen up to the moment of execution.

Poles, who held passes to the ghetto, also took part in the *Aktion*. Particularly, recently appointed janitors caught Jews and brought them to the *Komisariat*. Naturally, they did not forget to take away from them all their money. They searched the pockets of those they caught, ripped open their suits, grumbled while doing it, and complained, "Where is your money? Give it to us. The Germans will take it anyway!"

Is there a man who is in a position to describe what the Jews went through before they were shot? It is difficult to imagine it! A part of the ghetto was already inhabited by Poles. Women were straightening out the apartments, where the not-quite-cold bodies of the owners were lying about. Others were peeling potatoes in front of the houses.

Jews had to look on all this, the last image fixed in their minds before death. Their Polish fellow citizens began a new life in their apartments, inherited their possessions, while they themselves, with this beautiful world created before their eyes, awaited their own death. They were, after all, Jews—no? At a certain moment they had to lie down on their stomachs and await the "savior" bullet to the neck that silenced their aching heart.

Mass executions belonged to the daily order. Every few days, when several hundred arrested people were assembled, ten gendarmes would arrive assisted by the Polish police. Before that, Jewish workers were brought out of concentration camps. They prepared large, common graves, most often near Reymont Street.[140] They buried there about two thousand people. They also buried people near the sanitarium Marpe in Otwock. Individual graves could be found without exception in every air raid shelter on the territory of the former ghetto. We should not forget that in Otwock they shot about four thousand Jews. I know about this because I witnessed it.

At night, before the executions, we, the Jewish policemen, watched over our Jewish brothers. We knew that they would all be shot next morning, and, for that matter, the condemned knew it, too. Should I describe those nights? I will never forget them.

I see a small square before arrest. It is fenced in by a screen, and there are several hundred people crammed together on the ground. Men, women, and children, they all sit together, all close or distant friends from their earliest years.

I wrote that we guarded them, but this is not true. Nobody counted them, and a majority of them could have quietly run to Kołbiel or wherever their eyes and legs could carry them. Although no one interfered with them, rarely did anyone run away. The Jews were broken spiritually as well as physically, mostly the former. The majority lost their desire to live.

Behind me are many nights spent with my Jewish brothers. I lived through them threefold: as a Jew, as a human being, and as an animal led by the instinct for self-preservation. These three entities were linked by the fear of death. We were never sure that we would not be shot the next day. Still, we did not run away, so why should we be surprised about the other Jews?

All of us spent the nights crying. The condemned cried; we, their overseers, cried. Some wailed loudly, reminded God of all their good deeds, displayed their small children, and asked God if he had no pity even on these creatures.

Others scorned God and laughed at those Jews who wore *talesim*,[141] sang psalms, and recited prayers for the dead the whole night.

Still others, in a fit of insanity, laughed at themselves, remembering their efforts and hardships to live better, to gain wealth, to build one more house in Otwock. . . .

The poor, on the other hand, could not forgive themselves that during the three years of war they had done without almost everything, had eaten only dry potatoes for fear that they would exhaust all their resources. Now, impoverished, they were in a situation where someone would inherit what they had had.

But as the nightly hours of prayers wore on, the weeping and the wild, uncontrollable laughter weakened.

When the condemned wept, I wept with them; when they prayed, I prayed along with them. Like the other policemen-guardians, I joined in the familiar Psalms. Sometimes I stopped in the middle, struck by a sudden thought.

Why am I doing this? I asked myself. Is there anyone to pray to? Sometimes I fell into a semisleep, and it seemed to me that I was sitting in a movie house where some terrifying sound film was turning the blood in our veins to ice.

When the cries grew loud, I woke up and looked around. On all sides, in the dark of the night, I saw the shadows of people crying, cuddling the children to their breasts. What did happen to children in that cursed night? I did not see children from two to ten years who cried loudly. For the most part they huddled with their parents, did not grimace, did not demand food.

Was it the spirit of resignation or the wisdom of the old that they absorbed? Were these children or hundred-year-old dwarfs?

I remember a little girl who resembled my daughter. Struck by her appearance and especially her resemblance to my Aluśka, I took her from her mother to the opposite side of the enclosure. I sat her on my knee, cuddled her, and thus we passed the night. When I heard that the gendarmes were arriving, I understood that I had to part with her. My charge, whose name I did not know, cried loudly and did not want to be returned to her mother. She sensed that death awaited her on the other side of the screen. She tightened her arms around my neck, and I had to forcefully tear myself away. When I returned her to her mother, I felt as if I killed the child with my own hands.

I hear her voice till today. My own thoughts as well: Is there a God? Is there some higher justice that rules this world? If so, why is it silent? Why doesn't thunder roll down from heaven? Why doesn't the earth open and swallow up the executioners of women, old men, and children?

The gendarmerie appeared as usual at eight. In the period between dawn and their arrival most of the police went away under one pretext or another. It was better not to be near the condemned at that time. If the gendarmes did not like something, couldn't they shoot the policemen as well? Only those remained who had to be there—fulfilling their duties at the arrests.

The arrival of the gendarmes does not signify the start of the executions. Before that comes the raid. The Germans, with Polish assistants, search different apartments. Every once in a while a shot rings out. A single one indicates the death of a person; a salvo, the deaths of ten people; followed by a single shot announcing that someone is being finished off. This happens rarely. The executioners have plenty of practice not to miss the right spot from the distance of one or two meters.

I can hear the shots as I stand before the arrests. I am not allowed to cry—because they might take notice. After each shot I ask myself whether they caught my aunt Góralska and her son, Mulik, if maybe that shot cut off their lives. I am cheered by the possibility that maybe they were not discovered. One can be driven mad!

The Gehenna begins for us, the guardians, the helpers of our brothers' murderers. Jews did not run away at night, although they knew very well what the morning would bring. Only from time to time I glimpsed a shadow, individual escapees getting through the opening in the fence. Usually there were no more than five, ten at the most. At the coming of dawn, when the gendarmerie moved about the entire ghetto, the condemned seemed to have renewed strength. They all wanted to run away. Surely from a psychological aspect it was a well-understood phenomenon, but we had our way of looking at it. For what could we have done, being poor victims of our own baseness? Allow them to try to escape? They were condemned to fail from the start, and for us it would have been a sentence of death.

I know very well that there is an easy justification. I can say, after all, that I was not standing alone on my watch, that no fewer than three policemen took part in the arrests. It would have been a self-justification, and I have decided to write this diary not to justify myself but to give truthful testimony.

I don't know what were the attitudes of those policemen who saved their wives. The ground was burning under their feet; they thought only about escaping. Those who remained could be divided into two categories. Those whose suffering had ennobled their hearts sympathized with all Jews without exception and disinterestedly helped others. Others were embittered, and these not only sought but also found comfort in the misfortune of others. I remember the lawyer Sołowiejczyk, an otherwise quite decent man, who on hearing the weeping of Jews did not have a penny's pity.

"Our wives," he said to them, "were to die and not you?"

My arguments did not help.

"Other Jews," I repeated, "are not guilty because you brought your wife to the square."

He never answered me, but threatened the condemned men even louder.

One time when I was on duty, there were about ten people under arrest, and Gendarme Irlicht was informed about that number. Before morning I turned to one of the workers, Karczewski, to watch them. I went to have breakfast. The condemned man asked him for something to drink, and so he went to get water, leaving those arrested unattended. Old Krochmalnikowa took advantage of this and ran away. When Karczewski saw this, he sounded the alarm. I came right away, as did Sołowiejczyk. This escape did not bother us particularly. She ran away? Too bad, may she be well. God willing, there won't be a "stink."

After a half hour two Polish watchmen appeared, escorting Krochmalnikowa. They caught her at the boundary of the ghetto and did their "patriotic duty." When Sołowiejczyk saw Krochmalnikowa, he threw himself on her and, cursing, hit her repeatedly in the face. This opened my eyes, and the truth practically blinded me. How impoverished you are, Jewish nation. You have been sentenced for extermination by your German enemies, by your Polish friends, by your disgraceful Jewish sons and brothers.

The worst hour came when I had to stifle, together with my colleagues, the inclination to help save Jews. It could not have been worse. I felt that my heart was being torn to shreds. That's why it was with a feeling of limitless relief that I greeted the arrival of the first gendarme. At long last at least my own torment was at an end.

It was another matter when the first gendarme did not come at all to carry out the sentence. He declined to participate in the *Aktion* not because his conscience didn't allow him to kill innocent people but because it was a lucrative business. The money found on the corpses went to a common pool, so such a fellow wanted to steal it, to appear before the arrest and tell the condemned, *"Alles Geld, Geld mysem zi awegeben, aznyt werd ir derszosyn."*[142]

Magical word, *derszosyn*,[143] as if they would not be killed in an hour anyway. Magical because they all run quickly to him, give him all their money, tell him that they are ready to work eighteen hours around the clock if only they are not killed. They address him as *Unserer Gott*,[144] and maybe they are right because he does indeed dispose of their lives. The gendarme listens to all this, urges them to hurry, looking around fearfully to make sure his colleagues are not watching, and quickly disappears.

After a quarter hour the second one appears, after him a third, and so this tragicomedy lasts until the *Aktion* is finished. When all the gendarmes have appeared at the *Komisariat*, it is clear that shortly they will take the Jews to the resting place—naturally their eternal one. I tried, as much as I could, not to be at the executions. Generally I succeeded because I was off duty in the morning, having been on duty all night.

I nonetheless saw how executions took place; almost all of them followed the same pattern. From morning on Jewish laborers from the concentration camp dug a massive grave. In front of the pit they left some sand. An embankment rose up, to which they brought ten Jews. The people lay down on their stomachs so that the neck was higher than the head. At that moment, ten gendarmes who up to that moment had been in the background, on command from one of them, turned, took aim—and a salvo fell. If they didn't aim at the neck but at the head, it happened that we found pieces of scattered brains at the distance of even twenty steps. Those who still moved were killed with single shots.

After each salvo, Jewish workers who stood in the back searched the pockets and then quickly threw into the pit the still-warm corpses. The place was cleared. The next ten could approach. Of course, this was done before the eyes of successive groups of ten of the condemned. And also before the eyes of the Jewish workers. More than one of them threw into the pit with his own hands the now-cold remains of his wife, mother, or children. No one betrayed by an outward expression the finding of such remains. All moved during the executions like wound-up automatons.

Sometimes it seems to me that it's a fairy tale—the assertion by the medical world that the heart is a chamber of delicate membranes that cannot stand suffering or emotion and that they burst, causing death. Today I would advise those who construct fighter planes to build them out of heart membranes. They will certainly not burst and will outlast the most enduring steel.

In the meantime, tens after tens of Jews go to their deaths. They go passively, slowly, clinging to each other, wives to husbands, older children holding onto their mother's dress, small children carried in arms. Every inch of ground is moistened with tears, tears of pain, tears of fear, tears of resignation, but never tears of revolt.

The Germans stand calmly, fan themselves with helmets; they are sweating—the days are so warm and humid. They do their own "work" automatically. Aim! Fire! Aim! Fire! What's the difference whether it's at the head of an old man, a younger one, or a small child? Aim! Fire! Aim! Fire! Each bullet brings deliverance and freedom. For Greater Germany, for *Vaterland*! Ach, are there many more of these cursed Jews? They multiply like vermin that have to be utterly exterminated to save the very ancient European culture. Every bullet allows one to bravely come into possession of Jewish gold, which will enable children to live a life of luxury. Aim! Fire! Aim! Fire!

Before the Jews is spread out a beautiful aspect of an August day in the health resort of Otwock. In front of the *Komisariat*, not far from the place of confinement, stands a group of Poles. Among them is a local physician, Dr. Mierosławski. (It's curious. Why did he come? To confirm the "correct" deaths of the victims?) There are also administrators and women clerks of the criminal police in wind-swept dresses and white hats. They have large bags hanging over their shoulders. This is the latest style, the so-called *berlinki*.

The faces are full of smiles, happy. They carry on a loud conversation; they do a lot of flirting—we should not forget that we find ourselves among the intellectuals. The Poles are content with the beautiful weather. They have slept well, are in good humor. They are ready to forgive other people everything.

How do the condemned react in the last moments of their lives? The Jews have a worse character than the Poles. When they look through the wire screen at their faces, they probably strongly resent those smiles. They don't want to see this and turn away their heads. Then they see, far from the border barrier, the curious faces of those Poles who have no admittance to the ghetto, although they want to see how Jews are led to their deaths. The condemned turn away their heads. They see their apartments occupied by other Poles, they see Polish women peeling potatoes in front of houses, they see new hearths built on the ruins of their lives. Then they direct their eyes toward heaven. There at least they don't find anything.

If there is a God who is silent, let their curses reach him at last.

"You have chosen us from all the nations; you have loved us."

"What can a man do to me if God is with me?"

"In every generation there arises an enemy lying in wait for our lives, but God, blessed be His name, saves us from his hand."

So have prayed all the generations of Jews since the creation of the world. With what bitter irony must many of the condemned remember their own prayers. . . .

Jews push themselves at the gate; they want to go as quickly as possible to the place of execution. Every minute is precious for them. Quickly! Quickly! They're practically running; they throw themselves on the ground to let the bullet of salvation reach them and quiet their aching hearts. For them death is a deliverance. Others delay; they want to be the last ones to go. Some because they want to pray more, others because they are awaiting a miracle. In no way do they want to go through the gate of the fence that surrounds the detention area. Even in the last moment they rush to the toilets and have to be brought out of there by force. The Polish police train their rifles on them.

"Are you going? Because if you don't, you'll get shot!"

They have copied the Germans and have learned to threaten instant death. Every moment I hear voices.

"Give me the money because if not, *werst du derszosen.*"[145]

"Lie down on your bellies because if you don't, *werst du derszosen.*"

If you lie down, well, all is in order. Aim! Fire! Aim! Fire!

There was no Jew who loudly cursed his executioners before his death. They were all passive, resigned, without hope for life, and, what is worse, overcome by one thought—only not to suffer cruelty before being done away with.

I remember the death of Mokotowska and her sister-in-law. The gendarmes found them in the basement, robbed them of their gold, and rounded them up for arrest. Some Jewish policemen returned with them to the cellar in order to take the dollars that were hidden there. A Polish policeman nabbed them there and took everything. The day before their execution, these young, beautiful women sat calmly in front of the police station and talked to the policemen, who, after all, had known them for many years. The Mokotowski family was one of the wealthiest and best known in Otwock. I stopped by them, listened to the story of their last days, and asked why they didn't run away to Kołbiel, or wherever their eyes and feet would carry them—after all, here they would be killed.

"Eee, there," they answered, "we don't have any money. We're in summer dresses; wherever we will go, the gendarmes will come. We will hide in the police station."

The following morning, when the execution was coming to an end, I crossed Reymont Street and saw the two Mokotowski girls. Holding hands, they were marching in the direction of the place of execution.

"Girls," I asked with a shaking voice, "you, too?"

"Yes," they answered. "Kronenberg told us to leave the police station."

They walked faster. The last fifty feet they began to run. They ran to the embankment, kissed each other almost in flight, and threw themselves on the ground, still holding hands. Aim! Fire! Brains scattered, their hands clenched in their last convulsions. Not being able to separate them, the workers threw both bodies together into the pit. I was never curious about executions, but this time I stood by and watched as they ran to the embankment. I could not understand why they ran to meet their deaths.

I also remember well the death of an unknown woman. I came to the police station around four o'clock, long past the executions. Unexpectedly, a gendarme stopped me and ordered me to bring a woman to the square. It couldn't be helped; I had no choice and I brought her. I cursed my carelessness, but what to do? We walk, we walk, but in no way can we reach our destination. The woman stops at every moment, promises me thousands of złoty if I let her go. She asks; she begs, beseeches, and finally begins to curse me.

I explain myself to her. I would let her go without taking money, but, after all, we are surrounded by the Polish police and under observation by the gendarmes. I ask why she didn't run away at night. The woman gets hysterical, starts to struggle, curses and cries that I will be responsible for her death. If I could, I would have run away from her curses. A Polish policeman appears, takes her by the hand, and leads her by force to the square. I am very lucky that I don't know her name. But what good is that? To this day I hear her curses. Did I deserve this or not? My conscience tells me yes.

Executions took place twice a week in the course of four weeks. I could write a great deal about them, but I want to end this theme—it costs me in health to write about it. I will only recall episodes that made the strongest impression on me.

During one of the last mass executions, they led to death [Tobias] Mokotowski. Around him, like a spinning top, a policeman by the name of Noj kept jumping and insisting, "Take off your jacket. What do you need a jacket for? Give it to me!"

Mokotowski walked erect without uttering a single word. Noj circled him like a crazy man, tugged at his sleeve, but it didn't help. Thus, one Jew walked away insulted by another Jew because he wanted to be buried in his jacket rather than give it up.

Mathias Noj, how do you justify yourself before your conscience? I know; you will tell me that it made no difference to the other one and that you need money to save your wife and child. Assuming that your wife and child are presently secure, I wish that the silent blessings that Mokotowski bestowed on you before his death be fulfilled.

Another time, a German Jew, an old-time acquaintance of Gendarme Schlicht from Berlin, was brought to the police station. We were certain that he would not be killed, particularly since Schlicht greeted him and talked to him for a long time, like to an old friend. But he killed him personally, together with some other people. After the execution he yelled loudly and cheerfully to Kronenberg, *"Der Berliner!* Bury him on top. After all, he is my friend!"

Ah, how good it is to have German friends!

I also remember the story of Wajdenfeld, a Jewish convert to Christianity, and his daughters. They had been born Catholics. They lived all the time in the Polish neighborhood. One of them was married to a Pole, had a small child, and was pregnant. Gendarme Irlicht brought them personally from beyond the ghetto.

We were 100 percent sure that they would be executed. In the meantime there was a hue and cry among the Poles, a priest intervened, a magistrate interceded enough so that the gendarmes did not kill them. They were sent to another ghetto, to Wołomin. It was understood that they would escape from there.

After this incident, there wasn't even an attempt from the Polish side to protest. I understood then that the murder of Jews took place, if not by a silent agreement, then at least with a general *désintéressment** on the part of the Polish public opinion. Perhaps that's why they picked Treblinka as a place of torment even for Jews from France, Belgium, or Holland. Apparently, "climate" conditions did not allow the Germans to build prisons on those territories.

A successive episode that left a memorable impression on me was the execution of a group of eighteen Jews of both sexes who ran away from the ghetto and, having no place to stay, sat in a field not far from Karczew. Among them was old [Jankiel] Braff and his daughter, who was in her last moment of pregnancy. Probably because of the emotional shock, she went into labor. The old father delivered the infant and placed the fetus on the grass.

Several hours later a gendarme crossed the field, saw the group of Jews, and told them to lie on the ground. One shot fell, second, third, and the rifle suddenly refused to obey him. It turned out that he had no more bullets in the magazine. He sent a Polish youth to the Karczew *Komisariat* with an order to send him the necessary ammunition. He then sat down and waited, completely unarmed, because—as I have said—he had no other cartridge with him.

---

*"Disinterestedness," "unselfishness" (French).

What did the Jews do then? Did they throw themselves on him to avenge the death of their closest ones? They continued to lie down with their faces to the ground and waited, waited more than half an hour for the supply of bullets—obviously the bullets of deliverance. At last a Polish policeman came with the ammunition. The gendarme shot the rest of the Jews, killed the mother, and killed the two-hour-old fetus. The workers from camp buried the murdered; more than one buried his wife, more than one his brother. What is the difference? Now in Karczew near a small rise at the mill lie the remains of eighteen Jews. This grave, hidden from sight, is testimony for all time to German barbarism—or to Jewish cowardice?[146]

Finally, I will describe the death of a Jew to whom it was given to die in those tragic September days in ignorance of his fate. This was Frajbergier, the owner of a big real estate business in Otwock, near Mickiewicz Street, an older man suffering from stomach cancer. On the day of the *Aktion,* a Ukrainian left the old man in his apartment when he showed papers that he was the father of a policeman. After the *Aktion,* his son Michał, an engineer in radio technology, a good friend of mine, placed him in the Jewish hospital Marpe, where at first they left the sick alone.

After two weeks they brought all the patients to the detention area in order to shoot them. Michał, with my help, prepared medication for his father, after which we went to the detention area where the elder Frajbergier was lying on a stretcher.

"Papa," said Michał, "I spoke to Dr. Mierosławski. He agreed to take you into the local sanitarium, where you will stay for the duration of the war. You only have to sign over to him half of your villa."

"I agree, Michał," replied the old man, "I thank you. . . ."

"Well, then, drink the medication that the doctor sent you," directed the son. "You will sleep, and at night they will transport you to the sanitarium. Calek will help you."

The old man looked at us with a grateful eye and, full of the best thoughts, drank . . . a large dose of Veronol. He fell asleep and slept for twenty-four hours. Then his heart automatically stopped beating. We buried him near the villa of the police station grave.

What was at that time the relationship between Kronenberg and the Jews? Before the *Aktion* he had limitless power. Nonetheless, he did not exploit it to the fullest, keeping in mind that after the war he would return behind the counter of his haberdashery. Now, however, when he realized that there would be no more Jews in Otwock, he ceased to take anyone into account.

He did not feel sorry for his own father, whom he had lost on the day of the *Aktion*.[147] Who would feel sorry for an eighty-year-old man? He didn't lift a finger to save him and didn't even go the square to bid him farewell. During the first days of the *Aktion* he did worry about his own skin and planned all sorts of escapes. As time passed, the gendarmes treated him better and better. No wonder. He paid them off lavishly with gold found among the Jews. Then he settled down. His wife, Tola, circulated calmly among the gendarmes. She was not even ashamed to brag in front of all the policemen that the commandant of the gendarmerie once addressed her, *"Guten Morgen, Frau Kronenberg."*

All this had a positive impact on Kronenberg's feelings and aroused in him the certainty that nothing would happen to him. I remember that when they brought out those who were condemned to die, Kronenberg sat calmly in his chair and with a pencil in hand noted the successive "tens." By then he had probably forgotten that he was a Jew. Neither the tears nor the moans of his fellow brothers found a response in his heart. What did he have in common with those Jews? Only his wife, Tola, cried loudly day and night, "My poor Nelly, my dearest daughter!"

Jews going to their deaths heard her cries and gritted their teeth in helpless anger. Jewish policemen, on seeing Tola, turned away their heads so she would not read the hatred in their eyes. Grinding curses between their teeth, they were silent. Wherever a group of policemen gathered, sitting usually together in the evening, crying over their wives, Tola would appear and yell, "My poor Nelly, they killed her!"

She left after a while, still calling loudly, "Poopsie, Poopsie! Where are you, you unruly scamp? Come to your mother!"

Her cries grew louder. They could be heard in the detention area and even in the Polish neighborhood. More than one Pole stood wondering whom she was calling in the dead ghetto.

"Aha." After a moment he dismissed it with his hand. "That's the Kronenberg woman calling her dog to dinner."

The wife of our commandant compared the loss of her fox terrier Nelly to the loss of our children, and what was worse, we had to listen to her and be quiet. The greatest skill in this vile world is to be quiet when the heart is bleeding and the fists tighten.

The ghetto was becoming more desolate day by day. There were no more people hiding there. There were no more apartments to rob. Everything was carried off by the German gendarmerie, stolen by the police, or pillaged by the Otwock rabble. The time limit was fast approaching for sending out to camps all the Otwock Jews who remained alive. For everybody, that is, except those like my father.

At the time of the *Aktion* my father's lot turned out to be quite a different one. On August 19 he ran away with my mother to the Polish neighborhood, to an acquaintance who happened to be a court official.[148] He spent the night there, and in the morning he ran to the ghetto to see what was happening. He didn't find me at home, and my sister, Rachel, chased him away quickly. It was understood, although she didn't think of this at the time, that even she, a wife of a policeman, was still in danger.

Hardly had my father returned to the Polish neighborhood when shots were fired from all sides. When he reached the apartment where Mother was hiding, he found her in the courtyard. After the first shots in the ghetto, the owners showed her the door. Father and Mother had no other way out, and so they hid in the grass near the ghetto. They saw from there how the gendarmes were moving about and how the Jews who wanted to go to the Polish neighborhoods were grabbed. They witnessed how the Polish mob organized a hunt for the Jews, who—after being robbed—were handed over to the gendarmes.

My parents were lucky. An "acquaintance" managed to get hold of them and, allowing himself to be begged, took one thousand złoty and did not turn them over to the gendarmes. They lived through a Gehenna of fear, particularly when a small dog stood by the bushes where they were hiding and barked loudly.

They sat there the whole day, uncertain as to what was happening to their children and other inhabitants of the ghetto. In the evening, they asked their former maid, Małgosia, if they could pay her to let them sleep in the barn. In the morning, they went farther away. They wanted to live and had to find a place where they could hide. But where?

Driven by force of habit, they made their way to their former villa on Kościelna Street. They were counting on their old Polish tenants. Those had lived under that same roof for practically a quarter of a century, so they thought they could rely on them for shelter. When they got to the villa, my father placed Mother under the stairwell in the garret and alone began the nightmarish journey among the tenants. These were afraid to even let him cross the thresholds of their apartments.

"Run, Mr. Perechodnik," the first one said, "because they'll kill us."

He was greeted by all his friends and former tenants with these words in a hundred variations. My father, disheartened, finally knocked on the door of Miss Dąbrowska, a tenant who had moved in in 1940, that is, before the ghetto was established. Of necessity, there were really no proper relations between her and my parents. O wonder, Dąbrowska agreed and didn't even want to hear about a monetary reward. She decided, however, to leave her apartment (room and kitchen) because she was afraid to live with them. She hoped that in the event of some bad break it would look as if Father, as a former landlord, had a key and had taken over the apartment without permission while she was away. The tenant bought for them a supply of bread and, without waiting for thanks, left the apartment.

My parents thanked God that He had inspired them to build such a house and that they had built it solidly; the walls were thick, so no sound came through. They could sleep peacefully. In the evenings Miss Dąbrowska appeared, always bringing bread. They were only tormented and fearful about what was happening in the ghetto.

One evening, Father decided on a foray into the ghetto. He found me in the police station. Because it wasn't possible to talk safely there, we went quickly to his old apartment. Then I found out where my parents were hiding and what had happened to them in the last few days. For my part, I told Father about the tragic fate of our family. I also recalled how the office messenger Franciszek stole Father's belongings from Janek's and Rachel's apartment. Father listened to me and was hardly able to restrain his fury.

"How could you have brought your wife to the square?" he yelled. "You know from the past that the Germans cannot be trusted."

I had the impression that he was more furious because of the incident with his belongings, which I did not watch carefully. Still, as an energetic man, he got over that and quickly got back to the needs of the day.

"Calek," he declared, "it's necessary to watch the remainder of our things, clothes, bedclothes, pillows. Someone who's alive has to have something to live on, something on which he can sleep."

I opened my eyes wide: He had just learned of the death of his daughter, sister-in-law, grandchildren, and he talks to me about pillows. Is this an animal or a human being? I am supposed to watch his bedding, as if the entire ghetto isn't piled high with pillows. What's the point? Who thinks of life in the future? I didn't say anything to him, gave him a few shirts, and led him to the boundary of the ghetto. This first visit did not leave me with feelings of happiness. It's true my parents were safe, but a distaste stifled a son's feelings. There remains only a sense of obligation toward them.

Nevertheless, I had to prepare some things for them so they would be able to change into something and eventually sell something. I took a

suitcase from the police station, which I had brought the evening of my
unfortunate escapade in the gymnasium, and brought it to my room at
the Judenrat. I took out of the cellar two knapsacks that my wife had
thrown there before going to the square.

She hid the knapsacks in the cellar, but she herself . . .

In my father's apartment I found some small items and his suit. I gave
him all that, throwing the suitcase over the ghetto fence.

One evening, my father appeared in the ghetto in the company of a
young veterinarian, Staszek M.,[149] my old school friend. I greeted him
warmly, but with some amazement. I remember that he and his
brother Stefan, a graduate of the Agricultural Academy, were well-
known anti-Semites before the war. Both broke off friendly relations
with Jewish colleagues. Why, then, the contact with the older
Perechodnik? True, before the war Father was on very good terms with
their late father, an organist at the Otwock church. I didn't know what
to do, what attitude to take in a conversation. It ended with Staszek
taking my father's suitcase to his place. Mine remained with my friend
Niki Zemela.

After a couple of days, having regained his equilibrium, Father appeared together with Mother. It was obvious that her nerves could not
take it. She could not put up with the confinement, was afraid to speak
loudly, was almost afraid to breathe. On her own, without even asking
my father, she jumped out after him, slammed the door, and ran to the
ghetto. She explained to me that she would rather sit in the cellar, if only
to be together with Jews.

"With Jews one can at the most die," I replied coldly, "but one cannot
live with them."

I did not hear her answer because the trapdoor to the cellar slammed
behind my mother.

Father, on the other hand, did not have the slightest intention of hiding in a cellar. He said that he wanted to live and that he knew only a
bullet awaited him among Jews. He decided right away that he wanted
to go to Warsaw. Maybe he would succeed. His appearance is not too
bad. His hair is chestnut colored and graying; he has gray eyes and an
upturned nose. Unfortunately, his Polish expressions are a little weak.
He decided, however, that he would manage. Leaving, he said that he
would try to find a place for Mother.

Last night in the ghetto he hid himself in the Judenrat. I gave him
half of the money we had and a briefcase with linen. He slipped out in
the morning, unnoticed by anyone. He spent the day hidden in the

garden of Staszek M.'s parents. In the evening they bought him a ticket. He boarded the electric train and rode to find luck in Warsaw. Maybe his numerous friends will take him in and find a permanent place for him.

The first night he spent with a former reporter, P. When he came the following morning, they did not let him stay that night, and their maid took away his sheets and a nightshirt. The next few nights he slept in various cellars. He met Miss K. in the street, who welcomed him and possibly would have let him stay longer if not for her brother. This seventy-year-old chairman K., who had played an important role in community life before the war and was also an old acquaintance of Father's, dissuaded his sister from keeping a Jew. Father tried to persuade him, but without success. The elderly K. explained that it was not possible to live without a Polish *Kennkarte*. He promised that he would arrange for one and took one hundred złoty for starting costs. But whenever my father arrived, the maid always said, "The chairman is not at home."

Willy-nilly my father searched farther until he was able to rent an apartment from some old lady, a droshky driver. He spent several days there until he heard a quarrel among the neighbors and shouts.

"The old one is keeping a Jew from the ghetto!"

Hearing this, he did not return to the apartment. He went to another old acquaintance, one Michalski, the owner of two houses and a laundry in Warsaw. He was made to feel very welcome.

"We will gladly help you," he heard. "Our nephew lives in a big, single house in Żukow. You can go there and stay there for the duration of the war."

They agreed that Father would sign over for the nephew a building lot for after the war. The thrifty Michalski verified that my father was the actual owner of the real estate. My father sent me from Żukow a lengthy letter. The same Michalski brought it to me.

If I had not involuntarily spoiled it all, my father would have spent all of wartime there. But it happened otherwise. When I saw in Otwock the familiar figure of Michalski, whom I knew from before the war, I immediately felt confidence in him. I knew he was very wealthy. I took him to be an honest man, and without hesitation I asked him if he would take a suitcase for my father. I knew that I had very little chance of surviving the war. Besides, we didn't know if we wouldn't be shot right here in Otwock. I wanted to protect my father. Michalski kindly agreed, took the suitcase that was packed by the Magister's sister and my father's winter coat, and left.

After several days, Michalski's nephew brought me the next letter from my father from Żukow. The young man's face did not inspire in me confidence, but I gave him additional things to carry. I gave him my own coverlet, happy at least that my father would have it.

Today I think that both Michalskis first looked over the contents of the suitcase and came to the conclusion that it was not worth keeping the Jew. Better to divide up the contents and show my father the door. This is very likely what happened. Suffice it to say that young Michalski, after returning from Żukow, told my father a "fairy tale about the gendarmes."

Father, forced to abandon the apartment, made it to the ghetto in Parczew.[150] (There was also an *Aktion* there, but those who hid themselves remained free for a time.) Some Polish woman from there brought me a third letter from my father, who asked me to send him winter boots and a sweater. I understood that his things at Michalski's were lost, taken by the gendarmes.

It was too bad. I prepared another package: shoes, sweater, shirts, sheets. These things also did not reach my father. He heard another fairy tale about Germans who seized everything on the train, "recognizing" that there were Jewish possessions.

In the meantime, the young Michalski, not knowing that my father had informed me of everything, visited me for the second time. He told me that my father was forced to leave the apartment for a few days but that he was still ready to keep him. He wanted thirty thousand złoty. That he appropriated things for himself, he said nothing; that he also wanted to appropriate the money, I figured out for myself. When he realized that I would not give him such a large sum, he demanded that I pay him for taking Father to Żukow. I restrained myself with difficulty in not telling him to his face that he was an ordinary thief and a swindler. I was afraid that he would spoil things for Father in Parczew, and I promised that I would give him the money in a few days. I knew that in a few days we would be leaving and I would never see him again.

Like all policemen, I continued to live in the Judenrat building. My brother-in-law Janek at first did not want to live with us. Maybe he didn't want to tie himself to anybody; perhaps he thought I would be a burden. This changed when Rynaldo stole his jacket before escaping. (In general, each policeman was constantly robbed by another.)

When he finally came to live with us, the three of us[151] were bound by a real friendship. We made up a threesome based on intellect. Before this, my relationship with Janek had been correct but very aloof. We did not suit each other. He was, it is true, very good, sensitive in behavior, hardworking (although he did not show initiative)—but above all, he did not like to give an account of where and on what he spent money. For such a golden character he was loved by all—only not by my father, whose whole life, whole upbringing, was one loud protest against such behavior.

I had a character similar to my father's: I liked money. It's true too that I never desired what belonged to others. In that regard I was exceptionally honest, but I did not give away my money to anyone. I liked to count every penny, arguing that good and accurate accounts make for good friends. I was punctilious, but that was my father's characteristic. After the *Aktion,* suffering molded me and made me into a new person. I remember a certain episode, very unflattering of me and characterizing my old mentality. One time when I performed my early morning duty at the detention area, one of my father's friends handed me about two hundred paper dollars. The gendarmes were all around, and I was afraid to keep these bills on me. I hid them in one of the rooms in the police station. I could have given them to Janek, but I didn't trust him. They had not been counted. Besides, that would have made him a partner. God rightly punished me: One of the policemen found the money and took it for himself.

From today's perspective I can look at this matter twofold: as a sign of God's punishment but also as a sign given me by Providence. I had become convinced that if a policeman was wealthy, he would perish earlier. Money had only seemingly provided a greater opportunity for escape. Most frequently people chose an escape by car to Częstochowa or Kraków. But there death awaited them, not life. Maybe it would have been the same with me. Not having currency, tied to belongings, which were given to the Magister for safekeeping, I was forced to locate myself in a nearby place. On the other hand, these moneys—now particularly when I am writing this—would be very useful, and I wouldn't be facing death from hunger.

In any case, from that beginning I can date a complete change in my character. In the first days of the *Aktion* I was still keen for money and material things. After the story of the dollars, I experienced an upheaval.

Several days later an episode occurred after which I could not recognize myself. We were standing at the detention area when some woman gave me and my colleague a diamond of perhaps three carats. My friend tried to persuade me that it was a fake. I agreed to go with him to an expert, but on the condition that if it turned out to be false, I would keep it.

My colleague went to an expert on his own. Afterward he told me that the diamond was an imitation. He asked me to give it to him because he wanted to make a gift to his girlfriend.

I agreed. Did I believe him? Not at all! I just did not have the desire to fight over it or to care about the money.

From day to day I was interested less and less in daily routine. I fell into ever-greater apathy. I did not look as Janek took hold of the rudder that controlled our lives. He managed our joint cash, bought food, altogether took care of everything. I stayed in bed days at a time, looking, without thinking, at the sky. At night I went out to bring food to those hiding in the cellar and performed my duties at the police station. I didn't want to go on duty during the day; my heart could not stand the sight of murdered Jews, nor could I look at the swarming Poles, who surrounded the ghetto like vultures.

At that time, we could still go around the Polish neighborhood with the excuse of buying things without being punished. I took advantage of this opportunity. I no longer felt the pain looking through the curtains at safe and calm family gatherings. I just stopped regretting homes, wealth, possessions. I only wanted my nearest ones to be with me.

One day I saw in the Polish neighborhood a girl pushing perhaps a two-year-old child in a carriage. My legs buckled under me. I recognized my daughter's stroller. I looked at the child, the small, innocent child, and I had an irresistible urge to strangle it with my own hands. I couldn't get it through my head that an Aryan child had a right to be walked in a stolen carriage, and my Aluśka, because she had been born of Jewish parents, not only had no right to ride in her stroller but had altogether no right to live. This scene haunted me for a long time, and from that time on I avoided the Polish area as much as possible.

But I could not avoid walking into the ghetto, for which you had to have strong nerves. Empty streets and empty apartments, broken windowpanes, open doors, air raid shelters covered carelessly with sand, where human bones chewed over by dogs or picked at by birds protruded. In the streets there fluttered in all directions feathers from bedding, old ration cards, photographs, and identity cards. In the apartments remained only old, sacred Jewish books. Except for that, everything has been picked over: broken chairs, the worst rags, cracked pots, even clothes hangers. Every object had found a fan among the Poles, who dragged their loot day and night. Later on when there was nothing left to steal, they even began to take old Hebrew volumes, probably for waste paper. Tefillin[152] were much desired by makers of gaiters for their own products.

From day to day, the number of policemen diminished as more and more escaped. Grandowski, the well-known radio technician, ran away but returned after a few days. It seemed he went to Kosów, where he found out from Rykner about the circumstances of the Otwock death transports and also that Kronenberg was warned about that. This information caused Grandowski a mental collapse. He could not stand the thought that he himself, on orders of the Ghetto Polizei, had brought out his wife and daughter from their cellar. Feeling responsible for their deaths, he no longer wanted to live. He turned to Schlicht and asked to be killed. Naturally the German refused. They gladly kill those who want to live, but not those who ask for death.[153] Grandowski tried unsuccessfully to poison himself with Veronol, after which, close to madness, he decided to go on his own to Treblinka. He got as far as Malkin, where he was recognized by the gendarmes and shot.

My brother-in-law Janek was happy to go beyond the ghetto. He frequently visited his colleagues Staszek and Stefan M., about whom I have already written. He told me of the miracles, how well he was received, and especially how warm their mother was to him. I thought they must have undergone a great metamorphosis, especially since they were doing all this unselfishly. I convinced myself and I also started going there. For the first time I felt the maternal warmth of a woman who understood my tragedy, wanted to relieve me of my suffering and help me in whatever way possible. I took advantage of an opportunity, and I transferred my suitcase from the ghetto to Stefan. After a while, the Magister, at my request, took it to Warsaw. I assumed that if I left, it would be easier for me to maintain contact with Warsaw than with Otwock.

All this time my mother was staying hidden in the cellar together with Aunt Czerna Góralska, her son, Mulik, and some other Jews. I brought food to them regularly. However, I lived in constant fear that the gendarmes would track them down. I was not able to find any other place where I could relocate them. I proposed to Czerna that she risk a journey to Słonim, to her husband, who was probably still alive. She refused. Next I advised her to poison her son and go on her own to Warsaw, where she could live and find work as a Polish woman. That she also refused.

Finally Czerna went to a Polish friend, Miss Lusi, in whom she had complete trust. She placed many of her things there. Before the *Aktion* Lusi assured Czerna that she could always count on her, that she would help her, hide her, and would do more for her than for her own sister. When Czerna showed up in her apartment, Miss Lusi said that she could not stay with her because she lived close to the neighborhood where Schlicht was. She continued to promise help. My aunt left her money to buy provisions and returned with her son to the ghetto.

Several days later the new Polish janitors discovered her hiding place. They conducted a thorough search, took everything, even pulled rings off their fingers. Thank God, they did not notify the gendarmes. I knew, however, that the situation was hopeless; their fate had been sealed. I didn't want to be present at their deaths, particularly that of Czerna, to whom I was very attached. I didn't have the energy of a Frajbergier, to prepare for them a sweet death, to give them poison in their coffee. Besides, basically, I didn't want to deceive anyone, especially people close to me. In a most ordinary way I asked them what they wanted. Did they want to choose a quiet death with Luminol and humane burial in the ground or to go to Kołbiel with the expectancy of an inevitable journey to Treblinka.

They didn't even want to hear about Luminol. Mother chose Kołbiel. Czerna still asked for the poison to use as a last resort. Janek had the responsibility of finding honest guides in the Polish neighborhood. He finally found two boys who were ready to do it for two thousand złoty.

The day earlier, Kestenberg, the owner of the apartment in which my parents stayed formerly, also decided to abandon the cellar and make his way to Kołbiel. I gave him bread for the road; he said good-bye and went. He did not leave me any instructions for sure; it was not for nothing that he was a religious Jew with a red beard. He had a deep belief that he would return to his home and that he alone . . . but this will be explained later on.

The next day my mother and Czerna and Mulik went out. We gave them money, rucksacks, and they left without a good-bye into the dark night. I remember that evening clearly. I went to the police station to ask Kronenberg to relieve me of night duty. I told him that I had to send my mother to Kołbiel. Kronenberg's wife heard this and started to laugh loudly.

"What? You are sending your mother to Kołbiel?" she asked. "And maybe she thinks that she will stay alive?"

She laughed even louder. I was silent because what could I reply? Actually, I should have slapped the mug of that old woman and left. Her words and laughter must have been heard by the devil, and he too must have laughed.

My mother's journey went uneventfully. Only a *Volksdeutsch* caught them, took about one thousand złoty, and went on. This was a trifle if one considers that between Otwock and Kołbiel peasants lay in wait for Jews day and night in order to rob them of their possessions and money. They even took off Kestenberg's shoes. Other Jews did not fare any better.

When we received from Janek news of the lucky arrival of our people at Kołbiel, there emerged another problem: how to send money to them. Janek sent two hundred złoty with the son of the local shoemaker, Hieronym. Hieronym brought back a receipt. Janek sent two hundred once more, and he received a receipt, but for only one hundred fifty złoty. Later it turned out that the first receipt was a counterfeit and that for a sum of four hundred złoty they promptly received one hundred fifty. Probably Hieronym would not have handed over even that sum if he hadn't wanted to pull us into a bigger game. I shouldn't have to mention that he was paid separately for every favor.

In the meantime the last deadline approached for going to camp. We were supposed to go to Piekiełko, a place near Legionów. A group of policemen had left already and taken up administrative positions in the camp. The rest remained in Otwock for the time being.

Seeing how things are, we decided with Janek to send to Kołbiel one thousand złoty and a suitcase with valuables. We began to search for an honest acquaintance to whom we could entrust this. We were prepared to offer two hundred złoty and a nice present for the service. This was undertaken by one P., a friend of my brother-in-law. Janek guaranteed his honesty. I believed because I had to. We gave him one thousand złoty, took away from Michalski the suitcase with various things that my father put away even before the *Aktion*. We left with him only my mother's seal fur collar and my father's otter fur in case my parents showed up there. We gave the suitcase to P. together with a letter containing a list of all the things we were sending.

P. left for Kołbiel. He brought back an authenticated list in which Mother and Aunt confirmed that the things and one thousand kisses had been received. I was full of admiration of P., such a decent man. Janek gave him two hundred złoty, a new scarf, and sold him a new pair of shoes for three hundred seventy-five złoty. At that time they were worth at least three times that. Today their value has grown tenfold.

Both Janek and I were satisfied that we had finally come across an honest man. Janek was worried, however, about whether P. had handed my mother a new leather bag and gloves, which he had forgotten to note on the list. I cheered him, arguing that surely P. could have taken everything, so why should we be greedy for a silly bag?

But P. did not hand over the bag and the gloves. Moreover, he repacked the things and did not leave the suitcase with my mother in Kołbiel. Another problem was that Janek forgot to write what things were in the suitcase; it was supposed to be understood. I personally feel for P. a deep gratitude that he gave my mother the money and the various items. I am not a lawyer and don't know under what paragraph falls the deed of the bag and the suitcase. If a lawyer, not knowing about life, guided solely by the law code, recognizes P. as a thief in spite of everything—that's not my fault.

A more obvious problem concerned the school messenger Franciszek. Everybody laughed at me after I ran away to him. As it turned out, on the day of the *Aktion* Franciszek did not let in the wife and daughter of the policeman Noj, even though it was arranged ahead of time. Of course, he took all the things that were left with him. (Noj's wife saved herself only thanks to an unknown priest who hid her in his apartment.) The same thing was done with the possessions of the fabric store owner Pironicz. I have the impression that after the war old Franciszek will not want to be a messenger in the gymnasium. Now he is wealthier than any of the teachers.

One day he accosted me with a claim that I had besmirched his good name in Otwock by telling everybody that he had taken my things. He informed me that everything was, after all, at my disposal for after the war. I didn't answer him, waved him away, and walked on.

Janek proposed that I conduct a search of Franciszek's home jointly with a Polish agent, take away the things he had stolen, and divide them up with the inspector. I categorically rejected that out of regard for the Magister. If the problem became known, it would come to light that the Magister had visited me at the gymnasium, and then he would have no end of unpleasantness.

I met with the Magister often enough and even introduced him to Janek. Once I went to his office; in the corridors the officials were walking around lightheartedly. From the windows it was easy to see my movie house, Oasis. The Polish officials asked me with great curiosity about the *Aktion*. Probably, talking to a Jew they felt like Nero in the Roman circus: *Morituri te salutant.**

In my room there was a grand library with many books in rich bindings. The owner had died in Treblinka. I wanted to make a gift of it to the Magister, although, after all, I had neither a de jure nor a moral right to them; one could smell human blood on these volumes. How to make a gift of these to someone with clean hands? I asked the Magister

---

*"Hail, Caesar, those who are about to die salute you"—the greeting of the gladiators before combat.

whether he would accept them. He refused—did not want such a token from the ghetto.

Not everyone is so sensitive. Another Pole, an official at the Arbeitsamt, comes to me with a request: Would I let him take those books?

"Why, one can't eat them," he laughs, as if from a good joke.

Of course, I don't reply, but I expect that he will pack up the books and quickly remove them. But he takes his time, looks at every book, and tries to discuss with me authors and contents. I am afraid to insult him, but I would happily throw him out the door. Do I have the mind to listen to his philosophical wisdom? For four long hours I endure his presence as the worst of tortures, and he finally departs.

I would like to see him another time and settle scores. In his mind he hasn't done any harm. On the contrary, he recognizes me as an intelligent person and wants to discuss with me a theme as important as literature. What of it if shots are heard in the street? Indeed, they only kill a few Jews. In the refined life of a person, culture and poetry are most important.

In the meantime, our ghetto no longer exists officially. The last "inhabitants" have to clean up by themselves all traces of Jewish life. They tell us to dismantle the barrier. We remember our conversations in times when the ghetto was being set up. We used to say that this would be how it would look after the war. The barrier would be removed; Jews would dance in the street and celebrate their regained freedom. Such an end of the ghetto as that of today no one expected. The times of the prophets have gone, never to return.

In the area of the former ghetto Poles walk around peacefully. There is nothing to rob; now they're coming to buy. They're ready to buy everything, especially when it's dirt cheap. When they see a Jewish policeman dressed in a decent suit, they would like to tear it from his back.

"Why do you need it?" they ask. "In camp you will get a suit made of paper. For this one we will pay you."

I personally did not make any transactions. I was simply incapable of selling things whose owners had died in such a tragic way. Janek was a specialist in these problems; he had the patience and never got upset. I remember when he sold my wife's winter coat. Throughout the transaction I thought I would go into a rage. When the shopper touched the coat, I had to restrain myself so I would not hit her. I felt she was dishonoring the memory of my wife. It was as if she had committed a sacrilege. The coat went for five hundred złoty, and I was not able to eat anything that day.

Janek appealed to Miss Lusi to return four hundred złoty and the things she had taken from my aunt Czerna. I found out that the money was in the hands of Lusi's friend. Salted bacon that had been bought for that sum had to be resold. This product had now fallen in value, so it was necessary to wait. In addition, Lusi would take everything to my aunt, and in a little while she would bring her from Kołbiel to her place. Janek was barely able to get a negligible portion of the things she had and one hundred złoty. The rest Lusi was to return personally to my aunt. She even began to write a letter to Kołbiel: "I will shortly come to you, my lady, but in the meantime don't send me Janek or Calek." Surely she would have arrived; it's just that earlier they had deported Jews from Kołbiel to Treblinka.[154] It seems to have been foreordained for Lusi to receive a trousseau gratis from my aunt. After six weeks, when I told her of the death of my aunt, the poor girl broke into tears. Crocodile tears flowed. Well, the ordinary sort of morality . . . but with the crazed pretense of being a decent person.

In the last days before departure we had a small sensation. Under the room in which my parents lived they found buried goods worth several million złoty. These had been buried by the owner of the apartment, Kestenberg, who pretended throughout the entire war period that he was a poor man. Neither he nor his sick wife ate anything better than bread and potatoes. He ran away to Kołbiel, where he continued to suffer from hunger, and in the meantime the Germans continued to pull up piles of his goods. News of this reached the camp, but no one felt sorry for the emaciated Kestenberg. People only asked, Whom did he want to cheat? God or the devil, others or himself? Kestenberg's luck was that the quick *Aktion* saved him from death by starvation. Besides, he who was not a man while alive couldn't be helped by anyone after death.[155] I leave him with a sad reputation—one he has completely deserved.

In the meantime, twenty policemen were detached to the hospital Zofiówka. They didn't have to do hard work, but in spite of that, I didn't want to go there. I didn't want any contact with the Germans. I decided to transfer with the rest of the policemen to Piekiełko.

My brother-in-law Janek was able to get some fillings for his teeth before we left. Our former tenant, Lidia Wolańska, received him kindly and did not ask for any money. I did not go to her because it didn't seem to me normal to have teeth filled if one is bearing the stigma of death.

Before departure, I visited the court officer Alchimowicz, with whom I had left some things for safekeeping. I told him that if I didn't notify him in three months, he should take everything to the Magister. In this way I made him, although he didn't know anything about it, the executor of my estate. I gave proof of my absolute faith in his decency and—as it turned out later—also proof of my stupidity.

At the same time, I gave to the Magister thirty-five hundred złoty for safekeeping. I also wrote a letter to my father and mother.

The next day, the Jewish Day of Atonement,[156] a truck came for us. The police commandant Kronenberg, his deputy Ehrlich, the brothers Gurewicz, one of whom was the president of the Judenrat, the other a commandant of the fire department, and their wives were transported to the camp at Wilanów.[157] Kronenberg was appointed commandant for the camps of Wilanów, Piekiełko, and Saska Kępie. For all of them it was a ride to a summer resort. The majority of the policemen, on the other hand, took a road from which there was to be no return.

I would like to characterize the attitudes of Poles toward Jews and, in general, toward the acts of extermination of Jews. The lower classes of the townspeople as well as the peasants oriented themselves to whichever way the wind was blowing. They understood that they had an opportunity to enrich themselves, one that came only in a great while. One could pillage without penalty, steal, kill people, so that many using the slogan "now or never" got to work. They raised their hands to heaven, thankful for the favor that they had lived to see such times. . . . They considered themselves innocent. After all, the Germans were responsible.

In every town where there was an *Aktion*, the ghetto was surrounded by a mob that participated in a formal hunt on Jews, a hunt according to all the rules of hunting—with beaters. Did many Jews perish at their hands? Countless ones! In the best case, the beaters took money from Jews, resigned to lead them only to the gendarmes. It was in any case a sentence of death. What could the Jew do without money? He could go to the gendarme himself and ask for a bullet. I myself saw and heard from the mouths of Poles about such cases.

Our janitor, Jan Dąbrowski, caught Jews by force and delivered them into the hands of the gendarmes after first robbing them. The mob acted in unison, the nameless mob. When the conductors on trains noticed a Jew, they communicated to one another, "I caught a bird." A bird naturally had to be "plucked." I know about this from others, and I witnessed it myself, that the conductor checked the documents of women with "doubtful" appearance. In ninety-nine such cases, the conductor exposed himself to shame.

"What? Do you take me for a Jewess?" He heard then, "that's interesting. Do you look for Jews as an official or for your private purpose?"

But in the hundredth case, the discovered Jewess had to pay the conductor with interest for all past embarrassments. In Warsaw there was even a new occupation: a tracker of Jews. Still, one should not throw stones at these people because they work for the German service. After all, it is only the mob, but the fact that in Poland half the people belong to these lower classes, that's another matter.

It's a peculiar thing: Jews did not even dream that the order to kill Jews would apply to all Jews, while the Poles realized right away that no Jew would survive the war.

In general things happened that the greatest genius would not be able to describe. Tragedies took place that people never dreamed about, and in spite of that, they were not even an interesting topic of conversation. The Magister, who daily rode the electric train to Warsaw, told me that even in the worst time of the *Aktion* he did not hear comments about Jews in the train or that someone should have had pity for them.

In a word—not an interesting topic for a general conversation, but surely an interesting topic for a family discussion. Indeed, it happened that a Pole had a Jewish friend who gave him things for safekeeping. If he then obligingly went to Treblinka, the matter was finished. Possessions increased; the conscience was clear—*tout va très bien.*[158]

It was worse when a Jew appeared to be "bothersome," wanted to live and remind them of his possessions. Then there was something to talk about to others. Indeed, the Jew will not survive the war anyway, and so he will not be able to repay the favor after the war. He will not be able to lodge charges before a court, will not cast a shadow on an unblemished name. To give anything back to him is simply a sin. If we give things back to him, others will come and take things away. Majority found an easy answer.

"The gendarmerie took it away. Please don't come to us anymore."

There were also those who demanded from the Jews the return of thousands of złoty, claiming that they had to ransom themselves from the Germans, being judged guilty by them for the Jewish possessions they had. Usually, after a couple of months, everything was in order; the Jew perished.

I don't want to say that there weren't Poles who willingly helped Jews, some of them unselfishly. The best proof of this is the fact that I am still alive; if they had taken all my things, I would not be in this world. It's true that with the things they took away from me I could have lived to be one hundred, but that is really a small difference. It only amounts to two foolish zeroes.

Interesting are the changes in the mentality of many Poles in their relations with Jews. I know a Pole, our former tenant, who considers himself 100 percent patriot and a decent man. And, indeed, he is a decent man. I can trust him absolutely. He is probably the only tenant in 1943 in all of Poland's territory paying rent to his Jewish landlord. This man, in a conversation with my father, could express himself in the following manner: "I traded with that Jew for so many years, and think about it, he gave me nothing for safekeeping. They took him to Treblinka—and what did he get from that?! If only he had left me his goods."

But let us put aside the material questions; these are dirty matters. It was reasoned plainly. From where did the Jews get such wealth? Wasn't it from the Polish soil? The time had come for them to repay their debt to Poles. Everything, then, is in order. Moreover, *pecunia non olet*.*

I will now describe two other occurrences.

Miss A. belonged before the war to society's elite. At the start of war, when she lived in my house, she could have discussions with my wife for hours. She addressed her always as Dear Miss Anka. We considered her an educated patriot, a democrat, a person with a noble heart. That is why I was very surprised when after the *Aktion* Miss A. didn't even approach me and ask me what had happened to "dear Miss Anka." It became clear only in the fall. Dr. Lidia Wolańska told me that in a conversation with Miss A., she explained, "The one and immortal favor by the Germans toward the Poles is the fact that they had cleansed her of Jews."

What was more, Miss Lidia did not say this in an angry tone. She repeated what she heard and also added what she thought.

"Mr. Calek," she explained to me, "so many Poles are being transported to Oświęcim, so many thousands of people are being deported to work, and nothing has happened to the Jews so far. They have not suffered such sacrifices. Is this just?[159] The Germans, deporting Jews from Warsaw, behaved fairly. It's too bad that they have deported Jews from Otwock, for these are our friends. . . . "

This was how the lady doctor, the mother of two small children, with a clear conscience sacrificed 3.5 million men, women, and children as an

---

*"Money carries no odor" (Latin).

equivalent for the losses and sacrifices suffered by the Poles. It is necessary to add that she was not an anti-Semite; she expressed only the
opinion of the environment, accepting it as her own. Only her good
heart took pity on the Jews of Otwock.

' The reaction of prewar anti-Semites is interesting. I was surprised by
the actions of Staszek and Stefan M., whom I have mentioned. They
came from a Catholic environment. They had no social contacts with
Jews and even fought against them using means not sanctioned* by the
teachings of their religion. For them a Jew was a wealthy man who ex-
ploited Polish labor and was an opponent deserving of a fight.

When times changed, when a common enemy ruled Poland, even
though he sowed dissension among Poles against Jews, the prewar attitudes lost their significance. The human hearts of the brothers protested
against the extermination of Jews. The brothers, as much as possible,
saved their friends and those they did not know. I bow in honor to them.
That they were anti-Semites before the war means that their behavior
should be viewed in a special light. In these difficult and ungrateful
times, they behaved as real believers in Christ and as sincere Polish patriots. That is not to say that this is how all prewar anti-Semites behaved.
An overwhelming number now found a proper time to show their best
tricks. People such as Brothers M. are lost in such a mob.

What, then, was the position of the Polska Partja Niepodległościowa
[Polish Independence Party]?[160] Three months after the start of the
Aktion, in October 1942, an article discussing the deportation of Jews
appeared in *Biuletyn Informacyjny* [Information Bulletin].[161] It emphasized the barbarism of the Germans, expressed compassion for the Jews,
but in the end came to the following conclusion: The best class of Jews
were those who before the war did not want to be a parasite on a foreign
organism and emigrated to Palestine. They were destined to live; the remainder of the nation perished.

The Polish armed forces held to a prewar position of anti-Semitism
and had no intention of defending the Jews. If there had appeared in the
daily press even one communiqué with the following text—"The Special
Court has decreed a sentence of death on a functionary of the Blue
Police† for seizing and delivering Jews to the Germans. Sentence carried

---

*It may be assumed that Perechodnik is referring to acts of violence.
†A Polish auxiliary police, so named for the navy blue or dark blue colors of its uniform,
carried arms and assisted the Germans.

out on that and that day, in such and such a place"—the situation would have been different. Various Polish policemen or private trackers would have stopped such a disgraceful, although lucrative practice. Unfortunately, neither did such or similar communiqué appear,[162] nor did the armed forces proceed to enlist young and able Jews with the purpose of strengthening partisan detachments. Only in December did the Polska Partia Robotnicza [Polish Workers Party] come into contact with the Warsaw ghetto, furnishing arms for a price.[163] But it was already too late for Jews to save themselves or to inflict serious losses on the Germans. The last of the Jewish Mohicans could, however, thanks to that help, perish honorably with arms in hand.

It's difficult for me to write about Poles. What is happening today is the greatest disillusionment that I have endured in my life. I have lived for twenty-six years among the Poles, embraced Polish culture and literature, loved Poland, looked on her as another motherland, and only in the last year have I recognized the true faces of Poles.

I would gladly describe the facts of every noble behavior toward Jews, but I cannot be silent in the face of the vileness of those who, out of desire for profit or out of blind hatred, sacrificed the lives of hundreds of thousands of people.

One has to look truth squarely in the eye. Jews perished first of all because they didn't realize in time what level German cruelty and barbarism would reach. They were well aware, however, of the vileness of some Poles. They knew what it was that closed before them the gates of the Polish neighborhood and forced them to wait in the ghetto for the near and inevitable sentence of death.

I am not in the least blind. I don't consider it to be a duty of every Pole to hide, at the risk of his own life, every Jew. But I believe that it was the responsibility of the Polish society to enable Jews to move freely within the Polish neighborhood. Polish society is guilty of not strongly condemning the "trackers" of Jews.[164]

It's true Poles helped me, my father, my mother—they helped thousands of other Jews. Thinking of the base ones should not lead one to draw conclusions touching on all. Does the statistic of good and bad deeds have any meaning? No, this is not important. God on Highest took a position on this matter. In the Old Testament it is written that if one finds in a town ten righteous people, that place will not be destroyed. Probably in Warsaw and in every other city one can also find ten righteous people.

The Camp ⤳

WE LEFT OTWOCK exactly five weeks after the *Aktion,* on the Day of Atonement. I remember how we rode through Kościelna Street. Poles stood in front of our houses, the new owners of our shops, smiling, satisfied. . . .

I was sure that I would never return, that I was seeing my native Otwock for the last time. What did I feel then? The hell of a helpless revolt, but also my own passivity. I went voluntarily, no one forced me, no one was guarding me. I could have jumped off the truck and stayed in Otwock. I thought of the future, about what it would bring. Work and life or work and death? I felt it would be the second, but the majority were of a different mind. Indeed, Lipszer himself told us, "You will work through the entire war, and afterward, after the war, you will be freed."

We are riding through Warsaw. The ghetto, numbering at times seven hundred thousand inhabitants, is no longer. From accounts by eyewitnesses I know what happened.

At first, a certain portion of the population was sent "for the time being" to Treblinka or to the punishment camp in Lublin. For some it was possible to write letters to families in Warsaw. A few or several scores of such letters circulated in the ghetto with the speed of lightning and quieted the people. One interpreted for oneself that those who worked in shops would not be deported—for what does it matter to the Germans where the Jews work? Consequently, everyone tried to work and carefully held a certificate signed by an official of the SS.[165]

Frequent transfers, the creation of new workshops, attempts to find work, police roundups, blockades of homes and entire streets, personal tragedies, tragedies of the people as a whole—all that brought about such a tumult that everybody lived and moved about as if in a nightmarish sleep. Because the *Aktion* continued, the number of people who did not have "iron papers"* diminished.

Some of them worked in the Polish neighborhood, in the so-called outposts.† They went out in the morning and returned evenings under

---

*"Iron-clad" documents were issued by the Germans to VIPs such as the Ger Rebbe, who traveled from Poland abroad via Berlin.
†The Polish word *placówki* refers to areas where forced labor squads worked outside of the ghetto, a much desired job often acquired through bribes.

an escort. When blockades took place, everyone had to come to the front of the house and show his papers. Families of those who worked came out calmly. Their documents were examined; they were placed in rows, sent to the *Umschlagplatz,* and from there straight to the cattle cars. When the men came back from work, they did not find anyone at home.

Later they had selections in the workshops, this time under the pretense of checking if the number of people actually there corresponded with the written list. The workers did not hide themselves. They placed them in rows, some on the left, some on the right. Some they led back to work, others straight to cattle cars. Those returned to work were for the most part cripples and people of weak constitution. The strong hiked instead to wagons. At selections, for example, Germans especially exempted men and sent out wives. No pleading that he or she wanted to be sent out together helped. It is difficult to enumerate all the sadistic games of the Germans, but you could depend on them.

Earlier news came about deportations in other towns. People were surprised to find out that entire ghettos had been deported, together with workers in shops, officials of the *Judenrat,* and policemen. Did anyone conclude from this that Warsaw too might be threatened by a complete deportation? Not at all. Germans spread a rumor that three ghettos would remain with Warsaw at the head.

This was believed very willingly. Maybe they felt sorry for the remaining Jews. But every Warsaw Jew had enough of his own tragedy.

They gave a command that every Jewish policeman had to supply five "heads" to the *Umschlagplatz* daily.

"Boys," yelled the vice commandant of the police, the lawyer Lejkin,[166] "today is the last day for deportation. Do you want to save your wives and children? Then each of you must supply five Jews today."

The next day at roll call the same speech, and so on every day. There is no justification for the Jewish policemen in Warsaw. They cannot defend themselves by explaining that they had a mental blackout. This might be done in the course of one day, but not for three long months. Their hearts turned to stone; all human feelings became foreign to them. They grabbed people, they carried in their arms infants from the apartments, they robbed if there was an opportunity. So it was not surprising that Jews hated their own police more than they did the Germans, more than the Ukrainians. There is nothing like setting a brother against brother.

There was a corrupt handful of Jews who knew that it was impossible to exist legally. An "iron-clad" letter signed by the SD* meant to them *Hide yourself well!* They and all their families saved themselves until the last liquidation of the ghetto. But there were few of these.

Right before the Day of Atonement there was a proclamation about changing the boundaries of the ghetto.[167] They threatened with the death penalty those who wanted to remain in their old apartments. The entire population, numbering eighty thousand, was placed in—as it was called later—a "cauldron."† There, instead of home and work, a new selection awaited them.[168] The number of workers in every shop was reduced by half; workers in some of the shops were assembled *in corpore* and sent to the *Umschlagplatz.*

I don't feel I have the talent to describe all that was happening in that cauldron, although I have accounts of eyewitnesses. Eighty thousand men, women, and children crammed between several houses, sitting on the ground for days and nights. Every little while, a salvo of shots falls on that crowd. Ukrainians are shooting for the sheer pleasure of killing. They are also shooting so that Jews do not recover from the state of deadness and will not respond with some act. Frequently, in the dark of night, a series of shots falls; every moment one hears a drawn-out cry of pain. The wounded who were not finished off moan. Children demand from their mothers a piece of bread. . . .

Only the German Satan knows according to what rules the selection is made. Either the first or the last row goes to the cattle cars. It may be that the mothers are released and the small, abandoned children go to the wagons. Heroic sacrifice may be seen together with vile acts. A variety exists in this world: on one side of the wall, hell, and on the other—for free people, not for Jews—a beautiful September day.

The Jewish police, with their wives and children, had to be on hand at that cauldron.

---

*SD stood for Sicherheitsdienst, or "Security Service." Established in 1931 as an intelligence service for the SS to control dissent, the SD eventually became an important agent for the extermination process.

†*Kocioł,* "cauldron," also connoted a closed-off area, such as a street, an apartment house, or even a basement. Israel Gutman, *Resistance: The Warsaw Ghetto Uprising* (Boston: Houghton Mifflin, 1994), p. 140, referred to the "cauldron" decree that placed the Jews in the Warsaw ghetto in an area shaped like a cauldron. It was a word that, of course, had a sinister meaning.

"Boys," Lejkin told them, "do you want to save your wives and children? Then enforce the last blockade."

The boys went, and in the meantime their children and wives were loaded into the wagons. Half of these were servants of the Germans as well. Did the deportation of some of the policemen appear as a warning memento for others? Not at all. Every Jew was overwhelmed by a psychosis, everyone thought himself to be more worthy, everyone thought that for sure he would not be deported.

After all this, the ghetto was reduced. Those who worked in shops were left to live. Every workshop was fenced in. From six in the morning to five in the evening walking the streets was not permitted. Those who remained thought that they had been spared from a historical cataclysm.

In town the news is spread that all those deported to Treblinka have been murdered. People weep over their families, their children. They find comfort for their aching hearts in the misfortune of others. Everyone still wants to live, wants to survive the war, wants to see with his own eyes the end of the hated Germans, wants to lend a hand to the general acts of vengeance and punishment for German barbarity, and so all live on. It is not difficult to have money in the ghetto. Jews feed themselves well. They feel like a sick man who has survived typhus: He is weak, but he is certain that this same disease will not strike him. Warsaw is safe—happy is he who has remained there.

In the meantime in August and September 1942, regular transports of Jews from Belgium, Holland, and France arrive at Treblinka. It appears that an *Aktion,* such as shooting defenseless people, packing them into cattle cars, that is practiced cheerfully here is not to be considered in Belgium or France. Perhaps "climatological" conditions there are different.[169] Perhaps the character of Germans there does not allow them such similar barbarian conduct. Perhaps Germans are afraid of the voices of outrage of Belgians and Frenchmen, who would loudly manifest their contempt for German barbarism and would help their Jewish fellow citizens.[170]

In every case the Germans applied different tactics. A bank was established that sold to Jews parcels of land in eastern territories of Poland.[171] Jews have no other way out; they buy parcels and board the Pullman cars. They take considerable baggage with them, bah, even phonographs, which they play en route. Nothing bothers them; indeed they are riding to the east to work on the soil or to that industrial town, Treblinka.[172]

When the train passes through the station near Warsaw, where Jews work at the so-called outposts, there are often comments exchanged.

"Where to?" comes the commonly asked question.

"To the industrial town Treblinka," those in the train answer.

The Polish Jews make a short sign with their hand showing the loss of a head. The Belgian Jews smile. They don't believe these fools who want to frighten them. . . .

The train rolls along to that industrial town of Treblinka. Actually, this is an industrial town where they produce fertilizer from the bones of living people.

After this account of the fate of others, I return to my own. We are in Piekełko: a large empty square surrounded by barbed wire, two barracks. In the smaller one are located the guardhouse of the Jewish police, food storage, and the commandant's office. The larger one is for prisoners. In the square are a well and, farther along, a large hole surrounded by boards, serving as a toilet. Workers wander around the square, clad in rags. On the inside of the barbed wire hang, like flags, wet shirts, underwear, and other rags. Within a radius of one kilometer one cannot see any other buildings; only right near the camp there are three small huts, occupied by Poles.

When the truck stops at the square, we jump off quickly, throw our suitcases on the ground. The driver is in a hurry; he still has to take Kronenberg to Wilanów. He makes a farewell speech.

"Boys!" he says to us, "remember that we are bound up in a common fate. We can't all be generals, to be sure, some of us have to work with a shovel, but it doesn't matter. You are young, healthy, it's nice, you'll get a suntan, we will survive the war. All of us. We are all connected with Otwock; we will return to it and establish a new Jewish *iszuw*."[173]

And boys, like boys.

"Hurrah," they yell, "long life to our commandant."

And they throw him in the air. I stand from afar, feeling skeptical about the speaker, these words, seeing our future black.

Our commandant was Landsberg; the vice commandant, Kreisler, Ehrlich's brother-in-law. They both saved their wives, who were also in camp. There were about forty of us former policemen. They picked twelve for active service. These were ruthless people, with hearts of stone and strong hands. There were about three hundred fifty workers who came from the nearest ghetto in Legionów.

The *Aktion* had not yet started at Legionów. The workers who came from there were in the best of spirits. They worked in camp; for the rest of the time they were employed in the local barracks. The president of their Judenrat was told that Legionów *kommt nicht in betracht.*

I asked them why they were so ragged, why they didn't have quilts. They replied that it was still warm, so it was a waste to bring to camp better things, rather have them at home in Legionów. I try to persuade them to liquidate their apartments, bring their property to camp, and send their families to try their luck in the Polish neighborhood. They dismissed me with sneering laughter.

"Just the opposite," the workers said to me. "We intend to return to the ghetto. Here we have to work and we suffer hunger, and there in the ghetto the rich will continue to make 'great business.' We will settle with our president after the war for sending us here, while he and his bunch of relatives play the big shots in the ghetto."

"In the meantime," one of them explained to me in confidence, "we are looking for replacements. . . ."

For such *verba dicta** there was nothing left for me to do but to stop giving any advice.

We went to work every day at five in the morning to throw up a new dike on the Vistula in the vicinity of Zeran. At first we worked in two shifts; later, when the days grew shorter, only one, from eight until nightfall. We went out when it was still dark and came back in the dark. We had no time for anything; to wash and shave one had to wait for a Sunday.

The work was hard, demanding a great deal of strength and skill. One had to pour sand into special wagons, push them, and then unload them. It was hard for me to get used to those conditions. Luckily my brother-in-law Janek and a friend from Otwock, Michał Frajbergier, helped me out from time to time. Later I learned to look busy. I tried lighter work, and altogether—starting from the principle that every shovel of sand dug out is a sin—I "helped myself"[†] as much as I could.

The company "contractor" was in charge of the work; the supervisor was Polish.[174] We had Polish engineers, technicians as well as guards. A guard to whom we were directly subordinate, a Silesian peasant named Grudek, wasn't a bad person. He made noise, yelled a lot, cursed frequently, but did not particularly chase us to work. It was worse when we were supervised by the technician Nowak. He chased us to work with a whip, like cattle, yelling and mocking us: "Ny, ny, ny."

---

*"Uttered words" (Latin).

†From the Polish word *kombinować*, this phrase was a common wartime expression for making "deals," mostly illegal.

Later, when I got used to it, the work was not hard for me, but it was difficult to constantly bend my neck before those who ordered us about. Not only because I was not used to having someone chase me with a stick to work, but also because the supervisors were Poles. Often they threatened to notify the gendarmes if we did not increase our productivity.

At work and after work we would stick together with Janek and Michał and pool our money. The nourishment is not too bad. The food at camp is not the worst but because we have a wild appetite, we buy additional provisions in the surrounding homes. Mejer, the owner of one of these, makes a "great business"* with the police. But we have full confidence in him, and he takes care of assorted matters for us in Warsaw.

After work we play cards. I and Michał modestly play *Labotka,*† Janek the gambler plays twenty-one till late at night. I don't ask him how it went. Knowing Janek, I am sure that he is capable of losing his own and my last shirt.

"How is it," he said to me often, "that when Rachel was alive I had eczema on my face and lost at cards? Now, when she is no longer here, my eczema has disappeared and I win at cards."

Life in camp in general would be tolerable if it were not for the lice and our former colleagues who remained in active service. The policemen from Otwock have already forgotten how it was not long ago; again they believe that they are "better, privileged Jews." They beat the workers with the sticks put into their hands; indeed, "there must be discipline." They have lengthened the hour for drilling, as if it were the most important thing in the life of a Jew. I still hear that cry: "Dress right! Dress left! Attention! Rest! Mister commandant, I respectfully report all the ranks. . . ."

As if they didn't know that one day the gendarmes would appear and ask "that after the game" this entire army of marionettes lie down on the ground and . . . Only us, their old friends, they did not dare torment us with the drill or beat us excessively. They just tried to find fault with us wherever they could.

Envy dominated mutual relations between Jews. It was held against Kronenberg, Ehrlich, Landsberg, and Kreisler that they were able to save their wives. Everyone sought positions that afforded an opportunity for not working and assured a first-rate feeding; they envied those who ran away to Częstochowa, those who had a lot of money, those who already

---

Kokosowe interesy literally means "coconut business."
†*Labotka* was a card game; in French, *La Bête.*

had typhus, those who had a good Aryan appearance, and those who had Polish friends. One envied the other what he himself did not have. But nobody realized that the same fate awaited us all. Death. Nobody believed this.

The workers looked with pride at the results of their labor—a splendid new dike. Their confidence rose in proportion to its growing size. They felt themselves needed; everyone, after all, had poured nineteen meters of sand daily. And all this for a stupid twenty dekagrams of bread and a plate of soup.

Wealthy friends located their suitcases in Landsberg's room so that nobody would steal them. And indeed the suitcases there were safe from theft from the other workers, but not from Landsberg's greed. He took them all.

One day a rumor spread that there was to be an *Aktion* at Kołbiel.[175] Indeed, there, in a place considered up to that time as the safest. On Saturday, the Jews of Kołbiel calculated that it would take place on Monday, but in the meantime the *Aktion* began at four in the morning on Sunday.

What the gendarmerie will not do for Greater Germany—it is ready even to rise early in the morning and that on a Sunday. In Kołbiel, like everywhere else, the Germans did not have any special work. The local Jews considered the synagogue as a kind of camp, spent the nights there, and left it only to go to work. It was enough then to chase them out of the synagogue, assemble them in the square, drive them out to Pilawa, and then load them into cattle cars.

Some former policemen who had run away from Otwock to Kołbiel were also put into the wagons. I was sure that my mother and aunt also perished, but I did not allow myself to get into a state about it. For the longest time I was convinced that the deportations would not miss Kołbiel, and so I was ready for their eventual death.

In general, after the loss of two of my dearest beings, my wife and daughter, I was without feeling about everything. No death, not even my own, could now disturb my equilibrium. I felt that tears had dried up in me; if I could cry, it would be only to remember the luminous figure of my wife and the angelic likeness of my daughter.

That same day, on the second day of the Feast of Tabernacles, the president of the Judenrat of Legionów came to the camp and made a big speech.

"Workers," he said, "you complain that you are poor and that you cannot be ransomed from the work in camp. You blame me that all the wealthy men remained in the ghetto where they continue to make good business. You're not right! With your own work you are saving the town from deportation. The town then pays for the food that you receive. The Judenrat of Legionów remembers you and your needs; from tomorrow the daily ration will be increased. But you must work sacrificially, listen to your commandant, and nothing bad will come to you and your families in the ghetto."

The workers listened quietly to the speech, after which they began to complain of being mistreated in the camp and asked why they, fathers of numerous offsprings, were sent out and how their children would be able to survive in the ghetto.

I heard all this with enormous astonishment. Such speeches were delivered in the first years of the war, but not in October 1942, when practically every ghetto on Polish territory was liquidated and its inhabitants burned at Treblinka. Still, the workers appeared to believe the president. Even though they had before them the recent example of Otwock, they wanted foolishly to be deluded and to deceive themselves. A bunch of idiots.

I even wanted to advise the president that he and his wife and entire family should move to camp, but I was silent. I was afraid I would be stoned. Earlier, one of the workers who inadvertently insulted the president was immediately given twenty strokes with the truncheon on the order of the commandant of the camp, Landsberger.

Several days afterward came the news on total deportation of Częstochowa. They apparently deported thirty-two thousand people.[176] All of those who ran away from Otwock—Rynaldo, Klajner, Ehrlich's family, and many others—they also perished.

Just then, after hearing these news, I begin to grasp the truth about the method used by Germans: From times past I begin to assemble individual links that I can now connect into a logical chain, and there appears a monstrous picture, which I myself have difficulty believing. I share these conclusions with other friends, but they don't want to listen to me. Actually they are laughing at me. Indeed, they are not Jews; they are workers who labor for the Germans for nothing and who would get rid of a worker who works for nothing. Really, a bunch of idiots!

On the last day of the Feast of Tabernacles, early in the morning the *Aktion* at Legionów starts.[177] The town was not surprised, although at midnight the Polish police informed the ghetto of the impending *Aktion*. A large number of people ran away. They directed themselves mostly toward our camp, where their husbands, brothers, and sons were located.

The Jewish policemen, however, did not run away; they remembered the fate of the Otwock police, who became famous because they made a

pile of money after the *Aktion*. Also, the workers in the barracks assumed that nothing threatened them. Not true.

Lipszer personally killed the secretary of the Judenrat and the commandant of the Jewish police, although the last one struck more than
one profitable bargain with the gendarmes. All the remaining Jews were
chased to Radzymin, where there was an *Aktion* that day, and there they
loaded them into cattle cars. They loaded the Jewish police, too, only
twelve policemen—with the president at the head—were ransomed for
three kilograms of gold. Aside from that, after a few days the gendarmes
took them in a truck to an unknown direction. Gossip had it that they
were sent to the Warsaw ghetto, but I am sure that they were just shot. I
did not have any pity for the Legionów police, although in truth they
were not guilty. They did not help the Germans at the *Aktion,* but they
deserved such a fate as they met. After the *Aktion* they wanted to remain
in Legionów in order to inherit Jewish estates, and after that they were
ready to go to camp.

In our camp you can hear weeping and moaning. The workers are crying over their families. They suddenly realize that they are in rags, almost
naked, without money—and winter is coming. In the meantime ever
more refugees appear before our barbed wire, asking for hot coffee or a
plate of soup. Men, who until now paid for not going to camp, ask that
they be let in. They spend the night in the woods and come to the
barbed wire before dawn. The workers share their portions with them;
the police chase them away with truncheons.

"The gendarmes are on their way," they yell. "They'll kill us because of
you. Get away from the wires! Get out of here!"

The next day the deputy inspector of work, Frank, came and permitted the adding to the list of workers all men roaming around the camp.
There were twenty of those. Happiness was great. And the others?

When we go out for work in the morning, we see everywhere the emaciated faces of Jews, Jewish women, small children, and pregnant
women. It is hard to spend an October night in the woods. It is hard for
me to look on the death of my brothers, posing to myself only the question, How much longer will I live? One day, two, or a week?

After returning from work, I start talking to those Jews. I advise the
mothers of small children to go to Warsaw and to abandon their children. Maybe as orphans they will be saved in orphanages. I advise
everyone to get away from the camp, to try their luck in the village
among the peasants. I am convinced that here the gendarmes will exterminate them.

Nobody listened to me. The people had enough energy to vegetate but not enough to fight actively for their lives. But I write foolishly: To fight actively for life, why, yes—but by what means? A mother with a small daughter returned to the camp area. They took not only her coat but also her daughter's.

One evening there was an *Aktion*. We were certain that it was to snatch everyone from the outside of the camp and afterward to destroy them. But we were mistaken: The *Aktion* was conducted by the Polish police for the settling of their own scores. They took from Jews all their moneys and valuables, but they brought the people to the gendarmes. What "decent people!"[178]

More or less a week after the *Aktion* at Legionów, the gendarmes conducted a raid around the camp and snatched all the Jews. Twenty runaways, whom they had inscribed earlier on the list of workers, they also dragged out of the ranks. The gendarmes left those snatched, numbering around eighty, in front of the building of the Jewish police and left.

After we left work, we were afraid to return to camp. Some of us wanted to wait out the execution. The majority, however, thought that it was necessary to return, but to march in even ranks, so as to clearly differentiate ourselves from those who were snatched. This we did.

The uncertainty of our fate, the dread of a death that threatens, leads us into a funereal mood. Involuntarily I remind myself of the poem of Słowacki, changing its meaning slightly:

As a small girl mourns her mother's leaving,
So I, close to tears, look at the sun,
That casts to me from heavens its last rays,
Even though I know that tomorrow glistens a new dawn
It is sad for me, O God![179]

The gendarmes have not yet returned. Jews, Jewish women with children, some holding infants in their arms, sit on the ground near the barracks. Some old Jew with a white beard wears from habit a white armband with a star. All of them, crying, are waiting for a bullet. Among the detained is the wife of the president of the Judenrat. Before this, all of Legionów envied her: her wealth, relations with the gendarmes, that she surely would be the one who survived the war. Now "Madame President" is sitting on the ground and envying those Jewish women who work in our kitchen. Those Jewesses go around the camp in complete safety, and she waits for death at the hands of Germans whom she knows personally. So many times she entertained them at home. Indeed, inscrutable are the dispensations of fate.

Ten gendarmes came in the evening, all of them so drunk they could hardly stand on their feet. There was movement in camp. Jewish police-men stepped around, as if in boiling water.

"Quickly," they yelled, "ten people with shovels. Move quickly, sons of bitches; take a shovel and dig a pit outside the camp."

The policemen chase the workers with truncheons, while the gen-darmes wait and are impatient. The workers fear the truncheons, fear the gendarmes, so they take the shovels and go to dig a pit for their wives, brothers, and children.

The pit is ready. They take the Jews outside the camp, and there they tell them to get undressed. It's wartime, factories are closed, nothing can be wasted. Men get undressed; women get undressed. They lie down on the ground. The Germans begin the executions. Too drunk to shoot the rifles in rounds, they use pistols.

The shots are quiet. Often the victims are wounded, but they don't kill them right away. As the gendarmes laugh, they also kill the worker busy throwing the corpses into the pit; another one is shot with a bullet in the buttocks. Finally, they order that the pit be filled, and if they hear moans from the ground, they don't care. They examine only that the earth is piled smoothly, take with them the spoils of war, and depart.[180]

I was not at the execution; guarding my brothers was not something I wanted to do. I was lying on my bunk. Through my window I saw the gendarmes leading the Jews. I saw the deputy commandant of the camp, Kreisler, with truncheon in hand. I wondered if his remains would be here at the camp. I heard shots, then the cries of the wounded, and . . . fell asleep soundly. When I woke up, the gendarmes were gone.

Until today I asked myself the question, How I could have fallen asleep at such a moment? Was this the result of a heart turned to stone or a sign of a bad character? Or was this maybe proof of the monstrous-ness of our times? May the Germans be cursed for having brought about such a state.

In Legionów, a young girl by the name of Genia lived together with an older sister, Sonia. The father worked in camp. The night of the roundup they ran away from the ghetto. They lost track of each other while in flight. Genia wandered through the villages for a few days and finally took a chance and boarded a train to Piekiełko. The conductor saw immediately that she was a Jewess. Genia handed him ten złoty and—waiting for his decision—looked him anxiously in the eye.

There are ups and downs in life: The conductor was not tempted by Jewish money, but—purely from force of habit—robbed the German treasury. He gave as change nine złoty and twenty groszy and gave Genia a counterfeit ticket.* Then he opened a conversation. Genia, seeing in front of her a person whom one does not meet in our times, gained confidence and told him who she was. She said that she wanted to go to Warsaw, to a Polish girlfriend.

The conductor, apparently a good person, proposed that he would come the next day to camp and would drive Genia to her Polish friend Miss J., living in Warsaw. He also told her that he was hiding a Jewess, a Miss Irka, in his apartment in Falenica. He had found her in the field after the Otwock roundup. That was how they parted.

Genia did not attach importance to this conversation, but the next morning . . . the conductor comes and wants to take Genia with him. She does not hesitate for a moment; she would not expect to get more than one bullet. When they reach Warsaw, the curfew hour is near. Because of the late hour, the conductor takes Genia to a friend of his. They ride in a carriage, stopping for a little while at a shop. Genia pays, although she expects the worst. But it appears that the shop is arranged as an apartment: a clean room, a wardrobe, a table, a bed, a couch, and, in the back behind a partition, a kitchen.

"Hela," says the conductor, "give us something to eat quickly. This young lady will sleep over, and tomorrow I will take her away."[181]

Sleepy Hela gets busy quickly. She asks nothing. It is enough that her lover Wacław has come to her.[182] Of course, she realizes that this is a Jewess in front of her. They sit down; the three of them eat, go to sleep quickly. Genia sleeps peacefully, the fear of gendarmes is gone, the fear of death is gone.

In the morning Hela goes to work together with her lover, and Genia remains alone in the apartment. Leaving, they close the door with a padlock.

Miss Hela has worked for the past two years in the kitchen of some office. Her husband died at the front; her son she sent out to the family in the country. She lives a regular life. Gets up at five, goes to work, where she works until four, at times even until six. After finishing work, she comes home. Her lover Wacio visits her several days a week. Sometimes

---

*Lipny means in slang a "fake."

she rides to Falenica to his apartment. Wacław's wife is her friend and naturally suspects nothing. Except for that, Hela does not have any other relationships with friends.

Wacław comes frequently to Miss Hela. Every time he is supposed to take Genia to Miss J., it somehow does not work out. He either has work on the train or is busy in town. At other times he is busy with his daily work—and in this way Genia remains with Hela.

Genia spends the entire days by herself. She stops wondering why Wacław does not take her to Miss J. Miss Hela brings her every night a can with soup; there is no shortage of bread in the house. Genia inwardly thanks God and the good people; she just cannot get over being surprised about why they take care of her so selflessly. She knows that thanks to them she has escaped the fate of Jews who wandered to the camp. She even thinks that since she was saved from the *Aktion*, she may be able to survive the war.

We found out about all this in Piekiełko from that same Wacław. When the policeman from Legionów, Śrut, heard about it, he decided to find a place for his wife and her friend, the wife of the president of the Judenrat. For the time being they were with a friend of Śrut, the leader of the Polish police, Urbas.

Urbas, at Śrut's request, contacted Wacław, gained his confidence, and took care of the locum at Miss Hela's for the two women. Their stay was to be paid for—two hundred złoty monthly.

After a certain time, Śrut was supposed to join them. Who knows, maybe they would have remained at Miss Hela's for always, maybe their lives would have been saved, if it were not for the intervention by Landsberger.

Our commandant called in Śrut and "asked" him to leave him the top boots. He explained that if Śrut was willing to run away in clogs, he had nothing against that. This made his escape impossible.

In the meantime, Śrut's wife, unable to wait for her husband's arrival and not being used to going hungry (Miss Hela bought provisions very irregularly), decided to return to Urbas and later to go to the ghetto. They tried to persuade Genia as well, but she, not having acquaintances in Warsaw, refused.

Meanwhile days in camp run monotonously. Because our funds are slowly reaching the end, I decide to go to Otwock. Because of my appearance, I am afraid to pretend I am a Pole. I decide to ride wearing my police hat, with the yellow band and my tin number. I hope that all will assume that I have a pass in my pocket.

I inform Landsberger of my plans. He doesn't want to hear about them and does not allow me to leave camp. What to do? One day when we leave for work in the morning, everybody goes to the right, and I go to the left, to the train. I decide to go first to the Karczew camp to find out if I can show myself in Otwock.

I give the conductor ten złoty. Nobody stops me on the way; only the passengers look at me as if I am an apparition from another world. The first person whom I meet in front of the camp is my good friend, the baker and bicycle repairman in one person, Szmul Kołkowicz.

"Szmul," I ask, "what's happening? Where is the family?"

"It's bad, my brother; it's bad," he answers. "As you know, we all ran away from Otwock. In Falenica they took away my wife and daughter to cattle cars. The two remaining children I placed with a peasant in a village not far from Sobień.[183] When the *Aktion* began in Sobień, the peasant handed over the children to the gendarmes.[184] In Kresy[185] at Otwock, the Brothers Kwiatkowski robbed me completely of all money. I remained alone, but I get along. I have a false *Kennkarte*, have grown a mustache, go around the villages, and somehow I make a living. Calek," Kołkowicz ends his story, "the gendarme will not get me alive. If I have to perish, then before that I will get more than one son of a bitch. I will not wait for a bullet, like those who are situated at the camp."

Saying this, he takes out of his pocket a nice seven-shot Belgian pistol. I look at Szmul in wonder and with envy. He will not perish, and if he does—he will perish honorably and in "good" company.

"Szmul," I turn to him, "can you get me a 'barker'?"*

He agrees without question, we settle on a price, and I say good-bye to him. I go to a telephone, call the Magister, and ask if he would bring me five hundred złoty next Sunday in Piekiełko. Next I telephone Nisenszal,[186] the commandant of the section of Jewish police, stationed in the Otwock hospital Zofiówka. I find out that Jewish policemen do not have the right to move about without a daily pass, which is made out by an SS man. But since only gendarme Schlicht takes care of the passes, if I want, I can risk it.

On the train to Otwock the conductor recalls that in 1940 Jews were obliged to show a certification of being deloused. I give him five złoty,

---

*The Polish word *spluwa* refers to a handgun, or "barker."

and thanks to that small sum I am a clean, deloused, and legal passenger. In Otwock I direct myself right away to Zofiówka, trying still to avoid main streets. God be praised for the police hat, thanks to which I am not stopped either by Polish scamps or Polish policemen.

On the way, I decide to visit Brothers M. They are happy at my visit and with a mysterious expression lead me to the last room. There I see an older man with big gray whiskers, dressed in a black jacket. I open my eyes wide. . . . Yes, it is my father. He has changed unrecognizably during this time, is considerably thinner, but thanks to that has a first-rate Aryan appearance.

It turns out that he saved himself in Parczew during the second *Aktion*. He didn't wait for a third one but left for Otwock. During the raid on Jews in Łuków he almost fell into the hands of the gendarmes. He came to the M. family a day before I did; the moment I arrived he was getting ready to go on foot to Kołbiel.

It also appears that my mother lives and works in a camp for road building. She wrote a letter to Brothers M. to inform me that she is completely without money and is hungry. My father turned up at that time, and a day later I arrived. Doubtless, some unseen power was guiding us.

Not losing time, I give my father several hundred złoty, and I also take off my warm long johns, which my father is waiting to put on. We arrange that my father will go to Piekiełko in a couple of days and that we will leave our hosts' apartment. My father has changed so much that he moves about fearlessly on the streets of Otwock.

In Zofiówka he is received by his friends. They do very well here. They serve an eight-hour watch. Other than that they enjoy all sorts of civilized comforts. They have at their disposal nice rooms with central heating, beds with clean bedding. There is a kitchen; they even have a library. They have no contact with the Germans.

At first I intended to go to Piekiełko, but a bath and clean bed tempted me. I spent a night there and all of the next day. In the evening, with pain and envy in my heart I said good-bye to them, and I took the road back. On the way I met a local architect, engineer Szpakowski. In conversation with him I found out that he was commissioned to construct a coop for the *Kreishauptmann* with the help of the Jewish workers in the neighborhood of Greater Otwock. Szpakowski proposed to requisition me and Landsberg from the camp and even entrust me with the position as supervisor of workers. I thanked him heartily and went on.

A great deal happened in Piekiełko during my absence. In the evening Lipszer came to camp accompanied by another gendarme. They caught ten Jews who were still wandering around the barbed wire and shot them. Then after they were buried, Lipszer told all the workers to stand in formation and made a short announcement.

"All the money in your possession," he ordered "gold, foreign bills, you must hand over to me right away. Workers may keep for themselves twenty złoty, and the former policemen from Otwock may have fifty złoty. The commandant of the camp or policemen on active service are not bound by this rule."

As the evening came, all those who stood in the rear made small holes, threw their money into them, and covered them with sand. Only a few succeeded in doing that. Those who remained, even though they saw that Lipszer was not conducting a personal search, handed over whatever they had without a sound. The fear of him they felt was enough. The money was thrown into hats that the gendarmes held in their hands. If a góral (a five hundred gold bill) fell into a hat, it immediately disappeared into a pocket. Smaller moneys that remained went into a common fund.

Lipszer's visit did not cost my close friends Janek and Michał anything other than frayed nerves. Janek was afraid that I should not come then and fall into Lipszer's hands. Indeed, I would have received a warm welcome—for a good evening I would have had a bullet. It was not laziness but good instincts that directed me when I remained in Zofiówka for the night.

Right after my return I was summoned to the camp commandant. Using foresight, I left my police hat with Janek and went to Landsberg. He, not listening to my explanations, told me to turn in my police hat and armband and go outside the barbed wire. I did not even dream of carrying out such an order. I thought that if I had to leave camp, then I could go to Karczew or Wilanów, where they would receive me with open arms. But for that I needed a hat.

I did not have a chance to tell Janek and Michał about all this when the police on duty appeared, ready to execute the order. I refused stoutly. It would have come to blows if a policeman-colleague had not intervened.

"Listen, Calek," he said, "you know Florek. I am a whore but a friend as well. Give up the hat and stay in camp."

It was not worth arguing. I handed in the policeman's hat, and the next day I went to work in civilian clothes.

At about the same time, a girl from Otwock, Tusia Zolberżanka, came to our camp. She had saved herself from the *Aktion,* lived in a Polish neighborhood, but was short of money. All our friends organized a collection, and everyone gave her five or ten złoty. Likewise Janek gave her on our behalf, without telling others, an additional two hundred złoty. He had got this sum from a relative of Zolberźanka who had been arrested. Now he returned it.

Evidently, no one—except me—knew about this. I don't have to say that as Janek explained all this to me, I stood before him shamefaced, like a little child. I reminded myself of the affair with Rachel's money, compared myself to Janek, and found with shame that he stood morally higher than me. The money that my sister-in-law had handed to me I had planned to return at the earliest opportunity, but the fact of appropriation, even if only temporary, could not be hidden.

Likewise in those days came the news that the Rembertow gendarmerie, with Lipszer at the head, had liquidated around fifty Jewish specialists employed by them.[187] On a certain morning, all of them were told to board a truck and were driven out of town. The majority did not know that they were being driven to their deaths. The tailors thought that since they had not finished sewing uniforms for gendarmes, they were safe for the time being. The cabinetmakers, who had not finished their work, thought similarly. Only two Jews—guided by, I don't know, wisdom or the voice of the heart—jumped out of the truck at the curve of the road. For the time being they hid themselves; afterward they came to Piekiełko.

News about this plunged us into a deep despondency, but a majority quickly found a "rational" explanation: Those Jews must have robbed the gendarmes, caused some trouble; otherwise they would not have been killed. This would not affect us because we worked honestly; the dike grew from day to day. It was difficult to convince them, but I am not surprised at this. If they would come to the conclusion that they would also be killed, they would have had to decide to leave the camp immediately and go out into the world to a certain death. The illusion made them feel secure.

I was of the opinion that it was necessary to leave the camp. I proposed to my friends that we buy some grenades and revolvers with the money that we spent daily on cookies and cheesecakes. The weapons, in time of danger, would make our escape possible.

"One grenade would be enough," I explained, "thrown among the unprepared gendarmes, to enable a majority to get away."

But nobody wanted to discuss it or even hear about it. Those, however, who felt unsafe in Piekiełko decided to run to the Warsaw ghetto. The *Aktion* had been completed there and, with incorrigible Jewish optimism, would not be repeated.

Every night at least one worker ran away from the camp. These were mostly those whose families lived in Warsaw or those whose families were still wandering around the vicinity of the camp. Usually they made it to the Warsaw ghetto, which was basically fairly easy. It was enough to go to Jews working in the "outposts" in the Polish neighborhood, give them a few złoty, and lose oneself among them.

There were also escapes to Nowy Dwór, the town that was situated closest to the territory of the Third Reich. The prevailing opinion was that in Germany proper they would not kill Jews.

For every escape, Landsberg, the commandant of the camp, charged the police on active duty with responsibility, then the relatives of the escapees and their neighbors in lodging accommodations—in a word, he instituted collective responsibility.

He then applied preventive measures. It was enough to suspect that someone intended to run away, and then they took the shoes off the feet of such a person, took the clothes off his back, and confiscated his money. The unfortunate man in return received clogs to wear and a paper suit. In such a garb it was difficult to pretend that one was a Pole.

I cannot escape the impression that Landsberg was in the depth of his soul quite pleased with such escapes. Under the appearance of conscientiously carrying out his responsibilities, he pursued his own, usual robbery. The confiscated moneys he took simply for himself. After all, he had a wife and son located with some Poles, all this cost money, and from where would he get money if not from Jews? An elastic conscience allowed him to condemn others to a death from hunger or at least to make it impossible to save oneself.

Worse things happened. One day I heard shrieks coming from the police guardhouse. It appeared that the police, on Landsberg's orders, had caught the son of an escapee. In order to get from him his father's address, they hung the child by the legs and began to beat him mercilessly with truncheons. The tortured boy screamed piercingly but, in spite of the terrible pain, did not reveal the address. Black and blue, barely alive, he was finally let go.

When Róża, one of the first escapees who was able to settle down in the Polish neighborhood, came to the camp to get his things, Landsberg greeted him with blows and shouts.

"So it's you, you whoreson," he screamed. "You ran away from camp, and still you dare to show yourself."

The young man made a getaway, not remembering his things anymore.

The commandant of the Karczew camp, Wolf Kalkowicz, behaved quite differently.

"My children," he was accustomed to address his workers, "do you want to run away? Go ahead, please, but under one condition. I ask you for only one thing: Come and say good-bye to me first."[188]

All this time I was strenuously trying to talk Janek into running away to a Polish neighborhood. I explained to him that he had the requisite appearance and spoke Polish faultlessly. I told him that he had a 50 percent chance of surviving, whereas in camp and even in the Warsaw ghetto his chances were not even 1 percent. He didn't want to.

I didn't understand his behavior. There were occasions when he went to the Warsaw ghetto as a Pole in order to smuggle something. He risked his life to make a hundred złoty, and now, when it concerned saving a life, he was afraid. He argued that he didn't have the energy, that if Rachel had lived, it would have been different. He wanted to be among Jews as long as possible. It made no difference to him if he survived or perished.

In the meantime, the Magister arrived at camp. He brought us money and promised to make a genuine Polish *Kennkarte* for Janek. He also took Janek's suitcase and went away. Michał Frajbergier could not get over that a Pole came to us and brought us money. Those Jews who left their possessions and money with Polish acquaintances generally lost everything.

A few days later, my father arrived. We ate supper at Mejer's, and Father slept with me in the barrack. Somehow Landsberg could not refuse to let my father into the camp, though he fretted and fumed. Anyway, he was angry with me the entire time because I didn't ask for the return of my hat and I didn't accompany this request with a serious sum of money. I knew that at any moment I would be summoned by engineer Szpakowski to build the coop in Otwock, and then the commandant—whether he wanted to or not—would have to give me my hat.

At night Father told me exactly what had happened to him and what Mother had lived through after the *Aktion* at Kołbiel.

The *Aktion* took Mother by surprise in the apartment where she was with Aunt Czerna and her son, Mulik. The landlord ran away, as did the majority of the inhabitants of Kołbiel, to the synagogue. From there they went straightaway to the cattle cars. The landlady and Mother hid themselves in a small shelter under the floor of the foyer. From Mother's account it seems that Czerna refused to go down to the hiding place, saying that she didn't want to suffer any longer, and she went with her son to the square.

I read something a little different between the lines. Mother said that the shelter was quite small, so small that they almost suffocated lying there for three days. There can be only one conclusion: "There wasn't" room for Czerna. The people who had already entered did not take notice of those who were doomed, that someone else could hide there. That's how I figure it. I am sure that my mother as well as the landlady took the knapsacks with their things to the shelter because my mother told me that later everything was stolen in the woods. It is clear, then, that all their possessions were in the shelter. Whatever happened, a place was found for things, but as for my aunt—there wasn't any.

Czerna had a very noble character, very similar to that of my wife. I know she was too proud to enter where she wasn't wanted, and she would rather have gone to her death than inconvenience someone with her presence. The fact is that before departing, she handed my mother a gold watch. Perhaps it will always remain a mystery to me whether Czerna went to the cattle car of her own free will if there was a place for her in the shelter.

The image of a little Mulik crying haunts me: He is begging his mother that they hide, and my aunt answers him, "Come, Mulik, to the square. Don't you see there is no place? . . ."

Maybe my fantasy runs away with me. Maybe Czerna herself wanted to go. Maybe I do injustice to my mother with such thoughts. I could ask her about it, but I will probably not hear the truth. I have nothing else to do but be guided by my instinct and knowledge of human character.

Mother and her landlady spent three full days in that secret hiding place and finally took their knapsacks and went to the woods beyond Kołbiel. There they spent a few days, without food. All sorts of different peasants searched them, taking money and possessions. Even young shepherds approached them and called out, "*Jude*, give us money, or we'll go for the Germans!"[189]

Finally Mother had nothing to give up and resignedly decided to return to Kołbiel to perish there like other Jews. I can imagine what she went through before she got there. But this time, instead of a bullet, a surprise awaited her. Those Jews who had remained alive were not shot by the Germans but were gathered again en masse for return to the synagogue and then chased to work on the road. The German in charge was an older man and did not want to kill women with his own hands, knowing that anyway, sooner or later, they would die at someone else's hands.

Life in the camp wasn't bad if Mother had some money with her to buy some food. So she wrote a letter to Brothers M., the result of which was my father's arrival. He left her money, assured her that somehow he would take her away from the camp, and again returned to Otwock on foot. I was amazed at his energy, unusual for a man that age.

He slept the night in the stairwell because he didn't want to abuse the patience of the M. family, and the next day he went to Piekiełko. He spent a few days near the camp. During the day he traveled to Warsaw to find some locum, at night he returned to the camp. He made use of time. He made all sorts of contacts, arranged a false *Kennkarte* for himself. He also arranged *Kennkarten* for his friends, bought gold in Kołbiel, and sold it in Warsaw.

Altogether this took four weeks. Finally, thanks to Mejer, he got a permanent apartment with his relatives in Warsaw. He lived there quite well, even got breakfast in bed.

During one of his stays in Piekiełko, he met near the camp the above-mentioned Miss Hela in the company of the inseparable Wacław. They came upon the same policeman, who was acquainted with their charge, Genia, and asked if he would help her with some material means. Father does not divide people into those he knows and those he doesn't know. For him all are people he knows if he can only talk to them. He started to talk to them. It turned out that Wacław was a school friend of my brother's. One thing led to another, and Father took care of locating my mother in an apartment in Warsaw where one Jewish woman was already in hiding. After a short haggling, they settled on five hundred fifty złoty a month.

Because my father had no other choice, he did not make sure whether this hiding place was good or bad; in the end, it couldn't be worse than camp. He did not worry that they would rob Mother because she had nothing anymore with her. He decided to bring her to Warsaw right away.

Because this was the time of All Saint's Eve, he borrowed from Miss M. a complete mourning outfit, with a veil for the face. With my mother so dressed up, they went on foot to Celestynowa, and from there they reached Warsaw by train. When the train moved, Mother crossed herself. Seeing this, a young man gave her a place to sit. Happily they arrived in Warsaw and from there went straight to Miss Hela. From November 4, 1942, Mother lived in the store-apartment of Miss Hela.

Around the same time inspector Frank came to camp to take me and Landsberg to Karczew. When they came to the dike to inform me about my trip, I threw the shovel to the ground, rushed to camp, and in fifteen minutes I was ready—of course, the hat was ready for me. I said good-bye to Janek, let Father know from afar that I was going to Otwock, and got into the car. Landsberg was supposed to come by train the next day.

First we traveled on Długa Street, where the stores of *Wasserwirtschaft*[190] to which we belonged were located. It's difficult for me to describe what I experienced driving in daylight through the main streets of Warsaw. The traffic, shop windows, the smiling faces of the elegant passersby, women, children, everything made on me, a condemned man, a depressing impact. I knew that this beautiful world was not created for me. It would have been enough for me to leave the car, and the first policeman had the right to kill me like a mad dog.

In front of the headquarters of the *Wasserwirtschaft* I talked to the Jews from the Warsaw ghetto who worked there. Although they did not know me, they received me well and even treated me to lunch. I found out what was happening in the Warsaw ghetto, and we drove farther.

The car also stopped at Wilanów. I had occasion to greet Kronenberg and had to listen to his wife about how her fox terrier improved in the open air. I compared the wasted appearance of the workers with the shining coat of the dog, said good-bye, and we drove to Karczew.

I was assigned to Karczew for the duration of the construction of the coop, but during the day I had to guard the demolition of a house in Otwock. I figured out that the work would last three months and—in my naïveté—thought that no danger would threaten me at this time.

The workers in Karczew, especially policemen, could move about freely in Otwock. It was enough to say that one was working at the demolition. Because the stay in Karczew did not tempt me, already in the first evening I took my suitcase in hand and marched to Otwock. I left my valise at Stefan M. and spent the night at Zofiówka.

The next morning I started work, supervising five workers doing demolition of the house on Kupiecka Street. Once this was the busiest street in the ghetto. Now I did not recognize either the street or any other place. Almost all the Jewish homes were sold to the Poles for demolition. On the territory of the entire ghetto one could hear the crash of falling walls, and among the ruins burned fires at which the workers were warming themselves. Whole streets disappeared. In places where life had recently pulsated, where people had played, cried, worked, and rested—now, except for ruins, there was nothing. Jews perished, Jewish homes perished, the entire land fell into a tomb.

For those few Jews who survived, this was a terrible sight. Everyone remembered where he had lived or where his family had lived. Among the workers were those who had to tear down with their own hands a house built by their ancestors, a house that could have stood another hundred years. Near us, Poles were demolishing a house, carrying out of it sacred Hebrew books, and throwing them into fire. The fire from this was not the best, but it served to make fun of the Jews working across from them.

After a while my heart hardened to all these scenes. It was worse when work reminded me of times when I had been the owner of a lumber business, sorting out planks all day and sending them out with wagons to various buildings. Now at times I forgot in what sort of a world I was living; it seemed to me that in the evening I would return home normally. Once it even happened—that lost in thought I walked into my own movie house as if I still lived there. I came to myself on the stairs and wept bitterly.

I should have really returned for the night to Karczew, but I slept mostly in Zofiówka. There I breathed in the comfort that I had been used to, and thanks to that I felt like a newly born person. I ate breakfasts at the construction site, dinners at my former landlady Głaskowa's in my old apartment on Podmiejska Street. In the room stood my old furniture. Everything reminded me of my wife and child, of the whole period in the ghetto, which now, after the catastrophe, I idealized as the happiest time of my life.[191]

In fact, that was a happy time. I was together with my wife, daughter, whose white arms embraced my neck; the room was clean and cozy. Was I lacking in anything then? Every time I was at Głaskowa's, I promised myself never to return again to my former apartment. I suffered terrible anguish, and yet each time some force pushed me across the old threshold.

For the sake of justice I must add that Głaskowa made me feel very welcome, and I had to insist that she take money from me for dinner. Once she even suggested that I have a bath there, something that I did with pleasure. She kept on telling me that my furniture had not been touched and was always for me to dispose of. She understood how I suffered, knew what it was to be homeless, without a family, without a right to life. Although a plain woman, she had a better heart than some fine lady.

From time to time I visited Stefan M. Sometimes I met Father there, but in general I avoided that house in order not to awaken suspicions that the owner had contacts with Jews.

When my teeth hurt, I went to Miss Lidia Wolańska. She was always happy when I visited her. She received me well, did not charge me for the fillings, and each time she treated me to lunch or dinner. Only her assistant felt uncomfortable when I visited; she was the daughter of the school messenger, Franciszek Stańczak. On each one of my visits she covered herself tightly with a white apron so that I wouldn't see a sweater or a dress that she happened to be wearing that belonged to my wife.

I pretended that I didn't see, but the dentist, always feigning ignorance, asked why she wrapped herself so tightly with a dust coat, or she expressed "surprise" about a sweater in my presence. She would ask the Stańczak girl maliciously if she had made it herself or if she had bought it. The girl blushed deeply, but inside she was probably laughing at us.

"You're making fun of me," she might say to herself, "but I know that I am dressed well. Why should one get upset if these were things stolen from Jews? The owners will not rise from their graves, and those who live must be silent."

I felt a deep gratitude to Miss Lidia that she received me so kindly, but I cannot forget a few facts testifying to her character.

"Drink, Mr. Calek. Allow me to give you one more glassful," she would try to persuade me. "Indeed, I do have to get along with you. Your father is already old, he will probably not last too long, after the war you will be the landlord. So I have to get along with you."

And so, as I was accustomed to, I heard her out in silence, how light-heartedly she consigned to the grave my still-living, and still-craving-to-live, father. I reminded myself how in the past she had haggled with my father for the cost of a room, and I listened further.

"You see, Mr. Calek, the reason that your sister perished was because she testified against me falsely in court. It's a deserved punishment from God that she finally met up with."

I open my eyes wide. I feel as if I have broken out in a cold sweat. Finally I have an answer as to why my sister perished: It was for having been a witness for the opposite side in a case concerning ten or twenty złoty of a monthly rental.

On the second Saturday of my stay in Otwock I suddenly longed to see Janek and Michał, and making a quick decision, I took the train to Piekiełko. While en route, one conductor threw me off the train, but another one put me back on for the payment of twenty złoty. In the camp everyone was happy with my arrival. Because my father also arrived at that time, I wanted to meet him outside the wired enclosure. Luckily Janek warned me that a car was coming in our direction. My father ran away to one side, and we ran to the barracks. We didn't even have time to get settled when we heard a shot. We were certain that they had caught my father and killed him on the spot.

Later it turned out that Lipszer saw a lonely Jewish woman as he was arriving and that he killed her with his pistol right away. They did see my father, and even though he was chased by another gendarme, he managed to get away. This enraged the Germans.

Lipszer (accompanied by Landsberg, who went to Piekiełko legally every Sunday) directed that a grave be dug outside the camp for the Jewish woman killed a moment earlier. He demanded that it be bigger, which the workers readily complied with. Then he ordered that three former policemen be summoned: Gutner, Krumarz, and Felner. When they stood before him, he asked them in a mocking tone what they were doing at the moment when he was arriving. They were all in Mejer's house in front of the camp, but they weren't able to run away quickly enough for Lipszer not to be able to see them. No explanations helped. A short order fell: *"Umlegen!"*[192]

The three were led out of the camp, and they were told to lie down in the grave where they were to be killed. Majer Gutner was a man of exceptional character, and I am sure that if he had had a weapon on him, he would not have hesitated to use it. But because he was defenseless and didn't want to die without opposition, he started to run away. Krumarz followed him. Only Felner, a young and weak boy, sat on the ground resignedly.

Lipszer quickly oriented himself, ordered Landsberg and the workers to chase Krumarz, promising that they would be shot if they did not catch him. With another gendarme he chased after Gutner. Rifle shots quickly followed one after another. Soon they succeeded in wounding Gutner. A gendarme brought him back and again tried to get him to lie down in the ditch. Gutner gathered up his last strength and began to run again. This time the bullet found its mark, and he fell dead. (His brother Biume saw his battle from afar but could do nothing to help him.)

So perished Majer Gutner, the strongest of the strong, the best of the good. Before this he had often told me that if he knew where the partisans were, he would gladly have volunteered. Unfortunately, it was not given to him to die a hero's death—but in any case he didn't die like a coward.

In the meantime Landsberg was chasing Krumarz. He, sensing that he did not have the strength to get away, stopped and proposed that they both run away to the Warsaw ghetto. Landsberg would not hear this and brought him quickly to Lipszer. He took a rubber truncheon and began to beat Krumarz wherever he could. In the end, he threw the almost unconscious man into the pit and shot him. Before death, the unfortunate managed to cry in Hebrew, "Hear, O Israel, God is ours. God is One."[193]

Only Felner remained, who sat at the edge of the pit as if insensible. Lipszer sized him up with a sadistic look.

"You remain," he spoke quickly. "If the others had not run away, I wouldn't have killed them either."

What did our commandant do? Lipszer had hardly left before Landsberg appeared in the barracks in order to "inherit" the possessions of the dead.

I returned to Otwock with a strong conviction that I would no longer go to Piekiełko. Tension was the order of the day, with the expectation that December 1 would bring a complete liquidation. More and more of the workers ran away to Warsaw; more and more policemen arrived in Otwock to find for themselves a place to hide. Janek also came. The commandant of Zofiówka agreed to take him in for money.[194]

In Zofiówka I met Berek Kejzman who told me how he had jumped out of the cattle car where my wife was and how he had fortunately got to Falenica. The following day he was again grabbed in the *Aktion* there, but he somehow managed because he was taken to the Najwert sawmill for labor. He ran away from the sawmill, and now he intended to get to the Warsaw ghetto, where his wife and child were. They also saved themselves in the Otwock *Aktion* as well as from Kołbiel and Wołomin—and at last they settled in the Warsaw ghetto.

In mid-November an announcement appeared in the official newspaper that on December 1 new ghettos in Warsaw, Kałuszyn, Sobolew, Parczew, Rembertow, Kosów, and a few other places would open. Those who after that date were found outside of the ghetto were threatened with death.[195]

This time the majority of Jews were certain that only death awaited them in the newly established ghettos. In spite of that, numerous people went there, thinking that they would pass the winter peacefully and that with the coming of spring they would look for a safer hiding place. There was no shortage of naive people who argued that the new ghettos were being created because of the pressure of public opinion or for propaganda purposes.[196]

I reacted negatively to those ghettos. I knew that this was a trap, but I didn't have the energy to run away immediately. Janek, on the other hand, argued that every day of survival among one's own was another day won. He was convinced that he would be able to cut and run before an *Aktion* or jump out of a cattle car.

It also appeared that around fifty people would spend the winter in Karczew and in Piekiełko. In Karczew they paid the commandant two thousand złoty per head to remain in camp, with the result that all the wealthy ones remained. In Piekiełko it was just the opposite: The rich ones left for the Warsaw ghetto, and the poor people remained in camp.

Landsberg looked with envy at the commandant of the Karczew camp, Kalkowicz, who collected fat thousands, where he was offered only hundreds.

In the meantime Landsberg and I finished our demolition in Otwock, and we began to build the coop for the *Kreishauptmann*. Every day I wandered ten kilometers from Zofiówka to Greater Otwock, and I returned evenings. I ate a lot, although irregularly. Physically I felt well.

Only at the last moment did I realize that the *Kreishauptmann* had not received permission for the use of Jewish workers. As quickly as I could, I said good-bye to Landsberg and made my way to Zofiówka, where I had reserved a place for myself. Naturally, "not for my beautiful eyes," I was ready to give—and did give—a large sum, if only to spend a peaceful winter. I was also able to settle a place for Janek.

During the entire time of my stay in Otwock, I saw the Magister fairly frequently. Thanks to his friends I had the opportunity to get the use of an authentic *Kennkarte* for Janek. We visited him in his office of November 30, received the papers, which Janek had to sign and deposit in the municipal government in Warsaw.[197]

The next day the building Zofiówka was surrounded by gendarmes, and the Polish police gave us fifteen minutes to get ready to leave.

I decided on the spot that I wasn't going anywhere. First of all, I didn't want to go to the Warsaw ghetto; for another, I had on me the Aryan, false papers of Janek's, and I was afraid that they could be discovered. Not even saying good-bye to Janek—I didn't think I would ever see him again—I went downstairs, risking a bullet in my back, and ran away to the woods. From there I went to Świder to a janitor I knew and with whom I spent the entire day. In the evening I made my way to Otwock and, unnoticed by anyone, made it to the apartment of Stefan M. He offered me, unselfishly, his own room until such time as my father found something for me.

So ended another stage in my life. I ceased to be a worker in the German service. I had no right to remain in town. I knew that if I were recognized as a Jew, a bullet would not miss me. I tried to find Szmul Kołkowicz, but without success. I discovered only that he had found arms for a few butchers, who were caught after that and killed. A big affair was made of that, and Kołkowicz was afraid to show himself in Karczew.

In November I visited Franciszek Stańczak, who returned to me a portion of the things most precious to me and completely worthless to him. He returned to me photographs of my wife and child. The rest he promised to return after the war.

I would like to shed some light on my father's relationship to me and to my brother-in-law Janek. The attitude of my father to Janek, before and after the marriage of my sister, was exceptionally negative. After Rachel's tragic death Father continued to treat Janek very coldly, which did not stop him from benefiting from his material help. I was surprised at Janek's behavior. When my father returned from Parczew, he helped him get set up in a new apartment, he arranged for my mother's journey to Kołbiel, and from time to time he sent her money. As it concerns me, even though I was strongly indifferent in my feelings, I tried to behave correctly. I was not able to show more feeling— it is difficult to expect from a cold heart that it should suddenly become warmer.

To tell the truth, I didn't really feel that I could love anyone, but I believed that I had to fulfill obligations toward parents: share with them the money or possessions and help them in general. When Father set my mother up, I gave him a bedcover for her, a pillow, and a change of sheets. When he had himself settled, I gave him a similar sendoff.

I must add that Father was gripped by some sort of a craziness when it came to furnishing his place. The conditions in the apartment were quite good for him: They helped him; they did not take advantage of him financially. To put it briefly, he came across good people, and he knew how to put them to use. When he saw that I had some decent things—a silk shirt or pajamas—he wanted it right away. I didn't begrudge him anything. I even gave him my own Longines watch because I thought that it would be safer with him.

I asked my father several times to try to find me some sort of a hiding place, but he had no time to look. He was always busy with his own business in Kołbiel and Piekiełko. Although he knew that I could perish any day or find myself without a roof over my head, he didn't want to give me his or my mother's address. At first I thought that this was an accident, but later I convinced myself that he acted based on some deeper meanings. Finally he told me where he lived, but he didn't give me the number of the apartment or the name of the landlord. The M. family was surprised at his behavior and considered my father a terrible egoist.

At the end of November Father came to Brothers M. and very angrily asserted that he had lost his apartment because of me. It turned out that when he was sitting in his room, the secret police arrived, giving his landlord his assumed name. He barely had time to escape through the basement window.

"I didn't send the police after you," I answered calmly. "I don't even know the number of your apartment. Anyway, these were not at all the police but trackers sent by the landlord."

Father did not want to hear this. Naturally he was afraid to return to his apartment. Still, a couple of days later these same "policemen" grabbed him in the street, took four hundred złoty that he had on him, and told him that if brought them another thousand, they would return his *Kennkarte* to him. Willy-nilly Father brought them the next day the required sum. He received the *Kennkarte* with an offer of a profitable business. They proposed for him to track down and hand over to them rich Jews. Father declined to join in such a "good business," explaining that he did not know Warsaw Jews.

The landlord took away practically all his things and returned only a few torn shirts. I am sure that this was an arranged work among Majer from Piekiełko, who procured for him the apartment, his landlord, and the trackers. Father himself asked for trouble, letting himself be taken in by pretty words. He took many things from us, which he put in a new apartment (Kawęczyńska, 6/28). The landlords realized that it was not worth keeping Jews since it was possible to take away their things all at once.

After this story, Father enriched himself with one more experience—it is not permitted to be in an apartment together with one's things.

Because he didn't have another apartment, I agreed with Wacław that the three of us—Mother, Father and me—would live with Miss Hela for the cost of fifteen hundred złoty monthly. It didn't really appeal to me to be with them, but Stefan M. considered it his obligation to keep me until I found another place. Money would not tempt him. I planned then to confront him with an escape-proof situation. I wanted to tell him that he had to save my life since I have no place to go to and in support of that promise to sign over a portion of my villa after the war. Still, my father did not want to hear of this. He wanted not only to survive the war but also to preserve the property intact.

Whether I wanted to or not, I left Stefan's apartment, thanked him for a free week and a pleasant stay. I had no hope that I would see him again.

In the evening we went on foot with Father to Świder in order to take a train from there to Warsaw.

In Warsaw my heart was beating with an insane fear. While on the trolley it seemed to me that at any moment I would be recognized as a Jew. But luckily I arrived, and on December 6 I crossed the threshold of Miss Hela's apartment, where I am to this day.[198]

Warsaw ⤳

THE FIRST IMPRESSION was quite pleasant. As I entered, I saw an iron stove right in the middle of the room, and in a short while everyone looked flushed from its warmth. First I greeted my mother, whom I had not seen since the Otwock *Aktion*. She tried to avoid my looks, but I paid no attention to that. Then I saluted Miss Hela and made my acquaintance of Genia. Wacław was also present. We had dinner together, and I went to sleep.

The next morning while we remained alone in the room, I was able to evaluate our hiding place. One wall was a gabled end, which meant that another house adjoined there, and therefore from that side there was nothing to be heard. The rear wall was connected with a corridor and closets. Through there the neighbors could eventually hear what was going on in our room. They could assume, however, that it was the landlord. Later it turned out that there was no danger from that side either. The neighbors were always drunk. The other back wall was part of a coal bin. No voice would reach there. The front wall faced the street. Because the apartment had once been a store, the display windows had to be closed with shutters, as did the glass door. The door shutters were wooden; the top portion had double openings, which provided the only source of light. That was why it was barely light in the room, but even this did not last the entire day. We could hear very well what was happening in the street, but from the outside it was not possible to see what was going on in the apartment. The only appliances were the kitchen stove and the sink. There was no basement, so it was not possible to hide in the event it was necessary.

A plus to the apartment is that it leads directly to the street so that a janitor cannot control who goes in and who goes out. The landlady, after returning from work, opens the door widely so that everyone in the street can see what is going on in the room. At that time we are behind the wardrobe. Similarly, when someone is visiting Miss Hela—a janitor or some gossiper—we hide behind the wardrobe. Nobody ever finds out.

By a happy coincidence there is no one across the street. There is only a lumber business, and all day long they operate an electrical saw, the so-called *krajzega*.*

A minus to the apartment is the lack of toilets. One has to make use of a bucket hidden under the sink. Once a week Miss Hela empties it. It's not much fun, but it can't be helped. Miss Hela is not in all day, and so we are on our own. We can wash, do laundry, whatever is necessary, and there is no oppressive feeling of being cramped by others.

Behind the wardrobe stands a bed on which my father and I sleep. Mother is on a couch. Genia sleeps on a pillow on the floor near the stove.

My father goes into town twice a week. He leaves the apartment at six with Miss Hela and returns at seven. He also buys food. He communicates with Michalski, who blames his brother for everything. Father believes him because he has to. For one, he has to maintain contact with someone. Second, when he goes for the whole day, he has no place to stop in, and this way he can stay at the Michalski shop and do a little business with him.

We are afraid of only one thing: The "whole town" knows that Genia is hiding here. Piekiełko knows. The Jewish legionnaires† in the Warsaw ghetto know. We expect that if it "gets hot," other Jews will tear the lock off the door to get in here.

Later it turned out that such thoughts were only proof of our naïveté. We could not even get it through our heads that in Warsaw it would be so "hot" that this heat would literally burn all the Jews. The hiding place is a good one, and the proof of this is that Genia is already here ten months. And it is not especially costly.

After a week passed, I went to the Magister to introduce my father to him. I anticipated that from now on I would not be able to communicate with him personally. I asked that the goodwill he had shown me up to this time be extended to Father, whom I empowered to handle all my things. I only made an exception for a length of brown material for a woman's winter coat, as well as brown lining, which I left for Janek's disposal. Because of that, Father was furious with me, but I had no inten-

---

*This term is a hybrid of the Polish word for cutting, *krajać*, and the German word for sawing, *sagen*.
†These were widows of the veterans of Piłsudski's legion, holders of *Virtuti Militari* (for Military Virtue, a medal for valor that originated in the late eighteenth century), who enjoyed a special status.

tion of telling him that I did this to let go of a burden that had oppressed my conscience for three months.

My wife's white wedding suit, consisting of a silk dress, coat, shoes, bag, and gloves, I earmarked as a present for the Magister's sister. It seemed to me that I did not betray my wife's memory in bequeathing this beautiful suit to an unknown person, who nonetheless wanted to take in our daughter. I also wanted to leave our address for Janek, but my father categorically opposed it. I left only his Aryan papers with the Magister.

Although the Magister received us most kindly, I left him with my spirit broken. While we were there, someone was playing the piano in the next room. But it was not the pleasant notes of the music that so unbalanced me. . . . I was unsettled by the image of a house where the war reached to its very walls but could not breach them. Here my daughter could have been today, and if she was not, it was the result of my tardiness and lightmindedness. If it was intended for me to stay alive, it was so that I would do penance eternally. The image of my daughter brought up in such a noble family atmosphere as exists at the Magister's obsesses me to this day.

One more thing did not give me peace of mind and reminded me of my guilt. It had to do with being able to save my English suits and winter coat. My father was angry with me that I had saved so few things. However, I blamed myself that I had saved anything. If I had not regretted letting go of these things before the *Aktion,* I could have had enough money to buy Anka a *Kennkarte* and also save her from *Umschlagplatz.*

In the end my father sold the suits and my coat to a friend of the Magister, Dr. R., for the sum of eight thousand złoty. I gave a sigh of relief when they were sold. I came to hate them so.

Our monthly budget for Miss Hela's apartment came to three thousand złoty. We had ten thousand złoty in currency, and to that we added the money acquired from the sale of my property. We could sell other things that remained at the Magister's. We estimated that if all went well, it would last us for a year's life. It was necessary then to bring the rest of the things from Otwock to Warsaw.

My mother's fur collar as well as father's otter fur was at Dr. Mierosławski's, a friend of the Magister; mine and my father's small fur pieces were at the court official Alchimowicz's, a small suitcase was at Brothers M.'s, and a knapsack with some small items from camp was at Głaskowa's.

Because Father could travel to Otwock only in the winter, when the nights were long and dark, he decided to bring everything at once to Warsaw.

My father visited the doctor maybe ten times. At first he heard that another Jew, a Dr. (Michał) Kokoszko, who also had left some things with him, took them by mistake. Father explained endlessly that the one otter would enable our whole family to live for at least one month more. Mierosławski replied that he had sold his own otter for two thousand— as if this had any significance, except that it was probably my father's otter—and he just dismissed this with a wave of his hand. He told Father not to come to him anymore because his house was under police surveillance. Finally, after many requests, he returned mother's fur collar.

Dr. Mierosławski—I address him as if he were present—you are considered to be at the top of the social hierarchy in Otwock, but how are your morals different from those of the gymnasium messenger Franciszek? Indeed, I have more respect for him. At least he risked his head and robbed things worth around four hundred thousand złoty. You, on the other hand, a local doctor, our neighbor of many years, the father of my classmate, you were greedy for something worth one hundred times less.

It went a little differently with Alchimowicz. He returned to my father my small fur items with the gesture of a fine gentleman who would never covet someone else's things. He didn't let my father even cross the threshold of his apartment, received him in his dark corridor, and returned the things wrapped in a small pillowcase, as I had left them with him. At home it turned out that everything was in order except for one item. The most expensive item was missing: my gray squirrel lining.

I advised my father not to tell Alchimowicz about this because this great "gentleman" would feel insulted and in general would not want to talk to him, and it was still necessary to take away from him my father's fur lining. But nothing helped. When my father returned to recover his things, Alchimowicz did not deny that he had the fur, but he said that he would return it in the spring because his wife would wear it in the winter, and in general "he does not have a cloakroom." I am certain that he knew very well that my father would not dare come to Otwock in the spring.

When I heard about this, it really opened my eyes. I couldn't understand what had happened to a man who in his time had for safekeeping items worth hundreds of thousands of złoty and was now greedy over something worth several thousand. How could this man tell my father that there was "no cloakroom" in his place when all the furniture in his apartment was either mine or my father's? I will add that some time ago he asked my father if he would give them to him for safekeeping.

How could two years change a grown man, a captain in the Polish army? I always thought of myself as someone who knew human nature, and here is one disenchantment. Apparently the human soul reacts differently in the presence of a live person and differently when it has to do with live corpses. Then it seems he recites a prayer that the live corpse should change into a real one and stop bothering "decent people."

Only with Brothers M. was there no disappointment.

Everything that my father could collect he tied together and went to the station. He arrived in Warsaw after the curfew hours. When he was already on our street, two German soldiers stopped him. They examined my father's *Kennkarte,* and then they saw the night pass given by the railway to passengers of the late train. This they just waved off. They went carefully through his things and searched his person thoroughly as well. As an opportunity presented itself, they stole the three thousand złoty that he had and the new reindeer leather gloves.

As it was, the story ended fortunately. First of all, they did not take him to the *Komisariat,* and secondly, they did not recognize that they had before them a Jew. Thirdly, they did not notice my father's gold watch, and fourthly, they did not take all the things. This is the nature of a Jew that whatever happened, thank God that it wasn't worse. But Father had his full share of fear.

At that time Janek left the Warsaw ghetto for a few days. He liquidated his affairs in Otwock, submitted an application in the city council for a *Kennkarte,* and spent the night at the Magister's, where he enjoyed a bath. He probably rented a room somewhere in Praga. He could not communicate with us, but this was Father's fault since he surrounded our address with such secrecy. I would also add that he had more luck than we did; all his things were with Brothers M., and they could be trusted.

Because it was easy to get out of the ghetto, he returned for the time being to his friends, to that Jewish environment that created a *milieu favorable*[199] for a normal life. Father asserted that cards drew Janek to the ghetto, whereas I feel that it was a lack of family warmth that pushed him away from us.

The days dragged out in an impossible manner. Already at two in the afternoon I went to bed and remained there until nine in the morning. Most of the time I thought about one theme: how easy it would have been to save my wife and child. I went through thousands of combinations, one better than the other. It filled me with terrible sadness and feelings of guilt. There is nothing worse for a person than to be left alone with his own negative thoughts. Although I was not alone in the room, I didn't have anyone with whom to share my problems.

Genia was crocheting the entire time; she was certainly a decent enough girl, but she lacked education. She understood how to behave, but she did not have enough reasoning for conversations, discussions, for comprehending another person.

Mother was avoiding me in a most obvious way, was even afraid to look me in the eye. I could not understand this at all. It's true that there weren't particularly warm feelings between us, but . . . Then the truth came out. Because mother suffered from insomnia, I advised her to take one pill of Veronol for the night. She, remembering the situation after the *Aktion,* thought that I wanted to poison her. She could not forget that it was I who had suggested the poison. The fear, that it was possible to be poisoned by one's own son, she transformed into a mania that one could not knock out of her head.

She had shared this dread earlier with her husband, awakening in him an even greater mistrust of me. I was too proud to try to convince them that my intentions were always good. I thought that if I lived to be their age, and that it was necessary to fear that my son would dispatch the gendarmes to me, then I would no longer fight to live. Even now, as I write these words, I don't have my father's address, although I am here together with my mother.

I don't know if anyone believes this; it is so macabre. Finally, the year of our Lord 1942 showed that everything was possible in this vale of tears. Mothers poisoned little children so they would not be betrayed by their crying. Sons poisoned their fathers when they could no longer save them. Since everything was now possible, it was not difficult to imagine that my parents were afraid that I wanted to poison them. They were governed by the maniacal thought that I could not stand it that they were alive and that my dearest ones, wife and daughter, had perished.

All that I did for my parents did not count. The fact that in spite of everything, I saved my mother and sent her to Kołbiel, that I sent her money and provided my father with things, that I now placed at his disposal all that I had—thereby shortening my own survival chances if the war went on longer—all this did not have the slightest significance for them. In their own time they bore considerable financial sacrifices for me. I expressed my gratitude doing the same. That I shared with them my moneys, they had accepted as a natural thing. But that I had proposed to my mother the use of poison in a completely hopeless situation, they could neither forget nor forgive.

An even greater chasm than that which separated me from my mother divided me from my father. It is not just the fact that he would not betray his address to me. Any understanding between us was impossible not just because of his attitude on the Jewish tragedy in general but of that of our family's tragedy in particular.

I could not hear how a grown-up man, in addition a Jew, would argue that the murder of the Jewish people came as a result of sins committed by Jews toward God, that this entire cataclysm corresponded to the will of God and was foretold by the Jewish prophets. My father repeated frequently that everyone should do everything to save oneself but that one should not feel sorry for those who had perished.

But the crux of the problem was, it seemed to me, that he really could not forgive me for not taking care of his things rather than that I had brought my wife to the square. Ceaselessly he reminded me of what he had lost and counted what the cash value of that was. He did not reminisce once about the lost family.

His second most beloved subject was to consider how the Jewish policemen enriched themselves after the *Aktion*. Frequently he remembered the names of the policemen and the sums of money that they had gained, while reminding me that I did not have enough presence of mind to even take care of that which was entrusted to me. After his monologue I was certain that if my father had been a policeman, he would have already secured his possessions by the time the cattle cars left Otwock with his wife and child.

It was quiet in the room only when we did not talk at all. As soon as some conversation started, it would get deflected onto such subjects that they had to end with a quarrel. The hottest theme was the question of divine justice. I blasphemed openly. Frequently, for example, I asked Father with a mocking tone what he, an observant Jew, was guilty of that God, while saving his life, bestowed on him a plague of boils. I suggested that maybe God confused Germans with Jews.

But to be truthful, it was quite different. At first we were all troubled by an itchy skin infection, which Genia probably brought from camp. After a month Father brought some medication, and all of us were cured. But then Father, Mother, and Genia were affected with another plague. They had on them boils the size of fists. I did not have that. Father bought up an entire supply of *Hansaplaster* in several pharmacies, but they did not get cured of it until April 1943.

Writing such a severe criticism of Father, I don't intend this to be in the least an attack on his character and his faith. He is not a bad person. Quite the contrary—he is helpful, sacrificing, good to people. He is distinguished by energy and honesty. He always denied himself everything, but there was never anything too expensive for the family, for us the children, or for Mother. Still, the attachment to material things and cunning, on the one side, and, on the other, a fanatical belief in God and obedience to Jewish dogmas, also a terrible egotism and the desire to save mainly his own life—all this perverted the character of this man.

Now, when we are in hiding, I am convinced that a person needs many things for survival but absolutely indispensable—in our situation—are a pillow and a coverlet. When I realized that, I recalled my father's words when he saw me the first time after the *Aktion* and reminded me to look after pillows. Even though I have understood what he had in mind, I continued to condemn him for those words and am satisfied with myself that I hardly saved anything.

Janek was still in the ghetto while useless debates went on day after day. But one day he decided to finally abandon it. I don't know if the time limit had come to pick up the *Kennkarte* from the town hall or if there was another purpose to the escapade, but suffice it to say he wanted to go to the Polish side together with the workers from the outposts. Unfortunately, the sentries stopped him. Basically the gendarmes were supposed to let him go after a certain period of time, but this time they sent all the ones they caught to the *Umschlagplatz*. He spent a few days there, not eating or drinking.

In the meantime a new *Aktion* exploded in Warsaw, lasting around thirty days.[200] Selections were made in every workshop, and first they snatched all those Jews who came to Warsaw from the provinces and camps. These were easy victims of the *Aktion*, not knowing the terrain, not having a place where they could hide. About ten thousand people were loaded into cattle cars with the designation of the industrial town of Treblinka.

Unfortunately, Janek found himself in the cattle car, along with Michał Frajbergier and many former policemen from Otwock; these were the ones who were the wealthiest, the ones whom Father envied so. In the wagon Janek met a friend from Piekiełko who tried to persuade him to run away. Janek refused. The other one tried and succeeded. He jumped out of the window of the cattle car, got knocked about badly, but for the moment saved himself. Why Janek didn't follow in his footsteps I don't know. Maybe the few days that he spent on the *Umschlagplatz* broke him physically and spiritually. Maybe he longed to join his wife, yearned for an eternal rest in a grave. Suffice it to say that Janek, strong, energetic, of good appearance, and with official Polish papers, went to Treblinka.

In this way, around January 20, 1943, I lost Janek and Michał—two of my nearest friends—and I felt alone in the world. I felt guilty. I needn't have listened to my father, and I could have left Janek our address at the Magister's. I know that he used to visit him. Maybe Janek would have left the ghetto earlier and come to us.

After this *Aktion* a calm settled over Warsaw, but I wasn't at peace. I came to the conclusion that no Jew could be so wise as to guess what the Germans planned. Before the January *Aktion* in Warsaw we were sure that nothing more threatened the Jews in the winter.

We found out about all this from Kronenberg, who together with his wife and the Górewicz brothers remained in Wilanów to guard piles of potatoes. Father, who traveled to Wilanów or to Piekiełko on business often enough, kept in touch with them. He bought and sold gold and different castoffs.

Father, in general, managed very well. He convinced himself that he had a first-rate appearance and that he spoke excellent Polish, believed that no one would tell him apart from a Pole, and, more than that, believed that he was a real Pole. No wonder that he moved around the streets more and more daringly, went into stores, bought and sold. He made many new friends, and it didn't cross anyone's mind that he was a Jew. He got acquainted with an old shoemaker from the street where we lived. He would leave with him the things he bought and spent evenings with him waiting for the arrival of Miss Hela.

All this had a positive impact on his feelings and self-assurance. He even signed up at a library, and twice a week he borrowed books for me. He didn't always make good choices, but at least it provided some variety for the monotonous routine of life. After a certain period Father came to the conviction that it was foolish to remain closed up in the hiding place when he could live "officially" in freedom. He reported legally under his assumed name in Otwock, paid the health resort tax for two months, and even received on his fake *Kennkarte* a real endorsement that he lived in Otwock. He got a Polish matriculation for Mother and also—through the good offices of a friend working in the municipal office—arranged her registration.

He did all this in order to leave the hiding place for good by spring, to live somewhere in the village, and to register legally on the basis of proof of registration in Otwock. He planned to take Mother with him, even tried to talk me into leaving, but I steadfastly refused.

All his plans were based on the fear that our money would not be enough to survive the war. I remained a fatalist, and I didn't worry particularly about what would happen later. I thought that in the final analysis Father would have to contact one of his tenants and sign over, without payment, a part of the villa. I would have sacrificed the entire villa for the sake of surviving the war. Father, however, did not dream of even giving up a piece of it. He not only wanted to live but also was 100 percent sure that he would outlive the war. He wanted his entire property to remain intact. Day and night he only thought about how to save money and where to obtain more.

He forced me to write a letter to Franciszek Stańczak proposing that we give up our claims to the things he stole from us for the price of returning at least a part of them. I threatened that in case of refusal there would be a follow-up letter, this time to prominent Otwock citizens with a request to intervene and, if that did not help, also to the gendarmes. Franciszek did not respond. I think that he hid or sold all the things and that he laughed at us. I also wrote a letter to the parson to influence Franciszek during the Easter confession—after which I gave up doing anything further. I believe that if anyone of us survives the war, he will settle with Franciszek, perhaps with the help of Polish courts.

Miss Hela was an entirely different human being. She was also greedy for money, but it was part of her native honesty. She took money from us quite willingly, but she was too honest to take it all away from us and throw us out on the street. Having learned from experience, we kept practically nothing in the room. Later I realized that this was an unnecessary precaution. Miss Hela was a straightforward country woman to whom a word was more important than money, which did not stop her from being willing to "hang herself for a złoty." She was happy when she was able to ride a trolley car as a stowaway. Both traits of her character—parsimoniousness and honesty—basically appealed to us, which does not mean that we liked everything about her.

Miss Hela was above everything a terribly nervous person, coarse in her conduct, and she possessed a goodly amount of inborn sadism. Never in my life had I seen such a nervous person. When she didn't find something to her liking, when Genia did not prepare crocheting in time, everything flew around the room. Genia did not crochet too well, and so often there were scenes out of Dante. She would lock us up or leave us without coal or without bread or with a full bucket. When she returned from such an escapade, lasting several days, the following dialogue would take place.

"Miss Hela, we have not cooked for two days and have not eaten anything. You left us without bread and coal."

"That's good. I am happy. So less goes into the bucket."

One time, during her three-day absence, not having any bread or coal, we ate her raw cabbage. When she came home late in the evening, she was able to buy coal, but there was no bread available. We informed her that we had eaten the cabbage and asked her if the next day she would come home earlier and buy some bread because we had not eaten for a couple of days. Miss Hela promised solemnly and came the next day at . . . ten at night. Naturally it was no use talking about bread, but there was a lot to talk about the cabbage that had been eaten.

"There was no need to take cabbage," she scolded us. "Wacław is coming tomorrow, and what am I going to give him to eat?"

About the "subhumans" who were closed in the cage for several days and had nothing to eat, she did not think. She inflicted on us all conceivable petty, daily harassments. It was just her nature.

It was priceless. On the other hand, regardless of what was happening in the city, regardless of the various rumors of blockading certain streets in order to find Jews, we never heard her say that she was afraid to hide us or that since we were sentenced to death, why should she die on our account? For this she made our lives miserable daily in an ordinary, kitchenlike style, not particularly refined, not as any fine lady would have done in her place.

The truth is that she kept us for the first few days only because her Wacław wanted it. At first she tried to oppose it, always reminding him that in his apartment all was nice and clean and she had in her own a "disorderly house"* and a small ghetto. After a while she quieted down, got used to us, and most important, keeping company with us. Her Wacuś gave her a more refined character.

First of all she stopped using foul language. Father sold her two nice skirts and a turtleneck of my wife's, and she began to dress more nicely. It was difficult for me to get used to the sight of Miss Hela dressed in Anka's things. I suffered terrible torture; my heart was in pain—only reason persuaded me that Miss Hela did have a moral right to wear those clothes.

Wacław was an entirely different type. The most outstanding traits of his character were delicateness and goodness. He was good when he

---

*The word Perechodnik uses is from German dialect. *Bajzel* refers to a cheap drinking place.

was sober, even good when he was soused. Before the war he had belonged to the PPS [Polska Partja Socjalisteczna, or Polish Socialist Party], and he remained true to his leftist ideas. His views on the war placed him diametrically opposite the majority of the Poles. When others saw the war as a suitable time to enrich themselves, to buy gold, to dress elegantly, in a word, to rise in the world even at the price of doing harm to other people, he did not have such thoughts. Perhaps he thought that the Germans, after liquidating Jews, would start next with Poles. He did not worry about anything. All the money he earned he spent on good food and vodka. He drank, but he was never completely drunk. When he drank, his soul was like an open book—clean, noble, without a trace of hypocrisy or perfidiousness.

For seven months I did not even once hear some curse from his lips; he was always happy, helpful, polite, smiling. As a conductor on the train he has many opportunities to make money. Not a few Jews, after all, ride the trains! But he does not look for such "birds." When he meets them, unasked, he tries to open for them the gate to set them free. He does this, as I have convinced myself, completely selflessly.

His slogan rang out: If I cannot help Jews, then I will not harm them in any case. When he brought Genia to his place from Piekiełko, he told her he would have brought with him all the women and children outside the camp. That real nobility and openness, so rarely met with these days, were what made him suspicious in Genia's eyes. Later on she became convinced that she had before her pure gold.

Before Genia he had in his place Miss Irka. In March, when his neighbors realized that he kept a Jewess, he transported her with an aching heart back to the Warsaw ghetto. That's why Miss Hela by agreement keeps Genia for nothing. Wacław is a child of the Polish people—honest, plain, noble, who has sucked from the Polish soil her best elements. Wacław was very much loved by us, and when conflict broke out with Hela, he was the highest court under whose care we placed ourselves.

As our relationship with Wacław was singularly direct, that with Hela was very complex. One fact cannot be questioned: In hiding us, she saved our lives. Because one cannot measure human life with the weight of gold, at the same time—although we paid her a very high rental—we did not square that account at all. We owed her lifelong gratitude, love, and attachment. Did she receive these from us? It is a difficult question.

My parents were from such a mold that they measured everything in terms of money. She hid them; they paid—everything then was in order. To owe a debt to such a sadistic person, that they did not consider. It's true that a living person cannot constantly remember that to which he owes his life. It was also not possible to avoid looking at the everyday life made up of the constant cruel harassments that Miss Hela allowed herself against us.

Still, my parents reacted with exaggerated bad behavior toward our landlady. They thought that they lived in "the old house," where there was an obligation for the protection of the tenant. If the tenant paid, then he could not be evicted on the street; if he lived there for a long time, then the landlord had no right to let out the apartment. The tenants could move out anytime they wanted, the owner could not do anything without their agreement.

My father, very confident about this, has carried on since March such politics toward Miss Hela, as if he intended to take all of us out of here. When paying for the previous month, he remarks at every opportunity that it is the last one. Of course, he doesn't dream of taking us out at all. Setting aside the inexpensiveness and convenience of this locum, there is just no other place to go to. Father only wants to scare Miss Hela with the possibility of losing an income that's not bad. This is the so-called Jewish hyperfinagling.

Mother told me that she didn't have the slightest intention of moving anywhere. She would rather be killed in the apartment than on the street or in the field. I also admonished Father. In spite of that, he did not desist from threatening to move. That's how confident he was of his knowledge of the world and human beings.

One day, Father brought the news that my eighteen-year-old cousin Aronek, alone of his entire family, remained in Warsaw, met Kronenberg, and told him that he wanted to communicate with us. I was very happy and wanted to bring him to us as quickly as possible. I believed that every day spent in the ghetto could be the last. Father was also happy, but for another reason. He found out in the meantime from Kronenberg that Aronek had a lot of money, and so he wanted to combine the pleasant with the useful: to save my cousin's life and at the same time to reinforce our supply of cash.

There began a long correspondence between us and Aronek. Father carried letters to Tłomackie Street, where Jews worked in the outposts. After a few days, he went there for answers, which he brought to the house. I edited the new letter, which he took the same way.

After the first few letters, Father cooled off quite a bit because it turned out that Aronek didn't have so much money. Now the threat arose that it might be necessary to take him and support him. The correspondence continued. I warned Aronek to leave the ghetto together with those working at the outposts and to personally speak to Father so as to leave the ghetto as soon as possible and come to us. I suggested that he live with us in our place—taking advantage of his first-rate Aryan appearance—live with Polish friends of my father's. His legal registration and work would be taken care of. Everything to no avail.

In order to understand Aronek's behavior, it is necessary to know the situation in the Warsaw ghetto in the period from January to April. Jews were doing well in the ghetto; they did not lack anything, had money in profusion as well as food. There remained after all only 10 percent of the previous population, so it was no wonder that they had a mass of things to sell. They did not expect a new *Aktion*, because the workshops were busy and received always millions of orders for the military. Whole train cars with metal sheets arrived at the ghetto, where they were converted into military equipment.

Good life and hope for the future cheered people up and did not incline them to leave the ghetto. People also did not believe that it was possible to find a place in the Polish neighborhood. Many stories circulated—I don't know how many were true or how many were false—about Poles hiding Jews. From whatever place, such legends are worth quoting.

And so a Pole invites his friend, a Jew, to relocate himself and his wife to his apartment. He assures him of all conveniences and safety; in addition to that he is a member of the party[201] and will gladly give his life for him if it should be necessary. The Jew leaves the ghetto, goes to his friend, and breathes a sigh of relief: He will be saved from the daily cataclysm and will survive the war. A few days spent in peace, as in the past, go by. The landlord breaks the idyll.

"My brother," he says to the Jew, "I would give up my life for you, but my wife . . . You understand: She dreamed of a graying hen. You know what this means: a certain death."

The Jew sends for vodka, snacks, cheesecakes, tries to persuade him that it is a superstition. Finally, the landlord gives in.

"I am a member of the party," he says. "For you I will do everything. Please stay here."

A few more days pass in peace, after which the landlord speaks again.

"It's bad," he asserts seriously. "My wife dreamed of a bird with its head shot off. A sure death. I am a member of the party, but what do you do with a sick woman?"

Again vodka and the most expensive snacks on the table; then all is quiet for a few days. Not for long.

"My lady is nervous," a communiqué comes as if from the front. "She is sick from fear. But there is a chance we can buy from Franbol half a kilo of chocolates; it's dirt cheap, for a silly four hundred złoty. Buy it for her. Maybe it will quiet her."

The chocolate not only did not quiet her; it also emboldened her.

"My dear lady, maybe you could lend me your coat." A proposition comes after a few days. "I will go to town to buy things for you. It's not becoming to make a lot of purchases and to wear a worn-out coat."

"Please, if you will"—there can only be one answer—"do take it for a while."

This does not last long.

"My dear lady, people are looking at me in the street. I am wearing an elegant coat, but with worn-out gloves and an old hat. I will not be able to go out and buy food for you anymore."

It is not difficult to understand what this is all about.

"But please, dear madam, you may certainly put on my gloves and hat."

It is soon well understood that shoes and the rest of the wardrobe will go the same way. The landlady is without scruples and expresses it.

"Dear lady, actually, you don't need anything right now. You do need something to eat, a chamberpot at hand, and you can quietly wait for the end of the war."

And in fact the lady keeps Jews in her room, sees to their food needs and the chamberpot, and, when it is convenient, takes the rest of the wardrobe and the money. And when she has taken everything . . .

"Quickly, quickly," the landlord runs into the room, "please get dressed. The gendarmes will be here soon."

He throws them his old rags, a worn-out coat, a shabby jacket, and quickly leads them to the ghetto.

Someone who is suspicious will say, "What kind of a fairy tale is this? It's all possible, but I will classify it as a fairy tale."

Be that as it may, for every twenty Jews leaving the ghetto, eighteen returned after a period of time and mostly without anything. And so a new psychosis overcame the Jews. Everybody, in order to avoid the *Aktion*, built for themselves shelters and bunkers. Underground apartments were created, with water and food provided for long periods of time. There were toilets, hand pumps, radios, and even telephones. The bunkers were often built under the ruins of collapsed buildings.

Entrances to these bunkers came from houses some distance away so that there was no way to track down those hiding there. At times Jews would go into the bunkers and brick themselves up—workers-bricklay-ers went down with them. No one knew about it, and probably to this day some of them sit there still and wait for the end of the war.

So it was that the majority of Jews, taught by bitter experience, did not fear a new *Aktion*. Everyone believed in his hiding place; everyone be-lieved that if he hid in time, nobody would find him. Aside from that, everyone agreed to a man that the liquidation of the ghetto was not a fi-nal act, that there would always be new selections. Everyone then be-lieved that he would be last and that finally, when there was no other choice, he would go to the Polish neighborhood.

There were, however, in the Warsaw ghetto people who thought dif-ferently. Their slogan was: If we must die, then we will die with honor, with weapons in hand and "in good company." We will die together with our enemies.

There arose the Żydowski Związek Wojskowy [Jewish Military Asso-ciation],[202] which cooperated with the Żydowska Partia Robotnicza [Jewish Workers Party].[203] These parties worked together with the Polska Partia Robotnicza [Polish Workers Party], which provided them with weapons for money. Used pistols and even machine guns were sup-posed to make it possible for Jews to resist in case of an *Aktion* and to save the honor of the Jewish people.

In the meantime, the Jewish organization "cleaned up" practically all Jews who collaborated with the Gestapo. Those sentenced by the Special Court for being overly eager to work with the Germans were shot: the commandant of the Jewish police, Colonel Szeryński;[204] the vice com-mandant, attorney Lejkin; and many other functionaries of the Jewish police. The sentence was read to the condemned, after which they were shot and the text of the sentence was hung on the gate.

Many of the flunkies of the Germans were afraid, the Germans themselves were fear stricken, and they were afraid to walk singly into the ghetto.

Now we can understand why Aronek did not want to leave the ghetto in order to hide in a locked room. He had a good hiding place, earned money, most likely had a girlfriend. Maybe he didn't even know himself what he wanted. It is worth noting that new pairs were created in the ghetto while people waited.

"You lost a wife; I, a husband," a Jewess said to a Jew. "Let's stay to-gether as long as we live."

Life in the ghetto was lived with intensity. Everyone wanted to use time to the fullest, aware that he might not have much more time to enjoy it.

In my next to the last letter I wrote to Aronek that if he did not intend now to leave the ghetto, I could give him an address in the Polish neighborhood through which he could eventually communicate with Father. Still, I absolutely advised him to abandon the ghetto. I received an answer, a part of which I reproduce word for word.

"I nevertheless intend to remain here until the last moment. That's why I am sending you a photograph so that your friend may recognize me when I come to him in that last moment. I used that photograph in the making of a Polish *Kennkarte* for myself. If you will be able to take me with you, then I have decided to go with you. In the meantime I greet you and I say good-bye."

I sent him one more letter in reply, which turned out to be my last. We never received a reply to that letter.

On Saturday, April 17, my father, still at the outpost, talked to Berek Kejzman and asked him to notify Aronek that he expected him in two days in the Polish neighborhood. On Monday, April 19—this was the eve of Passover—my father went out for Aronek. But in the outpost there were no Jews, the entire ghetto was surrounded by SS men and Ukrainians; shots were heard.

The Germans started the last liquidation of the Warsaw ghetto. As with the majority of the *Aktion* in other towns, this too started on the holiest Jewish day. Jews, as always, did not expect anything. Most of the Jewish women with children who had been permanently hidden in the Polish neighborhood had come to the ghetto to spend the holidays together with their husbands.

This time a surprise awaited the Germans. Jews opened machine gun fire. Because many Germans fell on the first day, they decided to change the tactics of battle. They retreated, broke down walls with airplane cannon fire. Airplanes bombed some houses. They began to cleanse the ghetto of Jews.

The Germans knew very well that the majority of Jews had hidden in such a way that it would not be possible to find them without first destroying and burning down houses. The buildings collapsed, burying underneath terribly burned Jews. Some jumped and fell into the hands of the Germans. They were taken in groups to the Umschlagplatz and from there sent not to Treblinka but to Poniatow[205] and to Trawniki[206] in the Lublin district. There large "work camps" were created from which they chose groups marked for—as gossip had it—burning. The last *Aktion* was conducted with the participation of the Judenrat and the

Jewish police. The representatives of those institutions were treated the same as other Jews.

On April 23, they brought to the *Umschlagplatz* the president of the Judenrat, Lichtenbaum. He is the one who, when Czerniaków committed suicide, signed an announcement calling on the Jewish population to voluntarily appear for transfer to the east and assuring Jews that no more than 10 percent of the people would be deported. Together with him were brought the engineer Szereszewski, the attorney Wielikowski, the engineer Sztolcman, and the leading officials of the Judenrat. To the last moment, these wise, intelligent, educated people did not expect that they would share the fate of other Jews, and now they were placed in ranks and shot on the spot. They died the deserved death of traitors of the Jewish people.[207]

The *Aktion* in Warsaw proceeded very slowly. A portion of the Jews defended themselves decisively. From morning to night one could hear shots from machine guns and the boom of dynamite, which was used to destroy houses. The whole sky was red; houses were burning with people still alive in them—men, women, children. Slowly everything changed into a pile of cinders and ashes.

Sitting safely at Miss Hela's, we lived through the whole horrible *Aktion*. I imagined seeing people being burned alive. I saw how they loaded others into cattle cars and how machine guns destroyed at one fell swoop thousands of unarmed people. I wasn't able to forget for a moment the Warsaw *Aktion*. Every once in a while the boom of the dynamite reminded me that they had set another house on fire and that now more people were burning alive. Through the hole in the shutters we saw Poles, standing for hours on the roofs of their houses, observing this unusual sight.

As I have written, everything that happened in the street, every conversation, was clearly heard in our room. The smallest event in political life, the price of food, discussions on whatever topic—everything reached our ears. But for the two months of the *Aktion*, we did not hear anyone express any pity toward the Jews. Only one street comedian, sitting on our steps, parodied the style of German broadcasts, and his best jokes were about the Jews.

"The High Command of the Jewish Defense Forces announces a communiqué, dated April 23. Heavy fighting continues. We repelled the enemy, inflicting heavy casualties. Our losses: six killed, thirteen wounded. According to plan, we evacuated Franciszkanska Street. Fighting continues on Nalewki front—."

Szmul Kołkowicz was in the ghetto during the fighting. He fought until he fell with his entire group into German hands. In the last moment before execution he was able to run away and hide in some attic. Afterwards jumping from roof to roof, he made it to the Polish area.

With the background of the burning ghetto, with people being burned alive, my father's behavior seemed out of place. I remember this was the time of the eighth day of Passover. It's true that father could not buy matzo for the holidays, but he was able to buy horseradish. He made a meal with the horseradish for the first day of Passover in memory of the Jewish sojourn in Egypt. For the eight days of the holiday, Father ate only potatoes. His was not a fast, however, pleading with God for mercy for the unfortunate, doomed, innocent people. Father behaved from habit. He wanted—with whatever means were possible for him—to observe Jewish traditions.

There was really nothing bad about it, but it unnerved me terribly. The times had passed when I might repeat after Mickiewicz:

But do not destroy the altars of old
Since a holy fire on them glowed
And you owe them honor.[208]

Then, as now, I ascribed the entire blame for all our misfortunes equally to German sadism as well as to the Jewish religion and traditions, which divided us as if with a Chinese wall from other nations and which commanded us to have circumcision that made possible the discovery and murder of all Jews.

Around April 24 I advised Father to go to Wilanów and to see what was happening with Kronenberg. Father went and found him in his place. To the question as to why he didn't run away, whether he was not afraid to be shot, Kronenberg replied with a long lecture.

It turned out, first of all, that he did not think that he would be shipped out in this *Aktion*. Moreover, he counted on the Germans forgetting about the four Jews who sat in one place, guarded piles of potatoes, and didn't bother anyone. Beyond that, he did not trust Poles, was of the opinion that wherever he went they would take away his money and hand him over to the gendarmes.

"I know," Kronenberg said further, "that if I live through the next week, it means that I will probably survive the war. If they come to kill me now, I will not even tremble. After I saw the death of my son, who was killed by a party of Poles on the streets of Warsaw, I too can die without sorrow or fear. But I don't think this threatens me. Now it is spring; more intensive work in camp will follow. . . ."

It also turned out that the other day the commandant of the gendarmes in Rembertow, Lipszer, had visited the camp in Piekiełko, criticized the Jews for making tasteless coffee, but didn't harm anyone. Kronenberg built his assurance on all that.

Father, hearing all this, said good-bye, indicating that he was going to a village and was leaving Mother with me in town.

And, indeed, April 28, Father went to a village. He didn't want to tell me where. No persuasions helped. He only wanted to be sure that no one would betray his new hiding place. He promised that he would return after a month, took with him a coupon for registering from Otwock, a small package, and left.

Aronek gave no sign of life; he had either burned alive in his hiding place, or they had deported him. He had had all the chances to save himself, but he perished. Some sort of fate dogged his footsteps, the same one that caused the death of my daughter: one day too late. Our Miss Hela also lamented his probable death. She therefore decided to save the life of one more Jew and also to gain for herself another tenant. Wacław readily agreed with her.

One day Wacław met in the street Szmul Kołkowicz, the runaway from the ghetto. They had known each other in the past; in the good old days they had played soccer. Kołkowicz told him that he had just escaped the burning ghetto and had no place to stay. Wacław, in his selfless way, took him to his own place for a few days. Kołkowicz told him his story, but this time he did not get angry over the conduct of a peasant toward his little children. Quite the contrary, he even said that maybe it was better that they went to the cattle car when they did.

Was it that he had become indifferent? Not at all! When he saw the extermination of the whole Jewish people with his own eyes, when he became convinced that the struggle was hopeless, he became resigned. He surrendered, seeing that he would not be able to save his children—at most they would have burned alive in the Warsaw ghetto.

More or less at the same time, that was at the start of May, like a bolt out of the blue came the news that Wacław had to go to Germany for labor. As a metalworker by profession he received a summons from the

Arbeitsamt with an order to report for work in an arms factory. At the same time he also received a dismissal from his train work. This was for him, as it was for us, a catastrophic event. For him, because he would have to go away, leave his family without means of support; for us, because we realized that without him Miss Hela would not keep us any longer. I am not even mentioning the fact that we had become sincerely attached to him and that his personal misfortunes were our misfortunes. The efforts at gaining his "release" took a few days, but they did not augur well.

After one thunderbolt, another one struck. On May 5, before evening, the gendarmes surrounded the camp at Piekiełko. The workers and the commandant were told to dig a pit, remove their clothing, and then all of them were shot. Only the commandant of the camp, Landsberg, was able to get away, in spite of the hail of German bullets. He hid himself temporarily in some nearby village; afterward he got dressed and rode to Otwock, where his wife and son were located. I get news of him to this day, and I am happy for the sake of his child that he survived. I remember, however, the death of Krumarz, whom Landsberg personally chased and handed over to the Germans. I remember the death of those workers whose money Landsberg stole and whose survival he doomed. When I think about all this, I come to the conclusion that there is no higher justice in the world. Kochanowski, in the midst of his own pain, wrote, "Whom once goodness preserved from an evil incident."[209] I would add and write, "Whom evil preserved from a fortunate incident."

Later it turned out that others were also saved, altogether nine persons, among whom were Genia's father and the deputy commandant of the camp, Kreisler. For two months they hid in a nearby village. Unfortunately, at the start of June the gendarmes discovered them, and all of them were shot. My father brought me the news about this.

Thus was also liquidated the camp Saska Kępie, where the secretary of the Ghetto Polizei, Ehrlich, and his wife were located.

On the final day of the liquidation of the Piekiełko camp, the last hour sounded for Kronenberg. I don't have exact information on how the execution took place. I know that Kronenberg could not tear himself away from his wife, that both of them wept. Kronenberg had long been proud of his service to the Germans. Her pride in her husband was of equally long duration. And now they waited like sheep for death at the hands of the same gendarmes who so often personally answered her greeting: *"Guten Morgen, Frau Kronenberg."*

Kronenberg told my father that he was certain that he would not be sent out in this *Aktion*. He didn't listen to advice to remove himself to the Polish neighborhood. Now at the moment of death he must have regretted it. To Madame Kronenberg, in the last moment, Satan very likely provided a reminder that my old mother lives, whereas she—the privileged one—had to perish.

They were shot together with the Górewicz family and buried on the spot. The gold—the aim of their life—about which they trembled with fear lest the Poles take it, fell into German hands. I don't feel sorry for them at all. They sacrificed the entire town to their egotism; the deaths of one thousand people did not move them. If I feel pain, it is only because the Jews of Otwock, when they were dying, did not know that the Kronenbergs would share their fate. Maybe it would have been easier for them to die in that case. *Qui le sait?*[210] The news about the massacre in Piekiełko traveled with lightning speed through the Karczew camp and the sawmill at Falenica. The commandant at Karczew did not imagine that he was a better Jew because he had the honor of talking personally to the *Kreishauptmann*. He broke up the camp and proclaimed the slogan *Sauve qui peut.*[211] All the Jews ran in every which direction. How many are still alive? How many have already perished? No one is in a position to answer these questions. It is only known that they did all they could to save themselves.

The Jews from the Falenica sawmill, whose commandant was Najwert, reacted completely differently. The millworkers, excellent craftsmen, knew that if they were killed, the sawmill would come to a halt. And who would be better able to lead the sawmill if not its owner of many years, Najwert? For that matter, the German administration many times assured them that they were irreplaceable. So they sat securely. Right up to May 7.

That day the gendarmes drove to the sawmill and killed everyone on the spot. To the last moment, Najwert himself did not believe that he, so irreplaceable, would be killed.[212]

Against the background of the burning Warsaw ghetto I saw with my own eyes the twilight of Polish Jewry. I saw the death of all those whom in time I had envied. I understood the futility of the struggle. It occurred to me that sooner or later I too would be forced to share the fate of all the Jews. I thought to myself that in such a case no one will be left to weep and to honor the memory of my wife, that no one would transmit to posterity her suffering, that maybe no one would demand vengeance for her innocent life, for the death of millions of Jews.

Then—on May 7 to be exact—I decided to write down these events. Maybe they will be preserved and in the future will be handed down to Jews as a faithful reflection of those tragic times and will persuade democratic nations to absolutely destroy all those Germans, to avenge the innocent deaths of millions of small Jewish children and Jewish women.

In the meantime the mood in our apartment was funereal. Miss Hela was going crazy thinking that they could deport her Wacław for labor, Genia was weeping over the death of her father in the Piekiełko camp, all of us felt defeated with this last act of German barbarism and despondent over the uncertainty of tomorrow. We were able to take a deep breath only when one of these nightmares disappeared: Fortunately Wacław was able to take care of the formalities at the Arbeitsamt and to keep his position as a conductor.

All this time Kołkowicz was locked in a closet in Wacław's house, where he was cared for by the wife of our benefactor. After a while, when he calmed down, he thanked them and started living on his own. During the day he went to Warsaw, and at night he returned by train to Jósefów or Świder, where he slept in the woods. His appearance was good, although he was somewhat handicapped by his inborn sloppiness. But since he slept in the woods, it was difficult for him to keep clean. I only know that from time to time he would drop into Wacław's apartment to sleep under better conditions, to bathe, and to launder his rags.

Kołkowicz was not looking for a hiding place, did not want to live locked in, and the life of a vagabond apparently suited him. Besides, he was not afraid of bad breaks and was certain that at least he had his faithful "Belgian," that his weapon would not fail him in the last moment. He was not afraid of the Polish police on the Otwock-Warsaw line. Hadn't he distributed bread to them in his day? Hadn't he repaired their bicycles? He only kept clear of gendarmes, but here he was convinced that in the event something bad happened, he would be the one who would shoot first and then be able to escape.

And so went day after day, week after week, and the ghetto was still burning. On May 12, from early morning to late night, one could hear the rumble of dynamite detonating Jewish homes. The sky appeared bloodstained; a fiery glow from the fire in which people were burning alive was reflecting from every direction. And even on that hellish day we did not hear anyone expressing pity for the Jews.

One night when there were constant rifle shots, we heard what sounded like falling bombs. At that moment the sirens sounded an air raid. The Russians were bombing Warsaw.[213] They had a first-rate view of

the target because of the ghetto fire, and it was light as day. Before we realized that this air raid might bring with it the bombing of our house and
our eventual death, Miss Hela appeared completely dressed, with a bundle in hand. We stood still without doing anything, didn't even get
dressed. Well, what for? Where could we have gone?

Only when a bomb fell across the street and tore off our shutters and
broke all the panes did we decide to get dressed. The doors stood open; the
janitor walked in and then another acquaintance of Miss Hela's, who—
seeing the torn-off shutters—asked if anything had happened to her.

Luckily it was dark in the room. We hid ourselves behind the wardrobe.
Miss Hela spoke with them calmly so that no one noticed our presence.

Finally the alarm was called off. We went to sleep thinking how little
value the life of a Jew had and how it depended on everything. If Miss
Hela had slept that night in Falenica, we would very likely not have remained alive because we would have had no place to stay.

In the morning, our lady somehow closed the shutters and went to
work, and we got busy cleaning up a room full of broken glass and covered with a thick layer of soot. Working for half a day, we restored our living place to its former appearance. All this time, discussions about the
raid, the extent of damage, and complaints about the bombing of the
civilian population reached us from the street.

At that time I was terribly exasperated with my father, realizing that he
had gone away without leaving us his address. If our house had been
bombed, even if we had found asylum for a few days, we could not have
let him know where we were so that he could have come and found us
another place.

In the evening, Mother gave proof of her own selfishness and desire to
live at any cost. Now many Poles, expecting new air raids, left on May 13
for places in the suburbs of Warsaw. Miss Hela also decided to spend the
nights in Falenica; in the evening she came to Wacław for her things.
Mother, practically on her knees and with tears in her eyes, asked to be
taken along. She was ready to do anything, if only not to be in danger of
the succeeding air raids. She was asking only for herself. She forgot that I
was also in danger. Still, even though I was afraid of dying, it didn't cross
my mind to leave. As a Jew I didn't want to be murdered; as a human being I am not afraid of death caused by a higher power. All this filled me
for a long time with distaste.

Finally the news of the taking of Tunis[214] inspired me with better
thoughts and faith in the future; I was convinced that events would flow
more rapidly.

For a certain time we were absorbed in the fate of Seweryn Buchalter, the son of an owner of a large real estate in Otwock. When he appeared at our place, he told us in detail what had happened to him.

He was able to save himself during the Warsaw *Aktion*.[215] He worked at an outpost, while he left his wife and a five-year-old son at home. They had a certificate of immunity because he worked for the Germans. On August 8, when he came home, there was no one there except the maid. During the blockade of the house, his family, confident of their immunity, stood in line with the others and were taken straightaway to cattle cars. The maid, because she had no certificate, did not go downstairs, hid herself somewhere, and for the time being remained alive.

He himself was caught several times after this and sent to the *Umschlagplatz*, but each time he was picked for some local work. An older sister and son and her whole family were sent to Treblinka; her husband was sent to an "outpost" in Lublin and there burned to death. Another sister, Mela, worked in a shop, thanks to which she and her older son survived all selections and blockades. A younger son was lost in the cauldron and was sent to the cattle car. Her husband perished in Russia at the start of the war.

On April 23,[216] the house in which Buchalter, his sister, Mela, and her thirteen-year-old son were hidden was burned down. When the house started to collapse, they jumped out of their hiding place and ran quickly in the direction of the Germans. They knew that it was better to get shot than to be burned alive. Still, the Germans did not kill them, only led them to the Umschlagplatz, where they passed three days without food or water.

On the way to the *Umschlagplatz* they passed by the burning Jewish hospital on Gęsia Street. They saw in the windows the live torches of Jews burning, calling in vain upon God and people for help. Buchalter saw his friend from Otwock, Stasek Broder, who, in spite of six bullet wounds that he had got from the Germans in January,[217] was still alive. His iron constitution withstood the bullets, but he was melting in the hellish fire. The hospital burned for more than twenty-four hours, and all the sick inside burned alive. Their cries were heartrending, but the time had passed when one took to heart the adversity of fellow creatures.

On April 25, on Saturday[218] evening, Buchalter and family were loaded into cattle cars, and the train made its way via Otwock in the direction of Lublin. Earlier the Germans robbed them of everything. Buchalter was able to save only a few gold dollars that he had hidden in his shoe, whereas his sister saved a large diamond that she later sold for thirty-five thousand złoty.

It was dark in the cattle car. One could only hear the weeping of people broken physically and spiritually. There were scenes that it is difficult to describe, that cannot be understood, that have to be experienced in order to feel the whole tragedy of Polish Jewry.

In the corner sat a married couple surrounded by three sons.

"My children," their father said to them, "I did everything to try to save you. Last year at this time we ran away from Lublin. We lived through all kinds of blockades in Warsaw; many weeks we sat hiding in cellars. Today we are still together; tomorrow we may not be. Forgive me, children. Your father begot you as Jews, you suffer because of him, but you must know that your father did everything in order to save you."

In another corner sat an elegant woman with a five-year-old boy, beautiful like an angel.

"My little son," she said, "your daddy was a lucky man; he perished as one of the first. I didn't follow in his footsteps. I thought that at least I would be able to save you. I hid in basements, in burrows, but I always kept myself clean, took care of you, always gave you everything. Now, my little son, we are going to see your father. Forgive me that I couldn't keep you alive. Maybe we will be better off in the next world."

Weeping could be heard from all sides, and the parents began to beg their children for pardon for not saving them, for giving birth to them— they blamed themselves for the children's Jewishness.

But not all were sorry that they had been born Jews. Some were proud that they were perishing for the sanctification of His Name. A group made up of ten men loudly recited the prayers of Passover. Resigned, but with pride, they awaited their death. From the crowd came a question addressed to the oldest one of those praying.

"Reb Id, where is your God? Why does he let you perish?"

The answer was immediate: "Gentlemen, I might as well say that I am ninety-five years old, and since I can assume I will die soon, it may be better to die now."

Indeed, with such true faith. there is nothing to discuss. Indeed, "happy is he who can pray or to whom he can say good-bye."[219]

About thirteen people decided to shake off this state of despair, not to give up the struggle. In the final analysis they were bound to die, so it would be death there—they decided to jump out of the train window. They did this in turn. Buchalter threw out of the window his nephew, then his sister, and then he jumped himself. Earlier they had agreed that they would try to reach Miedszeszyn, where they had a Polish friend.

The sister with her little son was stopped by two "extortionists"* who represented themselves as *Bahnschutze*[220] and threatened to take them to the police. She bribed them with a gold five ruble; pleased with their booty, they showed her the way. At the Świdrów bridge another extortionist stopped them; he took a gold bracelet and also let them go.

At the station of Świder an elegant-looking Pole stopped her. He quickly understood that this was a Jewess and that she had jumped off a train. Full of compassion, he opened up his briefcase and gave them his late breakfast: white bread with butter and ham. He also offered money.

Buchalter's sister thanked him warmly for the bread but didn't want to take the money. The elegant man showed them the road, once more offered them some money, expressed his sympathy, wished them a good journey, and went away. All of this—the man's extraordinary manners, elegant dress and behavior, his goodness, anonymous sacrifice, sudden appearance and disappearance—all this made him seem like a prince from a fairy tale.

Buchalter's sister, her spirit buoyed with this encounter, reached Miedszeszyn without any difficulty and was well received by her friend, Tadeusz S.

Buchalter appeared shortly afterward. They stayed with S. about a week, recovered, calmed themselves, and acquired energy for further struggle. When a rumor spread through Miedszeszyn that the gendarmes were coming, S. unfortunately had to bid a farewell to his guests. He received them with open arms, fed them, helped them to get their clothes in order—but he finally was afraid for his own skin. There was no way out; they had to go farther.

Buchalter broke down momentarily, wanted to send for poison to end that unequal struggle, but his sister was able to persuade him that there would always be time to perish. They decided to take the train to Warsaw, to another friend.

In the train compartment Buchalter kept his face covered all the time with a bouquet of lilacs. The conductor smiled at him knowingly but did not approach him. He came near them at the last stop, explained that he knew at once that they were Jews, and offered them help in going out. In

---

*The Polish word *szmalcowniki*, from the Polish word *szmalc*, meaning "fat" or "grease," is difficult to translate. The American slang phrase "greasing the palm" is certainly comparable but lacks the homicidal implication for Polish Jews.

the street the conductor met his friend. Buchalter's sister asked her if she would take her to Ogrodowa Street, which she gladly did.

I don't think I have to add that this conductor was Wacław and that his friend was Miss Hela. They agreed to meet the following day on Ogrodowa. Buchalter asked if Miss Hela could put them up for the night, but our landlady evaded the answer. Just the same, Buchalter's sister, out of a feeling of gratitude, kissed her and gave her the first random bank note. Miss Hela, when she came to the apartment, told us of this encounter, verified that she got one hundred złoty, and was very pleased with herself. We were certain that we would soon have fellow companions. It was May 1.

The next day, Wacław and Hela went to Ogrodowa Street. They waited about a half hour in vain. I was sure that Buchalter did not come on purpose, not having confidence in strangers. I ceased being surprised that people were perishing. How could it be otherwise since they could not take advantage of chances that happened to one in ten thousand.

The Pole to whom Buchalter presented himself was a casual acquaintance, Franek S., who had conducted various businesses in the Warsaw ghetto. They had made more than one deal in the ghetto, drunk together more than one glass. Franek S. was a type of nimble but honest fellow; he liked to eat well, drink well, make good money—but not while doing any harm to people. *Garçon débrouillard,*[221] a risk-taker. The war gave him a chance to rise in the world, to build up a fortune; he could lead a merry life. He let Buchalter stay in his apartment where two Jews who had run away from the same transport were already hiding.

The last person who jumped from their wagon, Mandelbaum, also presented himself at Franek's. His daughter Bogda had once lived in Franek's house and had even passed for his relative. She had fake Polish documents, giving every indication that she would outlive the war. Unfortunately, in April, her mother demanded of Bogda that she spend holidays with them in the ghetto. A good daughter listened, and an *Aktion* took her unawares at her parents'. At the *Umschlagplatz,* with her mother's advice, she pretended she was Polish. She and a few other Jewish girls who had Polish papers did not go to the cattle cars but were shot on the spot.

The wife of Mandelbaum, who jumped out, perished on the way. Mandelbaum, on the the other hand, who had the least chance, saved himself.

Fifteen-year-old Romek Gutman also made it to Franek's and later went to another Polish friend. Eventually, Mandelbaum as well as

Romek shared the fate of Buchalter's sister and her son, but this I shall relate later.

Buchalter could not come down to meet Miss Hela because the house was surrounded by the police. Jews who were escaping through the sewers from the burning ghetto came out at Ogrodowa Street.[222] The police organized a raid against them.

Buchalter spent twelve days at Franek's hiding behind a wardrobe and then in a newly renovated apartment that was vacant. All the Jews from the transport were locked in there. Franek's wife supplied them with food. To her neighbors, she accounted for her frequent escapades to the "empty" apartment by removing things slowly. Each time she ostentatiously carried with her a few plates, and in her bag she hid food.

As much as Franek was a pal and good-hearted young man, his wife showed herself to be an overpious and calculating hag who knew how to—as it became evident—extract money from people.

Daily, she told the people who were in hiding about the coming blockades of houses, pitied them, and whined that they would have to go out into the street, where they would surely be killed right away. Determined, she knelt before the holy picture, loudly recited her prayer, and struck the floor with her forehead. After finishing her prayers she said, "Let it happen what may happen. It can't be helped! Please stay here one more day. . . ."

She repeated this story every day.

After several days they had to leave the apartment when Franek moved in. As it was, his apartment was not a suitable hiding place because everyone knew that he did business in the ghetto and suspected him of contacts with Jews.

Before the departure, Franek told his wife to make an accounting and to return the difference between the money he had received from those hiding and the cost of their upkeep. Then his wife knelt before the holy picture and swore that she spent for their expenses more than five thousand złoty. In addition to that she was due a surcharge.

There was nothing left for Buchalter to do but to make the best of it, give her the additional payment, and say good-bye. Although Franek's wife embittered their stay there and made a lot of money on them, she did, after all, save their lives.

After their stay at Franek's, those in hiding went to Żoliborz, where a new hiding place was supposed to be available. But nothing came of it. Buchalter sent his sister and her son back to Franek. He hoped that some place could be found for the two of them. He himself remained on the street.

Accidentally he met another Jew, one Filip, who also wandered around the streets, not having any place to sleep. Filip had an advantage over Buchalter in that he was elegantly dressed, had a first-rate Aryan appearance, and was soon to receive a legal *Kennkarte*. He just lacked some minor things. He didn't have money and hadn't eaten for three days.

When he left the ghetto, he had a lot of money, but in his first hiding place they took it all away from him. All that he had was a small sum left with one of his Polish friends. Unfortunately, this friend went on a vacation, and all that he could do was to die slowly of hunger. But even though Buchalter and Filip had not met earlier, their common misery united them from the start. They made a good pair: One had nerve and a good appearance; the other had the money. They bought food, ate dinner, and spent the night in the bushes along the Vistula. During the night they were awakened by a watchman of the garden plots asking them what they were doing. He was mainly interested in finding out if they weren't by any chance Jews. Filip replied with his first-rate Polish accent that they had come for a spring outing and didn't want to go home after curfew. He also explained that if there were any Jews in the area, they would gladly join in the hunt.

"Right, Franek?" Buchalter asked loudly.

The watchman was pacified and invited them to his hut, but they declined. The next day they spent in Miedszeszyn and passed the night in the woods. In the morning Buchalter decided to return to Warsaw. They boarded a train, and the first person they came across was Wacław. Buchalter, overjoyed, reminded him about himself, apologized for not being able to meet him, and they agreed to meet that same day on a street in the center of town.

Buchalter found his sister at Franek's. It turned out that on the way from Żoliborz, they were stopped on the street by specialists in tracking Jews. The system used by these trackers was indeed brilliant. It depended on specially picked hoodlums, who would get a hold of any of the passersby and yell at him, "Jews! Jewess! Jew!" depending on sex and age. The trackers themselves stood at a distance and observed the reaction of those going by. If the reaction was a "normal" one, they chased away the young hounds, and in case there was something suspicious— they intervened. They politely asked them to step into the gate; there they took away all their money and generally let them go on.[223]

It was in just such a way that Buchalter's sister was trapped, but she kept her presence of mind and absolutely refused to go inside the gate. She told them that she wanted to commit suicide anyway, so they might as well take her to the gendarmes. But if they wanted something from her, they would have to settle it in the street. Little by little they struck a bargain. She gave them twenty-five hundred złoty, after which one of them took her to the tram stop, even kissed her hand, and left.

Franek had in mind for her a particular place, but it would cost, together with upkeep, seven thousand złoty monthly. This was a colossal sum, but there was no way out. Buchalter said good-bye to his sister, saying that if he didn't return, that meant that the conductor—that was how he referred to Wacław—had found him a hiding place, where he would remain.

On the way to the agreed-upon meeting, he was stopped by a policeman. Filip was able to get away, but the policeman took Buchalter inside the gate and started to search his pockets. When he didn't find anything, he began to threaten him with death on the spot. Buchalter did not lose his mind and politely told the policeman that such dirty work would be better left for the Germans, that he should let him go and take instead the watch marked "Doxa" and five hundred złoty. The policeman did not wait too long to be asked, took the watch, and absconded.

I think that after the war they will both stand before the judge accused of serious offenses: the policeman, that he committed a robbery on a Jew, taking advantage of his helplessness; the Jew, that he cheated the policeman because the watch did not have the Doxa markings. As an extenuating circumstance in the case of the policeman, the court will take into account the fact that the policeman earned very little. In the case of the Jew, the extenuating circumstance will be that he wanted to save his life and had such a watch rather than any other. It will be interesting to see what the judgment of the court will be.

Buchalter, seeing how dangerous it was to walk the streets, took the tram. From the platform he went inside, and right away he came up against a group of Polish policemen with an officer at their head. These were all older men. When they saw Buchalter, they smiled one at the other, after which they surrounded him and concealed him from two Germans sitting in front of the wagon. They advised him which stop to get off that was the safest. The lady conductor also smiled, realizing that she had a Jew before her. With a pleasant smile she expressed to him her sympathy as well as an encouragement for further struggle. He got off happily, and at the appointed corner he met Miss Hela accompanied by Wacław, who quickly reported on the situation.

"If you want to have a hiding place," our protector said, "there is a place, a shop that is closed up, where some Jews have been hiding for eight months."

This sort of place was not to Buchalter's liking. He did not believe that it was possible to hide safely in such a shop. But he had no choice, and when Wacław told him that the young Perechodnik was there, he no longer hesitated. He recognized that if it was good for Perechodnik, it could also be good for Buchalter.

As regards cost, Wacław presented the problem in a nice and honest way. He said that he had no intention of exploiting their situation and that Perechodnik was paying five hundred złoty per person a month. Because everything had gone up in price, he asked in Miss Hela's name for seven hundred złoty. He added that, although she took the money, she was absolutely trustworthy and kept one Jewish girl for nothing and even gave her food. He wanted nothing for himself. He explained only that he was happy that he could save people. The most that he expected—he added—was that if Buchalter wished, he could express his gratitude after the war.

Buchalter accepted these conditions on the spot, and they went right away to the hiding place. Miss Hela led the way, went first into the room, leaving the door wide open. After a while, the men, seeing that there was no one in the street, also entered the room and closed the door. At that time we were standing behind the wardrobe, not having any idea who was being brought it. Only afterward did we realize that a Jew was standing before us.

And so in this way Miss Hela earned seven hundred złoty a month, and Wacław could enter on his account another human life saved.

I think it would be appropriate to mention the further fate of Filip. The money he received from Buchalter enabled him to survive until his friend returned from vacation. He arranged for a *Kennkarte*, rented a room in Międzylesiu, and rode the train daily to Warsaw, where he worked as a maker of leggings. (In his own time he was an owner of a big shoe factory and, wanting to better learn the line of business, learn how to make leggings.) He earned a modest livelihood, but it was sufficient. He met often at the train with Wacław. They talked frequently about Buchalter. Filip thought that he had been killed by the gendarmes. Wacław agreed with him, not betraying that he knew where and how Buchalter lived.

With Buchalter's arrival, we entered a new phase in our lives. His assertion—that in the opinion of almost all the Poles he met lately the war would soon be over—greatly strengthened our courage. At the same time, Buchalter could not quiet his nerves for a long time. He didn't believe that he was safe, was afraid to speak loudly, was even afraid to breathe loudly. He didn't let us chop wood, knock, walk, or talk. He constantly jumped from fear that we would be discovered, for which he indeed had good reason. Our lady, naturally, did not replace windowpanes that had been knocked out during the air raid, and she did not reinforce the shutters. I thought that it was possible to simply push against the window and the way to the apartment would be open.

Actually, to this day I cannot understand how all these people, the worst riffraff in society, sitting daily on our steps, did not realize that behind these thin walls sat so many Jews in hiding. God, let them find this out, but only after the war. Then one will tell the other, "Look, brothers, their whore of a mother and company, money was lying in the gutter, you needed only to bend down and pick it up, and we watched these kikes, their whore of a mother, for nothing—."

And, indeed, sitting as they did the whole day, they guarded us. Thanks to them Miss Hela's apartment was free of all suspicions. Besides, involuntarily and without anyone knowing it, they taught us the real "grammatical" Polish expressions.

The steady habitués on our steps—we knew them only by voice and name: Jurek, Janusz, and Roman—communicated to us the daily events of the world and the neighborhood, informing us how much they made that day, how much they drank, and worrying that the English, their whore of a mother, were afraid of those sons of whores Italians.

One time when our lady came, she left the door wide open. After a little while, a conversation started between her and Roman, the wagon driver sitting on the steps.

"You should thank me, lady," the voice reached from the outside, "and pay me as well for keeping watch on your apartment. I sit here all day and I watch."

"And how do you make a living," answered Miss Hela, "if you sit all day on the steps?"

"Well, from the steps, my dear lady, here I meet my clients or pals. You know, lady, before the war, when a Jew tailor lived in this apartment, I watched the apartment for him so well that he went out and left the door open."

The conversation was carried on in the doorway to the room; the open doors invited all and offered testimony to the town and the world that in this single room lived one lonely person. In the meantime, behind the wardrobe, four Jews sat quietly, listening from deadly boredom and necessity to this strange conversation.

One had to get used to it; this was most difficult for Buchalter, whom all of us now call Sewek. After the "schooling" he received from Franek's wife, our lady was, in his opinion, a veritable angel.

Since winter Miss Hela has been bringing me newspapers regularly. It impresses her that every day a paper is set aside for her at the bar,[224] the same as is done for the stationmaster or the dispatcher. From time to time we even get the underground papers, which Wacław brings. It's quite another matter that this particularly irritates Miss Hela. After reading, she burns them immediately. To her mind, they are more dangerous than hiding Jews in her home. We can never laugh to our heart's content for this reason. Wacław, in a fit of good humor, tells her at times that she should have a radio.

"Waciu, what are you saying?" Miss Hela wonders every time, "I should have a radio? Even if they would kill me, never in my life!"

Except for these minor things, Miss Hela made colossal progress this past half-year; she simply blossomed, internally and externally. She carries herself like a great lady, and from her former life she retains only the habit of taking a złoty for the shopping basket from everything she buys for us. We put a good face on it and pretend that we don't know anything about it. In this way the basket money that she appropriates is not so costly to us.

Sewek Buchalter is glad that he hit on such a cheap and good place. Because he jumped from the train with only what he had on his back, I lent him a towel and a shirt. Bedclothes he doesn't need because he sleeps with me. From day to day he gains more and more confidence in our hiding place, worries only if he will have enough money to live through the war. In general he has on him about five thousand złoty as well as forty gold dollars. In the present circumstances it ought to last him for a year. It is worse for his sister, who has money for six months at the most.

I am very pleased that he is with us. For one, with a new person, a new atmosphere and a new life entered our room. Besides, I am happy that Miss Hela is more and more interested in keeping us. I don't discount the fact that I also have a companion for discussion and for the *belotki** card game with which we vary the monotonous routine of our life. In addition to that, Sewek takes care of my hair, thanks to which I now begin to look completely decent.

The first weeks of his stay passed pleasantly and calmly. During that time Wacław visited us frequently. I thought to myself, how blind love is. Wacław is a young man, good looking and masculine as a picture, fairly

---

*This was a bidding game, called *Dirdl* in Yiddish.

educated, very intelligent, and of an extraordinarily good character. Our Miss Hela is, on the other hand, forty plus, not educated, ill-mannered, plain, nasty by nature, and inclined to sadism. She does have a lovely shape and an inexplicable "fluid" that draws Wacław.

How do we pass the time? Mainly in discussion—when Tunis will fall, when Italy will collapse—and we beg God.

What should we, we Jews, beg from God? First of all that our lady should not lose her job and that Wacław should not lose his; that they should not quarrel and go their separate ways; that they should both remain well; also that Wacław's wife should not find out about their relationship; that our lady should not come upon a candidate for marriage; that there shouldn't be an air raid and that our house should not get bombed; that no one should catch us or find out that Miss Hela is hiding us; that our patroness should not spend money because if she has too much of it, she will not be greedy for it; that she should not spend too much money on clothes because if she appears too elegant, people will wonder where she gets the money; that all of us should remain well because it is not possible to bring a doctor to the room; that the money for the room and for food should last us to the end of the war—for all that we beg and, oh wonder, we are happy that we ask for so little. It is fearful to think what would happen if in addition we had to beg that our lady not have bad dreams, as, for example, a grizzled cow, a bird with its tail cut off—undoubted forecasts of a bad break; that she would not tell us fairy tales every day of houses being blockaded; that she would not play her daily comedy that she is afraid to keep us and that consequently she did not raise our rent; and that, finally, she should not get greedy about our property and, together with a Polish policeman, sweep us out at night.

For all this, thanks to God, we don't have to beg. The unblemished character of Wacław and the artlessness of Miss Hela guarantee us peace from those fears. In any case, there are enough things for which one has to beg God.

And what does a man do who does not believe in God?

Far, far away, on a big meadow, an old peasant herds a cow. He chases her with a stick, sits down every few minutes. No wonder—he is old, tired of life; his gray hairs are falling down. Suddenly, he is startled, raises his head high. A flash of the sun forces him to put on his cap, but he does not lower his head, staring at the sky in an easterly direction.

More than one of the peasants walking in the distance wonders, What does the old man see in the sky? At what is he staring? They shrug their shoulders, and they forget about him after a while. Others who pass him nearby also look heavenward and, seeing nothing, there call out quickly, "Praised be He!"

The old one looks at the sky as if bewitched. Only his lips are moving in silence. What does he see in the sky? Who is it?

It's an old Jew, his head covered, who is praying to his God. He is reciting the morning prayers.[225] He asks God's forgiveness because he cannot praise His name aloud; he begs the God of Abraham, Isaac, and Jacob to protect him and the few remaining of his family in these difficult times so they can survive until the moment when he can gratefully build for the Lord a temple to bless there the name of the God of Israel. His lips move ever more quickly, ever more silently; the fervent prayer flows through them, pierces the atmosphere of evil deeds, and approaches the steps of the Almighty. Loudly, on the other hand, every few moments, the old peasant calls out to passersby, "For a world without end, Amen."

That old Jew was none other than my father. He came to the village in the company of a shoemaker he knew, whom he introduced as his relative. Father maintained that he had lived in Kresy his whole life, from where he had gotten his specific accent and drawn-out speech. His shoemaker friend believed this fairy tale; the village landlords believed it and received him with open arms. Gray hair called for respect; his reasoning—naturally Jewish—earned him recognition. An inborn politeness and pleasant behavior resulted in his having bestowed on him the title "Gentleman from Warsaw." Every landlord first removed his hat before him and gladly allowed himself to be counseled in various matters. All received either advice or encouragement to settle according to their own plans—in the worst case a sincere sympathy. Father captivated his landlady the first day by curing her boil with the aid of the *Hansaplaster*.

In a word, he lived as one would "behind God's own oven." Living here in comparison with Warsaw was much cheaper. The rent was not five hundred but thirty złoty monthly. Everyday he drank a liter of milk, smeared bread with butter—in a word, to live and not to die.

It was worse, on the other hand, with the daily morning and evening prayers; he was supposed to kneel before the holy picture and, as was the custom with the landlords, recite the prayers loudly. Father was, however, too stubborn a Jew to say a Christian prayer even at the cost of saving a life. He therefore used whatever tricks he could. When the landlords entered the room, they always found him at the moment when he got up off the floor in front of the picture. It is not difficult to imagine that he did not pray at all before they entered.

In order to be considered a good Christian, it was necessary to show oneself in the local chapel. On the first Sunday, my father went there in the company of his landlord. He entertained him so with conversation, so often fixed the shoelaces on his boots, that by the time they arrived it was after the service. In front of the chapel Father greeted his peasant friends and returned home with them. From that time on he was considered a patented Catholic and a decent man.

It happened that a sentence was uttered for which he sought meaning: "The Germans killed that whoreson Chaim."

He interjected, asking if Chaim was a surname or a name or asking other questions of that type. He was quite legally registered—even the gendarmes checked his *Kennkarte*—surrounded by a general respect, and under the thoughtful care of his landlady. He could live peacefully and repeat after Kochanowski:

> *A quiet village, a happy village which your voice praises*
> *Whose restfulness, whose goodness all can remember*
> *A man can live under your care honestly and calmly*
> *A safe existence.*[226]

He could have lived securely if not for one small fact: He believed that he was a Pole, a native Pole of blood and bone. There could be only one conclusion: If he could make it, why not bring his wife here? After all, nothing could be found out about a woman. After being in the village for a month, he decided to return to us and take Mother to the village.

One night we heard knocking at the door. We hid, as usual, behind the wardrobe. Miss Hela opened the door—my father stood at the entrance so changed that he could not be recognized. He had improved a great deal, had an aristocratic face, very sunburned, contrasting with his gray hair. He had acquired the manners of a decadent country gentleman. On the whole he presented himself very well.

He greeted all of us as well as Sewek, whom he knew personally anyway. He brought us a few bottles of sour cream, a little butter, told us of his miracles from the village, but he did not betray where it was. He was very circumspect and cautious and didn't even let me handle his *Kennkarte* so that I would not be able to tell by the stamps where he was located.

He said right away that he wanted to take Mother with him. She categorically refused at first, afraid of any kind of risk. After several days, during which Father spread out before her a picture of a peaceful and safe village, where you could drink milk straight from a cow every day, where butter and sour cream were part of a daily diet, where impenetrable forests rustled all around, bringing with them a breath of fresh and clean air . . .

He also told her that in the village no one would notice that her nose was a little bit deficient or that her eyes were dark and her expression not very Polish. He reminded her that she had a school certificate, a coupon for an official departure, and that it would be enough to hang a medallion around her neck, pray twice daily before a picture, cross herself from time to time, and then everything would go smoothly, like a hot knife through butter. He also added that they would not live together but that he would take care of her from a distance.

Confident of herself and trusting Father, she became convinced and decided to travel. Father occupied himself with preparations. From the Magister's mother he got a black hat, dark glasses, borrowed a veil from Miss Hela, and the mourning outfit was ready.

Father proposed that I go, too. I refused to make that decision. I don't want to live legally. I am even surprised that I allowed Mother to go away. Maybe because I did not want to decide the fate of other people and maybe because I saw how Mother was getting weaker day by day. I thought to myself that maybe she would make it: She would recover, gain strength, and be a healthy person again. Or she would not make it—then it couldn't be helped. I knew that it was June 3, the war had not yet ended, and in the dark, narrow room mother's organism would simply collapse. The worries she lived through, the heartbreaks, lack of food, advancing age, lack of spirit, all this would lead her to a grave, not to life.

The next day Father and Mother went away. Before they left the apartment a characteristic incident occurred. The moment that Mother put the medallion on her neck, Father turned to her and said insistently, "Ask God's forgiveness!"

Mother was a bit too painfully wronged by the Jewish God to beg his forgiveness or to believe in Him in general.

This time Father left me—as an exception—his village address, a place situated in Radomsk, near Stachanowic, as well as the name of his landlord, which sounded like Władysław Słyk.

It was only when he was leaving that I saw that he was limping a little, the right leg not quite following orders. But it was not in his character to take notice of such foolishness. His energy and liveliness propelled him forward. The weakened physique had to keep up with the strong spirit.

I remain in the apartment with Sewek and Genia. It's a little sad without Mother. One has to cook alone, but the days pass somehow. I advise

Sewek to bring us his sister and son. The money will last her for a year in our place, she will be safe here, and it will be more cheerful for us. Maybe a little uncomfortable, but it will be more lively together.

Sewek agrees with me, but he explains that it is impossible to carry this out. He cannot go for his sister by himself, and if he sends a card to Franek for his sister to come, her landlord will simply hide it. They will not let her go until she gets money. There is just no way to help her.

For the time being we rejoice with the fall of Panteleria,[227] and carry on long discussions on the theme of our experiences. Sewek mourns bitterly his son's death, then that of his parents, and finally that of his wife. I can't understand all this. My greatest tragedy was the loss of a wife and then that of my daughter. Parents—let them live as long as possible—are in last place. But these are matters that do not lend themselves to discussion. They are questions of love and attachments.

We discuss military affairs daily: how the war will end and what will follow. Sewek is a decided optimist, believes in the might of England, in the greatness of America; he is convinced of a rapid defeat of Italy and the automatic breakup of Germany. I, on the other hand, see the matter in darker colors; such is obviously my character trait.

We are puzzled about where such hatred by Germans of Jews comes from, how much of it is the fault of the Jews. My opinion is that, setting aside inborn German sadism, the desire to murder for the enjoyment of killing, and the lust for gold, I ascribe the entire blame to the Jewish religion.

One cannot enjoy the hospitality of other peoples and consider oneself as a chosen people, better and wiser. One cannot in daily prayers repeat the words "You have chosen us from all the nations of the world. You have loved us." Perhaps God did choose us, but for what? So that we would be the scapegoat for all other people, to make us responsible for all the sins of the world? What do I have to do with Blum?[228] What do I have to do with Kaganowich? What do I have to do with Rosenman? What do we have to do with all of them?[229] What links them with us? Nothing more than what links us with the Chinese. After all, we all come from the same ancestor and probably from the same species of apes.

And yet we European Jews, we have paid with the blood of our innocent children and women, and with our own, for all these accounts. Cursed be the Bund[230] that ordered the Jewish workers to struggle for a better existence here and forbade them to emigrate to Palestine. Where are you now, leaders of the Bund? You were the first to escape to America so that you would spread the same rottenness among the workers there.

Cursed be the *Aguda,*[231] with her fanaticism, her leaders who are en-
joying themselves in America,[232] while the Jewish nation stupefied by
them perishes in Treblinka.

You, rabbis, why do you faithfully believe in the judgment "What can
man do to me if God is with me"?[233] Do you also believe that if thirty-six
righteous people are found in a town, that town will not perish? In that
case, why did you run away? Indeed, you could have protected the
Jewish people from extermination with your holy presence.

Yes, the Jewish religion had divided us from other people with a
Chinese wall, had inculcated in us a psychology of distinctness, had
commanded us to circumcise our boys. We voluntarily sealed ourselves
not with a sign of unity between us and God but with a seal of death,
which led us to Treblinka.

Daily we repeated the words of the prayer: "If I forget thee, O
Jerusalem, let my right hand wither away."[234] Alas, we did not remember
Jerusalem, and not only did our right hand wither but also our entire
body. Only two things could have saved the Jews. The first was an un-
compromising Zionism: a dry piece of bread but in one's own home; the
second, an absolute assimilation, not only in customs and religion but
also in the regeneration of our blood.

There wasn't, and there isn't, a middle road. I don't believe in any democratic slogans. The human being has in him a slumbering devil, and
he will have him in heaven as well. Twenty-six years I lived among Poles
and the devil slumbered, but he awakened in favorable circumstances
and showed his devilish face.

You, the Jews in other countries, don't make our mistake because
there isn't a middle road in a human life. There was a time when the
Jewish people had a chance to choose a better way. The people turned to
the prophet Samuel with the following demand: We wish to be like other
nations; give us a king who will rule over us. However, the prophet
Samuel, although he listened to them, convinced the Jews that divine
rules are better than human ones.

Today we indeed have proof of how good it is to find oneself under the
power of divine protection. And a time will come when the democratic
world will win, and fanfares will announce the freedom of peoples. Jews
will then be able to live freely, to go back to Palestine—although from
the 3 million will remain perhaps twenty thousand, a tiny number. But
the most important fact is that justice will again prevail.

Rabbis, these base cowards who ran away in good times, will praise
anew the might of God's name, who again brought His people from slav-

ery to the Promised Land. They will establish new Passovers but with one small difference: The Jews came to Egypt numbering some seventy men and left as a people numbering some 3 million souls. In Poland some 3 million were gathered, but no more than seventy whole families will leave it. Finally, however, what do numbers matter in terms of eternity, in terms of the victory of good over evil? For that matter, this mere handful will multiply. After one thousand years there will be new millions of Jews. Let us praise the name of God!

No! Jews, if you believe this, you are mistaken! We have lost the war. If maybe there is a God in the world, the worst for Him—evidently it is a God of the strong and mighty, not of the weak and persecuted. And if there is no God at all, well then there is nothing to argue about.

If I could return to prewar times, I would have gladly given up all my possessions and gone with my wife to Palestine. With the labor of my hands and the sweat of my brow I would have sought a satisfaction from my life. Now it is too late. Even if I should survive, I will not go to Palestine. After this that I have lived through, I cannot live a normal life and look at happy people. I will not remain in Poland, I will not build a new hearth, and I will never be a useful member of society. So what can happen to me? Neither Jew nor Catholic nor a decent man, not even a thief—simply a nobody.

If there were justice in this world, then there should be created after the war volunteer battalions made up of such wrecks as myself, Sewek, and other Jews. Patterned on the Ukrainian battalions, we should deport Germans to the same Treblinka—precisely there and not elsewhere.

In my whole life I never raised a hand against a fellow creature, but I feel that I would cease drinking, that my thirst would be quenched with German blood, especially that of small children. For my daughter, for all the Jewish children, I would take a hundredfold revenge. My heart is already pounding with joy; my pale cheeks are glowing with the thought of the physical and psychological tortures I would inflict on the Germans before their final death. And then, satiated with blood and revenge, I could perish together with my enemies.

On June 15, the day after Pentecost (Shavuot), after an absence of several days, our lady made her appearance. Several minutes after her arrival, we heard a knock on the door. Miss Hela opened it, and an older woman entered, dressed in mourning, a small suitcase in hand. I felt faint—I recognized my mother. A moment later my father appeared. What happened in the village?

Mother lived with a poor peasant woman, in a house situated out of the way. Father, unfortunately, did not behave cautiously enough, visited her often, and every time brought her something—enough that people began to surmise. The landlady actually said to my mother, "A woman whom I consider an enemy is convinced that you are Jewish and the wife of that man."

Hearing this, my mother feigned being insulted and said that if she was suspected of being Jewish, she could change her place of residence. She then went to "Mr. Michael" with a loud pretense and demanded that he take her away to her brother in Warsaw. In fact, nothing had happened yet, but Father was a cautious person and fearful of remaining there. Loudly he wondered if he too could be suspected of being a Jew.

"What is it, may cholera strike it?" he told his landlord. "One can immediately check if a man is a Jew or not."

The next night he packed his bags and got out in a hurry. Well, kielbasa is not for a dog, nor is freedom for a Jew! They lost several hundred złoty in the affair, but the important thing was that nothing happened to them. The worst was that Father could not return there. Could or couldn't —in any case he was afraid.

They came to Warsaw on June 13. When they reached our street, the doors, unfortunately, were closed from the outside with a strong padlock. There was no point in knocking. They understood right away that Miss Hela was spending the holidays in Falenica. They had no place to go to. They could not even dream of going to a hotel. To remain on the street meant certain death.

Not having any other way out, they went to the Magister, who received them as best he could. The apartment was not his, it was his brother-in-law's—who after a long absence returned for the holidays. The house was, from certain aspects, in danger of an eventual visit from the gendarmes, but the Magister did not hesitate for a moment.

"Since you are appealing to my sense of hospitality, madam," he explained, "then I have to receive you."

My mother spent the night in one of the many rooms; my father went to sleep at the shoemaker's whom he knew. In the morning, a servant brought tea and a cake to her bed. Mother did not know what world she was in. It seemed to her that everyone was jumping around her, while she was just given the normal respect due her gray hair and position.

Later, the Magister and his sister asked to be pardoned, but they explained that she could not sleep there the following night. They justified themselves by saying that they didn't want to cause any trouble to their brother-in-law. The Magister, understanding my mother's feelings, said in addition, "Look, madam, it is such a big house. Could anyone believe that in spite of our best intentions, we could not have found a place for you for one more night?"

My parents spent the day at the cemetery. They also visited Dr. R. It turned out that there was nothing wrong with Mother, that she just needed better nourishment. It turned out worse for my father. He was in danger of paralysis in one leg.

They passed the night, thanks to the protection of the shoemaker, at his friend's. Father put up a "fortieth" of vodka, and the matter was finished. Only by the third night could they come to us.

Our lady let them in, but she realized right away that she was their only plank for survival. She realized that she was on top and that she could do whatever she wanted to. She changed her tone right away. She said that she did not want to keep Mother altogether, that she really didn't want to keep anyone, that she wanted more money, etc., etc. Finally she agreed to take money for the next month, but she asserted that Mother would have to leave then. If you fight by the sword, you die by the sword. Father had threatened her so many times with leaving that she had learned to apply the same tactic.

When Mother recollected her stay at the Magister's, praising him without end, Miss Hela said that he had to be a little stupid; otherwise he would not be so good. What could I say? It has come to such a point that a true and disinterested kindness is compared to stupidity.

I calmly heard the argument of Miss Hela's and Mother's stories in order to separate the naked facts from the ornamental language. The Magister allowed Mother to spend the night, although he didn't know her personally, had never even seen her. The second night, even with his most sincere desire—which I don't doubt—he could not offer her. Miss Hela, on the other hand, made possible Mother's stay not for one night but for at least two hundred nights and—what is most important—made possible further rescue. I cannot understand why Mother will remember the Magister for the rest of her life and will bless him to her last moment, but she will not feel any gratitude in relation to our lady.

What it comes to is that very few people can evaluate events according to their real specific importance, without any embellishment. Because in no case can one compare the credit due our lady for what she did for

Mother with the credit due the Magister. It would be like comparing daily bread to a tasty cake for dessert.

I don't treat lightly in the least the Magister's conduct. We owe him a debt of gratitude, a debt that can't be repaid. Not only for what he did, but also for what he wanted to do. I cannot forget that he wanted to save my daughter from death.

Should I also be grateful that he took my things for safekeeping, that he was not greedy for them? That would be for him the greatest insult!

In the meantime our situation is not rosy. We don't have much money. Father cannot return to the village, although he sent a postcard there saying that he will return soon. He doesn't have the slightest intention of remaining at Miss Hela's. At the same time he is in danger of a paralysis of his leg and cannot walk too much. What will happen? Time will soon tell.

Some distance from Warsaw, not far from Grochowa, the garden plots are turning green. Work proceeds at full steam. The gardeners are digging and fertilizing the ground, watering the beds, staking tomato plants. Every few minutes they interrupt their work and run to the shed.

"Mr. Bogdański, please let me have a watering can!"

"Mr. Bogdański, do you need a lot of manure under the tomatoes?"

"Mr. Bogdański, sell me a stake for the tomatoes."

One hears such words all day long. Then old Mr. Bogdański answers all politely, gives them what they need, helps everyone. To tell the truth, he never had anything to do with gardening, but thanks to his intuitive skill he gives wise answers, although in a noncommittal form.

Everyone is delighted with the new worker and asks him how he feels. The president greets him daily, treats him to homemade coffee. The secretary has procured for him free dinners at the Main Council for Public Assistance.[235] Mr. Bogdański closes up the materials in the shed for the night, and he also sleeps there.

As we see, old "Bogdański" has not become despondent. Thanks to the protection of his friend the shoemaker, he has managed to get a job at the garden plots. It's true he makes very little, only ten złoty a day, but at least he has a place to sleep. He makes a little more buying fertilizer and then selling it to the gardeners. At times he carries a bucket for someone, and he gets a tip for the favor. The old tenement house owner from Kościelna Street does not draw back his hand. All his life he lived from rents he collected; in his old age he makes a living from tips. What can one do? Evidently such is the will of God.

It's important that out of the seventy gardeners hardly more than two have interested themselves in his nationality and ask why he speaks with a strange intonation. He replies that he comes from the eastern region of Kresy, and that has satisfied them completely. All other doubts are dispelled by a postcard that comes to Bogdański. The old man, not able to see too well, asks that the following be read out loud:

Łuków 27 VI 43

Dear Michał!

I received your letter. I hasten to tell that your cousin, the organist from Białegostok, Malecki, wrote to me this month that he received a letter from your wife. She is in Słonim, is well, and manages somehow. Write to me often how you feel and how you get along. We have had changes here. My wife has given birth to a son. I will write you about the christening. Maybe you'll be able to come. I kiss you heartily,

Your loving Antek

The sender was Antoni Wierzbicki from Łuków, from Wierzbicka Street, 12. It was addressed to The Honorable Mr. Cz. Nowowiejski, Warsaw, St. . . . with a postscript: for Mr. Bogdański. That was the address of the good friend, the shoemaker. The actual sender of the postcard was the Magister, who composed it and sent it at Father's request.

It was very likely that everything would turn out fine and that Father would have remained at that job for a long time, if not for a detail: The president wanted to buy a fur collar, and since Father had something like that, he proposed to be the middleman between him and an imaginary acquaintance.

They agreed on the deal readily, after which the following dialogue took place.

"Mr. President, if we will see each other after twenty years and you will be wearing this collar, then I will accept your thanks."

"Mr. Bogdański, you are praising these goods with the mentality of a Jewish merchant. You know, the watchman was telling me that you must be a Jew. You speak so peculiarly. . . ."

"And what do you think, Mr. President? Do you know the accent from the borderland?"

"Do I know? If you're alright without your trousers on. . . . If not, you have to be very careful."

The conversation ended at this point. Nothing really happened, but Father felt anxious just the same. He was very sorry that he did not follow the example of Dr. Feldhof, Szlamowicz, and other Jews, who underwent a surgical procedure to disfigure their male member.[236]

The operation was very painful and unpleasant, but in the case of Szmulewicz, it saved a life. When the trackers handed him over to the gendarmes, he denied that he was a Jew. A Polish doctor who was summoned confirmed after a short examination that he could not ascertain if he was dealing with a Jew or a Pole.

At Miss Hela's, the first days after my mother's arrival pass in an anxious state. We think constantly about how Father is getting on at the garden plots. Only after a while we hear a voice from the street communicating to us that for the time being everything is in order. That is Father, adjusting his shoelaces on our steps, who whispers to tell us what is happening with him. We don't answer because we are afraid that someone may be walking in the street.

Time again flows by slowly. We fill it with accounts of our fate and stories of Jews we know. Wacław told us of the sad end of our friend Szmul Kołkowicz.

He was riding the train where Wacław was the conductor. In Jósefów, a certain Sokołowski, in the company of another agent, entered at Otwock a car holding a platoon of Polish police. The police looked around the car, after which Sokołowski asked if that was not Kołkowicz sitting on the bench. Denials did not help.

The police approached Kołkowicz, took out their pistols, and told him to put his hands up. Kołkowicz was not especially frightened, did not prepare either to flee or to defend himself. He knew that nothing would threaten him from the side of the Polish policeman; at the most he would have to give him something for a vodka.

However, when he did not raise his hands and tried to joke, he was struck in the temple with the gun butt. As he blacked out, Sokołowski handcuffed him.

They got off at Świder. Kołkowicz, taking advantage of the concourse, tried to run away. It was difficult for him to run with the handcuffs, but as he got away a fair distance, a bullet found him. Wounded in the stomach, he fell to the ground. When the police searched him, they found the gun, and they drove him in a country wagon to be disposed of by Schlicht.

First they ministered some aid to him; then they examined him in detail to find out where he had got the weapon. What happened at the examination we don't know. We know instead that one nice day Schlicht took Kołkowicz in a carriage and drove him to the Otwock park. There he wanted to shoot him with his pistol. Luckily it jammed. Kołkowicz tried to run away. He would probably have run into the woods if the bullets of Polish policemen who were there to assist at the execution had not found their mark.

Thus, Szmul Kołkowicz perished at the hands of those by whom he least expected to be killed. He worked for so many years for the Polish police, not begrudging them the repair of their bicycles or the free bread. For all that the Polish police repaid him with a good portion of hot lead. Sokołowski in a subsequent conversation even bragged that he had personally caused Kołkowicz's death and that he would kill with his own hands every whoreson of a Jew that he caught. Another hero who has arisen among us!

At the end of June, Wacław received through the assistance of a little girl a postcard with the following text:

Dear Mr. Wacław:
I would very much appreciate it if you would communicate with me on a very important matter. I am the sister of Seweryn Buchalter. I live in Hotel Polski, Długa 26, room 68. Ask for Mela.
   Awaiting the disposal of this matter,

   Mela

That same day we learned through the mediation of our lady about the letter from Sewek's sister. We still did not know the contents. Sewek was completely despairing. He suspected that his sister had lost her hiding place, that they had taken away her money, that she had no place to go to. He wondered how to deal with Miss Hela so that she would agree to bring Mela to us.

After several days, when Miss Hela brought from Wacław the postcard cited above, we were as ignorant as before. It seemed to us that the whole thing was a dream. How did Sewek's sister get to Hotel Polski? She lived officially, did not hide the fact that she was Jewish. One could dare to visit her, and she herself did the inviting. Inconceivable! How did she get there? We were not in a position to know anything. There was nothing to do but wait until Wacław went there.

On June 28, Wacław met with Sewek's sister, and the mystery was solved. In Hotel Polski there were about two hundred Jews, citizens of foreign countries, who were supposed to be taken out to Vittel[237] and interned there. Some said that from there they would go out, via Portugal, to America.[238]

Sewek's sister made it to Hotel Polski, and she was supposed to go out shortly with the whole group. She was of the opinion, as she told Wacław, that Sewek should follow in her footsteps as quickly as possible. We didn't know what to make of this proposal.

I saw in this a trap created with the aim of pulling out those Jews who were still in hiding and finishing them off discreetly. Sewek, on the other hand, hesitated. He trusted his sister, who, being on the spot, had the possibility of orienting herself in this situation. He assumed that if she had any suspicions, she would not try to get him out. Not knowing what to do, he sent Wacław with a letter asking how the matter looked and who of their friends were still in the hotel.

On June 3 he received a reply. Below I am giving a fragment from that letter:

Dear Sewek!

I am happy that I got your letter. I am here together with my son for over a month. I will probably leave on July 6. I don't know exactly if it will be Vittel[239] or a place on the Bodeński Lake. Our protector is Lolek Skosowski (Jew, Gestapo man)[240] as well as Adam (Pole, Gestapo man).[241] I am despairing that we are not together now. Franek directed me here. Mandelbaum and Romek are also here. My heart pains me that I have to leave without you. If you do not find me here, my girl-friend Szochet, a citizen of Palestine, is here. Their group is not leaving yet. You can turn to her in case it is necesary. Try to get here.

Mela

Mandelbaum and Romek Gutman were Jews who had run away from the same transport with Buchalter. The letter mentioned a lot of Sewek's friends, who were in the hotel. These were wealthy people, possessing both money and Polish friends.

We began to debate the matter hotly. Sewek told us in detail about every Jewish acquaintance who was there. He evaluated many hiding places, 100 percent safe, in which these people had hidden until now. Some had legal *Kennkarte*, a suitable appearance. He drew only one conclusion from all this: If these people went there, it could not be a suspicious affair.

The matter in question was not altogether new. All during the war foreign papers arrived for a variety of Jewish families, who were subsequently interned in Vittel. The letters that came from there were of the best. The Jews who were taken there found themselves under the care of the International Red Cross.[242] When the Warsaw ghetto still existed, it was everyone's dream to reach Vittel.

We surmised that lately fresh papers had arrived for various Jews, and because these were for the most part no longer alive, other Jews began to make use of these documents.

Whatever it was, even if true, it didn't stand up under criticism. The counterarguments were as follows: During this war, there wasn't a Jew who succeeded in deceiving the Germans. On the contrary, all Jews, and among them the wisest ones, were deceived by the Germans. The Germans had to realize that this was simply humbug. If they agreed to tolerate it, this was only for objectives known only to them. How could you have a guarantee that you would not be taken someplace and, without publicity, shot? Who would take up for the Jews? Who in general cared about the deaths of Jews? Could Jews be protected by foreign papers? The answer to all these questions was one: If you were already a Jew, then the only thing you could do was to hide yourself well.

Sewek nevertheless decided to risk it, and he planned to go to Hotel Polski on July 5, to talk it over with his sister, and to decide right then and there—if it's possible—to remain there. Wacław, however, absolutely did not agree with this. He was afraid to let Sewek go because of the security of our hiding place. He had nothing against Sewek leaving and not coming back. But to go and come back carried with it the risk of being followed. Willy-nilly, Sewek had to remain.

That same evening Father came to our place. Because he carried some packages, we realized right away that he no longer worked in the garden plots. It turned out that he had given up the job earlier than expected. But he wasn't sorry. He did not feel badly about Mother's escapade in the village. In the meantime it turned out that it was forbidden to ride the train to Stachanowic.[243] If Father had remained in the village, he would not have been able to return to us.

Once again it was proof that this man was like a cat, always landing on four feet. He often repeated that in life things had to be accepted as they were and that it was never possible to know how things would be better.

This time it also proved him right. When he worked in the garden plots, he got to know a Polish woman who was employed for many years by an octogenarian professor. Because it was a large apartment, the professor sublet one room to a variety of tenants.

"If you don't have anywhere to live," the Polish woman said one day to my father, "then you can live at my place. You don't have to bring your bed linen because I have enough of mine."

They agreed on one hundred twenty złoty monthly. The sum was a bit too much to take from a Pole, but from a Jew—definitely too little. Father is very pleased. The Polish woman seems like a very decent person, and it also seems that she is not capable of recognizing that he is a Jew.

Later it turned out, as it has often before, that there are no limits to human naïveté. This very same Polish woman came from Rowno and had spent her whole life among Jews and recognized any Jew from a distance of one kilometer. As soon as she exchanged the first two words with Father, she knew with whom she was dealing. She decided to take care of him and rented him a room, actually a bed in the kitchen. She took from him more than she would have taken from a Pole but a lot less than she could have demanded from any Jew.

Later she told Father that if she could have done it, she would have saved not one life but tens of thousands of Jews. At the same time she wanted to be legally correct. That was why she rented the apartment to Jews who had Aryan papers. In that way she could pretend that she did not know that they were Jews. The rental that she took was only slightly raised.

In her apartment Father found three people of "Polish nationality." When they saw Father, they got frightened that they would be living in the company of a real Pole. They even suggested to the landlady that they would pay another one hundred złoty monthly if she would turn Father away. She, laughing to herself, naturally did not agree to it. Two days after he moved in, two female tenants, a mother and a daughter, moved out. One cannot exclude the possibility that they were afraid of Father. After a while, news came to the landlady that they had been discovered and killed in the village during a raid.

Father then remained with one other fellow tenant, a masseuse. In the house, one speaks of Jews as little as possible. The landlady corrects Father's Polish pronunciation, Father corrects the Polish pronunciation of the young lady, everybody is fine, everybody is pleased. The landlady can take care of Jews and be legally in order, the tenants live as if they were native Poles, and they don't have to watch themselves against an unguarded gesture or word.

Father was with us for a couple of days, during which time we told one another what had happened. He didn't want to hear of the matter con-

cerning Sewek's sister, saying that he had no intention of going there and
that if anyone wanted to ask, he would not offer advice. He said that he
basically did not trust the Germans and that this approach had never
turned out badly for him. He really did not trust anyone—sure enough,
he did not even give us his new address.

Before he left, there was a big uproar. Father wanted to pay the rent for
me, but our lady did not want to take the money. She started her old
tricks and demanded that we move out on the 16th. In general she was
angry at Father, mainly for the reason that when he came, he furnished
us with provisions for an extended time. Now it was not possible for her
to have an income from the purchase baskets. On top of everything, my
mother told Miss Hela that if we would not be here, nobody would be
here. These words smelled plainly of blackmail and rightfully made our
lady fly off the handle.

At that point Wacław gave her his full support, saying that the Jews
would have to be removed since they could not behave themselves. He
also had a long conference with Sewek. He told him that the old
Perechodnik tried to frighten them and so his family had to leave. Miss
Genia had someplace to go to, and he too had to get ready to leave.
Wacław promised that he would exert all his efforts to locate some place
for him.

All the persuasiveness of Sewek did not yield any results. He then told
Wacław that he intended—following his sister's example—to go to Vittel.
He asked him to take a letter to Hotel Polski. He wrote the letter, handed
it to Wacław, and with that the conversation ended.

The following day was a day of repentance for my mother. Her arro-
gance just flew away when she finally realized that she could lose the
place. She cried endlessly, was ready to pay a much higher rent for the
room, and did not broadcast any more threats. She was as if unconscious the whole day. She told Genia that Calek was calm because he
had a place to go to and that she had no place to stay. She would have to
poison herself in the street.

These laments were distasteful to me. For four months she and Father
did nothing except threaten our lady with leaving. She played with fire
so long that she finally got burned. I was calm myself because I took all
this as a sign that I had to go to Hotel Polski. If Mother wanted that, I was
ready to take her with me.

What saved us? First of all—an answer from Szochet to Sewek, which
Wacław brought. Sewek's friend wrote:

Dear Mr. Seweryn!

Mela, as she was leaving the hotel, informed me that a friend of yours would come. I was ready the whole time since I assumed that he would visit momentarily, even went downstairs frequently because it is so difficult to communicate with us. Now this, in summary, is how our fate looks to us. Although I do not know you personally, I am writing to you honestly. Right now there aren't too many of us in the hotel. Together with the transport from Pawiak, we are around two hundred people. These are all strangers. There are no families among us who might work together. Each of us is afraid of his own shadow. Heaven forbid that we should tell someone something or advise them. We are in the hotel as foreign citizens. Each of us has personal papers of his own citizenship. Your sister had Palestinian citizenship that she had arranged for herself in Warsaw. You have to apply to the hotel with papers prepared because the administration has to report your name right away, include it on the group list, and conduct an interview, although this usually succeeds. Everything has gotten a little worse, but people manage.

Don't wait for the departure of our group, which is to happen soon. The news of the first group has arrived, and so my feeling is 200 percent certain.

I don't want to stay in Warsaw any longer. I have the most important guarantee: foreign citizenship. The papers were done by Orbis, America line. It cost me personally a lot of money. Sister told me that her total costs, with the payment to the intermediary, were fourteen thousand złoty. All this is done legally.

Come to the hotel with your papers. Part of the group from Pawiak left, and a part has remained. The departure of our group is supposed to occur between August 5 and 10. Sister's wish was that you present yourself for the departure. I send greetings from sister and wish you a lucky conclusion of this matter.

Szochet

This letter explained a lot. First of all, everything now argued for getting to the hotel, and secondly, the attitude of our lady changed. When Wacław read her the letter and explained that we had someplace to go to, it turned out that Miss Hela did not want to lose tenants.

Well, she had got used to money flowing in regularly every month, to our presence, and, above all, to Genia's services. One also has to remember that our presence bound her to our moral patron, her Waciu, the way small children unite a marriage. I don't want to say that Wacław would have ended relations with her if we had left. But he surely visited her more often, being bound with a joint burden of keeping alive such dependent and helpless children as we became during the war.

Her decision was also influenced by a newspaper story about the Allies landing on Sicily[244] and, connected with it, a prediction of an early end to the war. It was not worth getting high and mighty and freeing the tenants of the debt of gratitude that they contracted during so many months of their stay.

The other thing was how I, and Sewek, hit the nail on the head. The letter was very convincing. Everything gave the appearance of a time when one could benefit from taking a chance. The hotel provided an alternative; either one would surely outlive the war, or he would perish unexpectedly. There was no middle way.

Very likely the hotel was not a trap. I was of the opinion that, although eventual journey abroad in time of war was doubtful, one could be interned there for the remainder of the war. I explained to Sewek that it was possible that great figures who had influential families abroad were freed as part of an exchange, but not a nobody, a mediocre man, who in addition pretended to be someone under an assumed name. Aside from that you have to take into consideration one other possibility: Before the end of the war disorders could break out in Germany, whose first victims could be Jews. Then nobody would care if these victims had foreign papers.

On the other hand, remaining in our hiding place, we exposed ourselves to the possibility of a slipup, an eventual blockade of all the houses conducted by Germans for the purpose of discovering Jews, all sorts of harassments by our lady, and finally, that we would lack money to outlive the war.

Sewek emphasized that last danger. He knew how much money he had, and he took care, considering the progress of the Allies, that it would suffice him. My situation was different. I had money and I didn't have it. What I had were "rags" then hidden at the Magister's. Who knew how much they were worth? One would have to sell them all, then perhaps buy a gold twenty dollars, and then one would know how much it was all together.

In the meantime Father was of a different opinion. Because he had lost much on the sale of clothes—mine as well—he decided to get rid of things at the last moment, when he would have absolutely no money. That was not for me. Father, in his egoism, did not want to think that some misfortune could occur, that he might be found out, that his leg might refuse to obey him and might confine him to bed.

I couldn't tell Father all of this because there would have been, without a doubt, a big brawl, accusations would have fallen, that I had said "that" because "that" was what I wanted. In any case Father had at his disposal an excellent argument with which he could close, and did close, my mouth: "Now that there is a harvest, there are no buyers."

I had to take into account one more danger: a misfortune involving Father and the likelihood of remaining without money. But I realized that by selling things through a third party, I would lose so much money that I wouldn't have enough for a couple of months.

Everything inclined me to go to Hotel Polski. I was determined to risk everything on the throw of one card because I did not have the strength to suffer longer. Still, I had to resign myself because Father did not want to handle matters and also because of Mother. Miss Hela would surely not keep her by herself.

Sewek, however, not dependent on anybody, felt that his fate rested only in his own hands. In order to make it easier for himself to decide, he sent another letter to the hotel, to which he received an answer. Szochet begged him not to delay and informed him that she had started preparing the paperwork for him.

Father visited us on July 21. As it turned out, he had escaped death by another miracle. One morning when he went out into town, three men came to the apartment, identified themselves as Gestapo agents, and ransacked the place. Alarmed by the noise, the neighbors called the gendarmes. A shooting ensued, with the result that one of the attackers ran away, another was wounded, and the third one was killed. The gendarmes conducted an examination to which they summoned all the members of the households, with the exception of Father.

Father told about this incident in a normal voice, as if it were nothing. He now considered himself a real Pole and that before all else he had a Jewish God who watched over him. I wonder at Father's indefatigable energy, his spirit, his luck with people—but it passes my comprehension that a man can be such an egoist. I wanted to ask him what would have happened if they had discovered him this time. How would we have been able to survive? But in the end I just dismissed it with a wave of my hand.

Sitting in silence, I looked at Sewek with envy as he explained to Father how he could arrange for him the journey to Hotel Polski.[245] But Sewek saw how Miss Hela accepted money for mine and my mother's stay and suddenly decided to remain in place.

He told me later that he reminded himself how they liquidated Belgian Jews, how they also gave them papers, how they brought them in Pullmans to the place of torment, and how with a smile on their lips they rode to Treblinka. He realized the German perfidiousness, thought about Sicily, and changed his mind. The future will tell whether he did the right thing.

Again a few days passed. Time flows slowly. Indeed, we don't live through the days; we vegetate, suffering terribly. In order to kill the monotony, we try to guess what the evening paper will bring. If there is some important news, the paper is grabbed on the spot, and in general we don't even hear the cries of the paper boys. If the *Nowy Kurier Warszawski* [New Warsaw Courier] is not interesting, then we hear the cries of the paper boys until it is late. In the evening when our lady arrives, we grab the newspaper, read the communiqué, and, depending on the text, the next day is either good or bad.

On July 26 we heard Romek's voice reaching us from the street.

"How are you, dark face?* They have fucked over Mussolini! Marshal, what's his name, that whoreson, is to take his place. It's the end of the macaroni eaters."

We did not believe our ears. Miss Hela came in the evening with the paper. We had to believe our eyes: Marshal Badoglio had taken over the government of Italy.[246]

We could not sleep the entire night for the excitement; it was both joyful and painful at one time. Joyful because we had lived to have the satisfaction that the war would soon be over, that our suffering would end—but at the same time our hearts wept at the thought that our wives had not lived to this happy moment. The same thought came to our minds: We longed for the end of the war, prayed for its early termination, and at the same time we trembled at the thought that the war would end. Where would we go then? With whom would we celebrate?

Today, August 1, Father visited us. I marvel at my own nerves that I could still sit quietly at a table and write. What happened? We had asked Father some time ago that he buy us some marmalade. Father went to Wilanów for this. A naive person might have inquired if it was not possible to get marmalade in Warsaw. But that would be asked only by a person who did not know my father. In Wilanów there was a store where you could buy marmalade for five złoty less a kilogram!

That store was near the Wilanów camp, so Father sought information about the details of Kronenberg's execution and altogether did not fear that he would be recognized as a Jew. He thought that there were few

---

*This reference is to a dark bread, *razówka*, or swarthy complexion (Jewish?) of the person so addressed.

people who resembled a Pole as much as he did. He often bought marmalade in that store and was always faithfully convinced that others looked on him as a native Pole.

I don't know if the lady of the store herself asked Father if he had something to sell, but they did agree that my father would bring a lady's suit. When Father appeared, there was an unpleasant surprise for him at the store—"trackers." Father's *Kennkarte* did not help; they knew well how one can tell a Jew.

"Show us your prick," they demanded.

They took the suit and several hundred złoty that they found on Father, after which they let him go. They were most likely not professional trackers but the family of the store owner. They took advantage of an opportunity that presented itself and robbed a Jew.

Father told me all this in a quiet voice; miserly by nature, he was accustomed to picking up a piece of fluff and not realizing that he had lost the entire feather bed.[247] He made fifteen złoty on the marmalade and lost on account of the marmalade fifteen hundred złoty.

He wasted the money only because of his recklessness, but even that he did not comprehend, as well as that he could have been taken to the gendarmes. That would have sealed his fate as well as ours. I am not upset in the least over the loss of the fifteen hundred złoty, although it represents the value of seven kilograms of butter. Father is practically swollen from lack of fat, Mother's body festers, and he throws into the mud thousands of złoty.

I wonder, Can we really not allow ourselves a better life? Certainly not if we want to preserve the house and places for "after the war." Certainly not if a man feels badly about selling his things, when instead of thinking of what he now needs to live, he thinks of what he will live on after the war.

One may be killed any day, and one's whole possession may be left to someone unknown—such thoughts do not occur to the pious Jew. I, deprived of the possibility of leaving the house, am helpless. Nothing is left except to believe in luck and the God of my father's, to suffer, go hungry, and be quiet, looking to the end of the war.

It's fortunate that in Father's house there are no more surprises. The landlady surrounds him with thoughtful care; he has acquired a ration card. His fellow tenant—the masseuse—fearful over the investigation conducted by the gendarmes, moved out. Her place was taken by a lawyer from Łódź, another "native" Pole, who—in Father's opinion—does not realize that he lives with a Jew.

Would to God that he does not find out that Father is a Jew. Would to God that Father should not find out that the lawyer is a Jew. Would to God that the gendarmes do not find out that both are Jews.

Today, August 18, I decided to end this memoir.

Tomorrow, my dearest Aneczko, I will read this to you, and my hand will not touch this again.

It seems to me that I have written about everything, regardless of whether it was pleasant for me or not. Rightly, I should have also written about Genia's experiences, although they do not touch me directly. But since she still lives among us and shares our lot, I must write about her. Just as the tragic death of every Jew has its own explanation, so every Jew after the war must give an account of himself, by what miracle he has remained alive.

How did it then happen that Genia lives to this day? Above all, she was saved by lack of money. This sounds funny, but the war showed that money for the most part resulted in losing lives rather than in saving them.

Because Genia was poor, she was forced even before the *Aktion* to leave the ghetto and to go to the Polish neighborhood "for smuggling." Hunger forced her to risk her life daily. Thanks to that the Polish neighborhood was for her not terra incognita. Not having money, she knew that there was nothing to look for in the ghetto during *Aktion*, that inevitably the Umschlagplatz awaited her.

She met Wacław by accident. If she had had enough money, this would never have happened. Earlier she decided to go to the village of a peasant woman she knew. Because she did not know the road well, she asked some girl to take her there. The girl wanted fifteen złoty. Genia, because she hardly had a few cents, offered her ten. Because of these silly five złoty, their paths parted. Genia returned when she was halfway there and then met up with Wacław.

She risked a ride with him to Warsaw, risked going to Miss Hela—because she had nothing to lose. Even if she had wanted, she could not have gone back to the ghetto because she did not have the money to bribe the guards or for her basic needs. Because she could not pay for her upkeep, she started to work right away, that is, to help Miss Hela.

As much as our lady first kept her out of regard for Wacław, later on she got used to her services and work. Genia made no demands. The food cost was practically nothing; there was no special risk since there were also other Jews being accommodated. Genia finished one sweater and started another. After a while she undid that which she had sewed earlier, making from a camisole a blouse and from a blouse, a camisole.

When Sewek joined our company, Wacław stated that from now on no one could leave the room. He was clearly afraid that the secret of our hiding place might be discovered. From that point on Genia was sure that she would not be shown the door.

But the food situation worsened for her. My father wasn't there, the only person who had the courage to admonish our lady about providing food for Genia. When Wacław agreed with Sewek on conditions for stay, he told him that in the room, aside from my mother and myself, there was a poor Jewess who needed to be supplied with food, and if Hela would not do it, then the Perechodniks would provide her with food.

Sewek was then in such a mood that he would have agreed to anything just to get into a hiding place. When he heard the above, he assured Wacław that Genia would get food from him. When he came to us, he confirmed that, also saying that if the war lasted a long time, he would anyway not be able to survive, and that if it came to a few months, he would have enough for everything. I am sure that he spoke honestly.

But after a few days, when he quieted down, when he heard that we had already been here nine months, when he became aware that one could sit here endlessly, he changed his mind. He now thought for sure that the war could last a long time, longer than a year, and he had money for only twelve months.

Not enough that he didn't give money to Genia, he also denied himself everything, content with only dry bread. In the meantime, our lady stopped bringing suppers, and Genia suffered hunger. Miss Hela ceased to feel any responsibility toward her, Sewek had no intention of defaulting on his promise, my mother noted that she was too poor. As for me, I did not say anything. Genia lived only on groats, which she received from Mother for redoing the sweater.

In June, when my mother wasn't there, Genia's situation improved. I was no longer under a constraint, and I gave her a portion of my food.

Finally—on top of fortunate or unfortunate circumstances, I myself don't know—a Miss G., in whose house Genia was supposed to live at first, appeared. Miss G., as it turned out, was a school friend of Genia's mother and was hiding her sister Sonia.

Sonia, together with the first letter, sent her sister a shirt as well as a blouse. These things made their way—as a matter of course—to Miss Hela's suitcase, who noted that every Jew was rich and if he could, should pay.

At the present time we are waiting—how will the matter resolve itself? Will she find a place for herself? What does fate have in store for her? I wish her and all the remaining Jews that they survive the war. If Genia as an eighteen-year-old had to see the deaths of Jews, let her, in the following years, be a witness to the destruction of the German nation. Amen.

Today, August 19, is the day of my wife's Golgotha. Tomorrow is the anniversary of Her death. A year has passed since I saw Her for the last time.

You see, Anka, I don't believe in God, and I will never believe, but there is one thing I believe in and must believe: in the immortality of the human soul. I cannot imagine that nothing remains of You. I know very well that Your body, so many times kissed by me, was burned by the Germans and used as fertilizer. Perhaps out of Your ashes grew the potatoes that I am eating just now; perhaps rye grew, from which was made the bread I eat. I don't want to think about it—I would go insane quickly—but I want to and must think and believe that Your soul lives and looks on me from afar.

These diaries—although I wrote in the preface that they should be accepted as a deathbed confession—are basically an account placed before You on the anniversary of Your death. I cannot share with others every evening my thoughts, my experiences. I had to commit it all to paper and read it to You today.

You see, Anka, I was terribly afraid of death—not before the Otwock *Aktion* but after it. Before the *Aktion,* I was a fatalist. I thought that whatever had to be would be. But I never imagined that You would perish and I would remain alive.

I was certain that we were inseparable, that no power would divide us. Unfortunately, I failed. The example of the crowd took hold of me, and I allowed you to go into the unknown and I remained alone. After that I began to be afraid of death. Maybe not death as that, but the shame that I died in such a way because I could have lived honorably and have sweetened the last minutes of Your life.

Today I am not afraid of death, and in a month I will not be afraid of anything. Listen from where this metamorphosis comes.

Once I wanted to have a child so that I would be remembered after death. Now, when I am completely alone, I cannot leave a creation that lives on after me; I had to beget a dead fetus into which I would breathe life.

These diaries are that fetus—and I believe they will be printed one day so that the whole world will know of Your suffering. I wrote them for

Your glory in order to make You immortal, so they will be Your eternal monument. Now, when our daughter no longer lives, this second baby must be nursed and protected until such time when no power can destroy it.

Our second fetus may perish with me, and so I do not wish to keep it near me. Shortly I will send it to the Magister so that he can take care of it and hide it until there is again freedom of expression in Europe.

I believe that millions will read these diaries, and they will feel sorrow for You, will feel compassion that fate linked You with me in marriage. If You were alone, if You had not so faithfully believed in me, surely You would have saved yourself. I have lost You, but I will avenge You.

Your second child, born in death pains, will avenge You. In a day, when I have placed this child with the Magister, my soul will regain its balance. Not only will I not fear death, but I also will not be afraid of anything. I will not be afraid of the life to come, and I will not be afraid that I have remained alive, that I betrayed You so cravenly in the last moment.

Now I feel an immortality in myself because I have created an immortal work. I have perpetuated You for the ages.

Surely, what I have written about the behavior of Poles toward Jews must have surprised You. You could never have imagined this. Doubtless You must wonder for what Your brother Mietek went to the front with such enthusiasm, a front from which he did not return. You are surprised why Your other brother Kencio hid his weapon in the ground, a weapon that in the future was to bring freedom to Poland and that because of the betrayal by a Polish woman brought death to three Jews.

You probably do not believe what I write about the behavior of the Alchimowicz family. You would never have expected anything resembling this from such people. But You see, Anka, fortunately not all Poles are the same; there are also many decent and noble people. You surely must blame me that I wrote so little about the Magister. But You must know that he is such an exception that one cannot offer him as a model. I had to react to how the masses behaved.

In the midst of the masses there are sometimes atypical phenomena. Old Dr. Mierosławski, who had injured my father so, has died. His son, on his own, voluntarily returned to my father five hundred złoty. He let him understand that he did not praise his father's conduct. It is not important that Father lost a great deal more. The son's gesture is simply decent and testifies well of him.

I probably still have to justify my relationships with my parents. You, Anka, did not know Your parents, but You always spoke as the good daughter You would have been. Small wonder that my parents loved You better than they loved me.

The truth is that in general I don't love my parents—but is this my fault? You have shut me off to other feelings. In the fire of my love for You burned up the possibilities of loving other people. I can sacrifice all for my parents—money, possessions, my work—but I cannot give them love.

In any case, You know, my mother particularly does not deserve it. She and I, these are two worlds. Lately this has changed as well with my father, with whom I cannot come to an understanding.

You know, Anka, that I wanted to give my mother poison so that at least she would have a better death. I admit that I had no right to do that. It appears that a person must fight to the last moment because it is never known in which direction his fate will go.

Try to understand how I suffer, how ashamed I am in front of Sewek, that Father will not give his address to me. I wish my parents the best, will always help them, but after the war I will not live with them, and I will not love them.

I have changed a great deal this past year. I used to be conceited and proud, often just repelling others in relationships with me.

Now I am quiet, humble. I learned to listen and be silent, not to show whether I am satisfied or angry. I have put on a mask of politeness in order not to cause harshness in everyday life. I have learned not to compromise people by telling them the truth to their faces.

After this I learned that money is necessary in life but only when one is not a slave to it. One has to learn to throw everything into the scale when it has to do with saving a life. What else can I tell You this day, the third anniversary of the birth of our Alusia and the first one of Your death? I remember both of You and will remember as long as my eyes remain open, but I cannot write anymore. I feel somewhat guilty.

Finally, I want to tell You what is meant only for Your ears. You see, Anka, I have deceived You. After nine months the organism could not stand it and led me to deceit.

It was on May 13, the night after the Russians made an air raid on Warsaw. As You know, we were saved by a miracle. Our lady went to Falenica to stay there overnight, and we stayed in place awaiting another raid.

For nine months I did not have any sexual relations. Others behaved differently. After the *Aktion* there followed a great laxity of morals. No one had any respect for anything, knowing that he would shortly perish.

Some young men right after the *Aktion* had relations with girls who were to be shot the next day.

I avoided this with disgust, but after a prolonged period the body did not stand up to the strain. I had done no physical work, was rested, thought that I would soon perish . . . in short, on May 13 I slept with Genia.

I also did it to spite my mother. When there was talk in March about bringing in Aronek, my parents were planning to go out to the village, and I was supposed to go to the camp. Then Aronek would have remained alone in the room with Genia. Mother did not want to agree, explaining that the greatest misfortunes could come of that.

According to her, it would not have been a misfortune if Aronek had remained in the ghetto and perished—and he did perish. It would have been worse if he had lived in a Polish neighborhood one on one with a Jewish girl.

When I reminded myself of that, when I saw that Mother, in order to save her own life, was ready right away to leave our hiding place and to leave me alone with Genia, then I showed in her absence that this did not bite, that no person had died from it.

I know that You will forgive me. Understand: I can assure You that I will not marry a second time, that I will not have any children, that I will always love You, but, after all, I cannot assure You that I will not have relations. I am only twenty-seven years old.

As concerns Genia, I don't understand why she gave herself to me that night, particularly since she offered me her virginity. Maybe she liked me, or maybe she came to the conclusion that she could get along without her hymen in the next world.

We have lived together now for three months, but the words *I love* have not passed between us and will not fall from my lips.

I conclude now, Aneczka. I have told You everything already. Know that You will be bloodily avenged. Know that the revenge has already begun, that daily air raids on Germany bring with them deaths to numberless women and children. It is a drop in a sea of blood that will be spilled in order to avenge You and millions of innocent Jewish women and children who fell at the hands of the German barbarians.

You know it all, Aneczko—perhaps You know if my brother, Pesach, the only person whom I love apart from You, still lives, or did he die as well?[248] If he lives, send me some sign that You have forgiven me. Your blessing is so important for me, more than daily bread, more than air. Anetka, have You really forgiven me?

Warsaw, May 7–August 19, 1943

Conclusion ✒

October 9, 1943

I AGAIN PUT PEN to paper, again sit at the table in order to write. The course of my family's downfall nears its end. The sad role of a chronicler falls on me as a last sacrifice. Only two months ago it seemed to me that maybe, God be willing, good people would help and the Perechodniks would somehow "smuggle" themselves through life. From where did this hope come?

Father has a first-rate Aryan appearance, is legally registered, and even has a ration card. His landlady knows and doesn't know at the same time that he is a Jew. It shows that she knows but doesn't want to know, wants to help him unselfishly to survive the war.

We and Mother are hidden in a good place. We have good landlords, the small misunderstandings were happily resolved, and we also do not lack funds. We find support in Father who moves about freely from place to place. All say that the war must be reaching an end. There are reasons, then, to be in good spirits. But it seems this is a delusion.

Father visited on August 20. He paid Miss Hela the rental for the month, brought us provisions and a successive portion of good news. Before he left, Sewek gave him a gold twenty-dollar piece to sell. He had, it's true, some money, but in any case if it were necessary to ransom one-self, or to leave the apartment, he wanted to have a large sum of money to dispose.

Father came to us again on September 6. He brought money for Sewek, provisions for us, and as usual shared with us the good news: the news of the invasion of Italy and information about the mood in town.[249]

He came back a few days later, but Miss Hela wasn't around, and there was no one to open the padlock on the door. The following week we heard Father's voice in the street daily, but there was no way for him to get to us. Miss Hela returned a bit late.

On September 14, in the evening—it was quite dark—someone knocked on our door. We recognized Father's voice asking if he should wait. Mother told him not to. It was not possible to count on Miss Hela's appearance. That was the last conversation; that was the last time we heard Father's voice.

Father had to return quickly in order to make it to his apartment be-fore the police curfew. It seemed to him that he was going to a light and warm room. He deceived himself that his landlady was waiting for him with dinner, that he would go to sleep in a clean and soft bed. Alas!

German gendarmes were waiting for him at home. Seeing the Germans, the old Bogdański for the first time in his life broke down. He understood that neither his gray hair nor the *Kennkarte* would help him. He had the sentence of death written on his forehead. He admitted that he was a Jew, and he spent the night not in his own bed but on a plank under arrest. They arrested his landlady as well. After a few days they released her because from a legal point of view she was in order. Father had good papers, and she was not obliged to look into his trousers. Before she left, Father asked her to tell the Magister everything, which she did.

Father spent two days and nights under arrest. Is it possible to imagine what a person thinks when at any moment he may be shot, when there is no power in the world that may save him. Perhaps it is only possible to beg God that the executioners give him an easy death, that they do not treat him sadistically before the execution.

What did Father think about? Surely about his whole life, about his whole family, about those who perished, and about those who still live. He remembered his toil in order to acquire wealth, the strain to keep it, the work to raise and educate his children. I think that he realized that, even though he was already fifty-five years old, he really had not yet lived. If life is happiness, then he dies in his infancy; but if life is misfortune and hard work, then he dies a very old man.

The man remembers his whole life, sees mistakes that can no longer be corrected. He thinks that now that Italy has surrendered, the war will end quickly. One stupid month and one can be safe.

One image follows another. The pain increases from moment to moment. He remembers suddenly that his wife and son are without funds. Who will bring them bread? Who will take care of them?

Maybe his son was right when he said that the villa, that material things are created for the person and not the person for them. The thoughts are tangled; the images from life are clouded. Vanity of vanities, you are made of dust and to dust you will return, said Kohelet. Good, good, agreed, only do it quickly, only not to think that one dies being blamed, that one dies because of his stubbornness and causes the death of his wife and son.

Should I describe the death of my father? No one has told me about it, but I know it down to the smallest detail. I see it as if on the palm of my hand. They bring him to the ghetto among the walls of the burned buildings. They tell him *laufen*[250] ahead. He barely takes a few steps when a bullet reaches him.

Old Bogdański falls to the ground, blood spills, and a living human being turns into organic matter. They throw him into a pit, but before that they take out with pliers his gold crowns. No wonder, every gram of gold now goes for about one hundred złoty. That is how Ussher Perechodnik perished.

Father, Father! You will no longer knock on our door, we will not see you again, you will not bring bread to us, you will not cheer us with your faith that we will survive the war.

What speech can I give over your grave? Whom can I hold responsible for your death? Was it a German barbarity or maybe that unknown man who fulfilled his "patriotic" duty? Who, after all, informed the gendarmes that in Warsaw, on 28 Leszno Street, apartment 3, on the first floor, there probably lived some Jew? Who did that? The janitor, an administrator, a neighbor, a woman neighbor, an acquaintance, or a stranger? That will be Satan's secret forever. You fell the victim of human vileness—and nothing will resurrect you.

If that stranger had known that with his denunciation he had oppressed not one but four others, he surely would have been happy. His service to God and to a future Poland would have been many times greater. He had served the national cause. He was a quiet, modest, anonymous hero. Such a deed is even better than killing a German, isn't that the truth?

And maybe you too, Father, are to blame for your own death. You chased after an ideal, a chimera, something that is unattainable for us Jews. It seemed to you, and you deluded yourself, that if only you acquired the good looks, that if only you were legally registered, then you would surely survive the war.

In your calculations you foresaw all possibilities, but you did forget one. You didn't take into account human viciousness, that which hunts the Jew not in order to rob him but in order to destroy him.

Father, you had fought for thirteen months, and nothing could break you. Many nights you slept in stairwells. Many nights you spent in the fields in outhouses in order to hide yourself from peasants. The many robberies did not break your spirit. You always sprang to your feet, always ready for another battle. You saved yourself, you pulled your wife out of the camp in Kołbiel, you placed your son in a secure spot, you saved, went hungry, and you still had hope that you would win. You thought that it was impossible that your efforts would be wasted. And yet!

You possessed an indefatigable energy and moral strength, strong faith in talent and reason that led you from youth always toward success.

You were defeated by the "anonymous hero" with whom it was impossible to fight.

I have criticized many of your character traits, and now I am ashamed. I wrote that because I was certain that you would survive the war. It is, after all, possible to criticize someone still living, even if he is your own Father. Now I don't know if I should cross out what I wrote or explain your actions.

You were the best of husbands, the best Father; you always sacrificed for us. You always begrudged yourself everything. Your character trait was a stubbornness and attachment to material things. Where did it come from? As a small, fifteen-year-old boy you came to Warsaw from the dull provinces. Without money, without a patron, with hard work and an uncommon mind, you acquired a factory of women's hats and, later, a large villa in Otwock.

Life turned out favorably for you, and so you took it into your head that you were always right, that you had to always follow your own reasoning. You worked hard all your life, you did not inherit anything from your parents, and so you always remembered how hard it is to make the first złoty. It seemed to you that money has to be respected and that squandering it is not allowed.

During this historical cataclysm you were not sufficiently flexible to understand the new conditions of life. You did not understand that now everything had to be sacrificed, especially one's property, in order to escape with one's life. You perished not only because of your fanatical belief in a better tomorrow but also because of your attachment to material things, which you could not renounce.

But regardless of the dark labyrinth into which you led us, regardless that we are condemned to death because of your cleverness by half, we forgive you. You did everything in the firmest conviction that you were saving our lives. May the earth rest lightly on you! You certainly fell with the cry "Hear, O Israel," and so let me, Father, reply with the prayer *Iskadal wiskadasz szmo rabo.**251

Was Father indeed to be blamed for his own death? There is no salvation for any Jew since we are surrounded by enemies, each of whom lies in

---

*"Magnified and sanctified be thy great name" (Hebrew).

wait for our life. One cannot guard oneself from one million eyes. Human swinishness is the greatest ally of the Germans in their war on the Jews. Jews fall into their hands with the least effort. Some on account of denunciations, others when they were robbed, still others by trackers, or even on account of friends to whom they entrusted their property.

On September 15 we did not hear Father's voice in the street. The following day we lived through an ordeal by fire in our hiding place. They were changing meters, and four linemen, an engineer supervising the work, the janitor, a concierge, and several tenants entered our room. Two hours passed before they finished their work and the doors closed behind them.

How did it happen that no one noticed us? We very simply took apart a bed and from the boards we made an artificial wall behind the wardrobe. There we spent two hours completely motionless. Only two things could have betrayed us: if one of us had coughed or if one of the linemen had come with a dog. Neither of these happened, and so we only worried that Father should not arrive while strangers were in the room. It didn't cross our minds where he would be at that time. . . .

By September 17 we were clearly alarmed over Father's absence, the next day we were all in a terrible mood, two days later we began to have bad premonitions, and on the third day we were certain that a misfortune had occurred. We suspected paralysis or some problem with a gendarme. Nothing else would have prevented Father from coming.

In the days that followed we became convinced that something bad had indeed happened. I decided to send a letter to the Magister, and Wacław took it. I asked if he had any news of Father. I described our difficult financial situation and I asked for help: Specifically, I asked him to sell the things left with him for safekeeping and remit to us the money realized from that.

Wacław visited the Magister in his Otwock office. He first heard the account of Father's fate. The Magister also explained that my property was available to be disposed of and that he would give it to anyone who came in my name. But he didn't want to be involved in the sale.

How did we react to the death of old Bogdański? First of all Mother. Should I write of the sea of tears that she spilled and is still spilling over the loss of her husband, of the sleepless nights, of the fact that in the course of a month she aged twenty years? Or maybe I should write of the heart of mother and wife that withstood that blow and did not burst from pain.

Mother had spent more than thirty years at the side of her husband. She was always surrounded with respect, love, and comfort. She enjoyed a good husband, talented children, and a beautiful granddaughter. The war came, destroyed her comfort, then took away her children. Her oldest son, with his wife and grandson, was lost in Russia. Could they be alive? Daughter, daughter-in-law, and granddaughter perished before her eyes in the course of one day. She lost her sister-in-law and her nephew. She herself became a homeless wanderer, condemned to death. Her heart did not burst.

Now they took away her husband, she remained without funds. This time she was condemned to death without appeal. Her tears flowed, her shoulders stooped even more, but in spite of everything her heart did not break. Where does Mother get strength to withstand these blows? What blame is hers that she must see with her own eyes the twilight of the Jewish people and the downfall of the entire closest family? For what sins does she suffer?

The old mother is of two minds. She wants to live and to see the defeat of the detestable Germans. More than anything she fears death. She sees, however, that she does not have enough money to survive the war. It might last for one person, certainly not for two. The old mother wants to sacrifice herself, wants to enable her son to live, but she has no strength, has no courage, has no moral fortitude.

Mother, I don't need your sacrifice. If we perish, it will not be because we lack money. If anything threatens us, it is the terrible fate of Israel. For now, we must fight to the last moment, even though I know this today: If we win, then the curse of our fathers will be fulfilled, we will envy the dead, we will be sorry that we have been left alive.

At times it seems to me that if Mother's heart suffers, withstands tortures, but endures pain and does not burst, my heart has ceased to react completely to the world that surrounds me. To tell the truth, nothing can disturb my equilibrium: neither the inhumane conditions under which I live, nor the laughter of children playing in the street, nor the advertisement in the paper of a missing dog or cat, for the return of which is offered a high reward, nor the tragic death of my father, nor the specter of my own death.

On August 19 of the preceding year something died in me. A living human remained, but one who is not capable of suffering. It is difficult for me to explain this, but I know this: Not one tear fell from my eye on account of Father's death. Even the knowledge of my own impending extermination will not throw me off balance.

Truthfully speaking, the survival of the war no longer has such great significance. I know that I have to fight. I know that I have to suffer. Why?

I only know that I will be needed as a witness after the war, that I will be needed as an executioner after the war. If my memoir fulfills that role, I can die without regret.

But if this memoir appears too pale in comparison with the Jewish tragedy, then I have to survive this war. Somebody has to remain in this world who will remember with reverence Anka's name and will pray for the repose of her soul.

Wacław showed himself to be, as one might have expected, delicate and noble. He told me not to worry that I had no money and that Miss Hela would willingly wait. Even though he was a little anxious about the security of our hiding place, he calmed us and encouraged us.

Miss Hela also behaved nicely. She expressed her sympathy and said that Father could have safely remained with us and not courted disaster in town, and in general her conduct toward us improved. We advanced from the position of domestic animals almost to the position of members of household.

In spite of the misfortune that befell us, the fact that Miss Hela treats us better means that our hiding place is completely bearable. We begin to have hope that we can survive the war here, but under one condition: We must have money. Not much, around one thousand złoty per person per month. If there is no unforeseen catastrophe, if the war ends as we have calculated it, we need with Mother at least twenty-five thousand złoty.

Unfortunately, the Magister refused to sell my things. That really did not surprise me. He belongs to that category of people who will make a great effort to save another person, except for the management of material things. Such people do not wish to be suspected of profiting in any way from their activities.

This is a very nice attitude, but if I don't overcome the Magister's distaste for monetary arrangements, if I am not able to induce him to lend aid in that matter, then our fate is sealed. I have to pay rent, and I have to buy food.

Because misfortunes come usually in pairs, we remain without any supplies: without groats, fat, bread; we don't even have soap. It's true that Miss Hela knows now that she has to buy supplies for us, but for that one needs money. A lot of money—enough to last for us and for Miss Hela.

Our landlady can "earn" even seventy złoty on purchasing six kilograms of bread. If she buys groats, then her price is at least ten złoty higher than the price in town. She very often makes "mistakes" and gives less than is owed.

Our requirements are nonetheless minimal. We are satisfied with five kilograms of groats monthly and fifteen kilograms of bread per person. We don't buy anything else, persuading ourselves that a person does not need any more to live on. If we buy little, then the "basket money" is not much, at the most two hundred złoty. Where is it said that rent must amount to only five hundred złoty and not seven hundred?

I asked Wacław if he would sell some of my father's things that he had for safekeeping. He promised to do it right away. But Wacek, as Wacek is, he has his own occupations. One night he must sleep in Falenica at his wife's; one night a week he must devote to our Miss Hela and another one to Jadwiga from Henrykowa. Aside from that he must sleep when he is on duty in Karczew or Jabłonna. All day long he works on the train—is it any wonder that the sale of our things is for him a physical impossibility?

After a month he was able to sell only one item: father's winter jacket. Actually, it was Miss Hela who achieved it. After deducting the provisions, I received nine hundred złoty. That's a very low price, but I don't worry. I am only sorry that I don't have in stock one hundred such jackets. Then our lady would have an opportunity to make calculations, once on the left, once on the right—and I would have money to survive the war.

These days I travel to the Magister. I want to ask him for active help and to leave with him my memoir. I would also like to resell father's real estate in Otwock. I will not spare anything in order to survive to that great day of revenge. And if I don't succeed, if on the road I am caught and killed, if the Magister refuses help, if I am not able to sell the real estate, then no one will shed even one tear on my nonexistent grave. I don't deserve it.

I ask only for one thing: Carry out faithfully my testament of revenge, and remember at times the luminous figure of my wife, Anka, and the angelic picture of my daughter, Athalia. What were they blamed for that they fell victim to German sadism? What were they blamed for that they fell victim to Jewish cowardice?

And I? I must go my thorny path with a refrain on my lips: *Zol zajn az majn szyf wet kajn breg nit dergejn.**[252]

---

*"It does not matter if my boat does not reach the shore as long as I pursue my course" (Yiddish).

The Last Days of Calek Perechodnik

IF I AM NOT mistaken, sir, you know of the death of your father. His death meant to us the loss of our hiding place. Calek remained completely penniless. Mr. Banasiuk would never have agreed that any one person might leave Miss Hela's apartment. That is why Calek was forced, a few days after his father's death, to contact the Magister with a humble request to raise some cash for the remainder of his belongings. It was then that Calek handed the Magister his memoirs.

Hunger, fear for tomorrow, and, what was the worst, the death of Father so affected Mother that had she a little courage, she would have committed suicide. She was very ill to end of her life. We wanted to join the partisans. Nonetheless, we resigned ourselves to look out for Mother. Hungry and cold, we served time in our prison until 1944.

Several days before the uprising, that is, in Warsaw, in the last ten days of July 1944, Mr. Banasiuk came to us. He directed Miss Hela to pack up the wardrobe, they bought for us some food, and he ordered her to provide us with a small supply of water because it looked like something was brewing. In the last moment—that is, before leaving us—he mustered some courage and told us that yesterday he had seen Russian reconnaissance in Falenica. I cannot describe our feelings at the time. Calek, who preserved his presence of mind, asked Mr. Wacław for permission to take Mother and me to Falenica or at least to Otwock. Calek and Buchalter wanted to dress up as conductors and make their way to Falenica, where we could have been free people that very day. Wacław did not agree to any of these proposals. They said good-bye to us, locked the place with a key, and left. . . .

For several days we did not know that Warsaw was fighting. In the middle of August, the Germans bombed the main water supply pipes. During those days we lived with the hope that the Russians were about to enter, and this gave us strength to struggle on. Can anyone imagine how it was possible to live several days without water, that is, to have enough only to cook a thick rice mash? The knowledge that we had

---

I am indebted to Paweł Szapiro for sending me these excerpts from a letter written by Genia on November 11, 1950, to Pesach Perechodnik, Calel's brother. Genia's reference to the mother's fear of poison, as mentioned in the memoir, suggests that she either read the memoir or discussed its contents with Calel.

nothing to drink was the final straw; we lay lifeless like corpses. Calek was least immune to hunger and looked like a shadow. I did not realize how very ill he was. He got up at night, felt that he could no longer stand the thirst, and together with Buchalter they knocked out the shutters and got out to the street. The central portion of Warsaw was already in Polish hands. The command post opened up our doors and windows and gave us permission to continue to live there. Then for the first time in two years we could breathe fresh air. We hardly had time to breathe when the Polish army started to evacuate Pańska Street. . . . We ran down several streets, our faces clearly marking us as Jews, for the Poles greeted us with the words "Where did you cats hide yourselves?"

We wandered together through cellars and bunkers until the start of September. Calek and Sewek joined the Armja Krajowa (AK). Mother and I remained together in the cellar. One day Sewek was wounded, and Calek was laid low with typhus.

In the meantime Sewek got to know a Jewess who lived as an Aryan on Złota Street. Calek was released from military service because of his illness. He could not come to us and was transported to the apartment of that Jewess. Her Aryan name was Ela Rutkowska. She brought a doctor to see Calek, attended to him, and, in a word, did all that was possible. Mother and I did not know about this. One day Sewek came with two cans of meat from an air drop. There was then a terrible hunger in Warsaw. He asked me to take them to Calek. That same day there were furious shooting and bombing, and Mother did not let me go. The knowledge that I was keeping the meat and that Calek was suffering from hunger did not give me peace. The following morning I got up early and went out without being seen by Mother. I ran toward Złota Street. . . . At last I reached my goal. Calek did not let me return. I was with him and Ela until the day of that disastrous defeat of the uprising, that is, October 1. Calek, Sewek, and I had cyanide tablets (Mother did not, for reasons made clear in the memoir), which we intended to use at the last moment.

In the meantime we sought shelter under the demolished houses, in bunkers, and in sewers. It all turned out to be useless because we had not supplied ourselves with food and water in the course of several days. It was October 3, very early in the morning. Calek woke me up with these words: "Genia, you will leave Warsaw, and today. . . ." I cannot express it otherwise: *He forced me* to leave Warsaw. He collapsed at the last moment; typhus had worn him out utterly. He no longer spoke but cried out that he had to perish and that he would not allow me to perish on his account. . . .

Calek gave me two shirts (one I am keeping as a holy talisman), took off his shoes (he was wearing his father's shoes) and a coat, and did not allow me to say a word. He was terribly nervous. The two of us wandered among destroyed houses, and suddenly we stood near the cellar where his mother was hiding. Calek did not want to go inside. He knew that he was not in a condition to do so, knew that he was not capable of helping her, and was unable to look at his mother with pity in his eyes. . . . Oh, what troubled moments these were! If this had been my mother, I swear I could not have done otherwise. I could not look at the death of a person close to me. We knew that in one way or another she would perish. In the last moment I ran alone to say good-bye to Mother. She was ill with abscesses and did not want to hear about accompanying me. I remember her words: "I have no strength for any more struggling. I want to die here."

I returned to Calek and Sewek. Around five o'clock Calek took me and Ela to the road that led out of Warsaw. Calek promised that on the return trip he would stop in to see his mother. He swore that at the last moment, that is, when there was no way out, he would use the cyanide pill. Mr. Błażewski was the one who provided him with that miraculous remedy. Knowing Calek's frame of mind, I am absolutely certain that the cyanide pills saved him a great deal of suffering at the last moment.

Letter to Pesach Perechodnik from Henryk Romanowski

I have received your letter of the 10th. Unfortunately, I can only report to you of the loss of your brother and my good friend, Calek. He perished in a bunker following the surrender of the Warsaw uprising. He was together with a group of twenty-two people. They were discovered by looters who were searching on behalf of the Germans.

A friend of mine, the only one from the whole group who saved himself, found the group from our bunker by chance at night, and we took him along with us. As he told it to me, all those in his bunker came out as the bandits demanded. Calek, having just been ill, could not come out and perished in the bunker and very likely burned to death; all those who came out were shot on the spot.

The following day, when I found out about this tragic event, I went to the place where it happened and buried the remains of my dear and good friend, whom I tried to save with all my strength during the uprising.

You probably know that he was ill with typhus and lived under most difficult conditions. All that was in my power to do, I did and brought a physician to him under the most trying circumstances.

Unfortunately, he now belongs to all that we have lost.

Dear friend! As to the place where it happened and where he is buried, I am not in a position to give you an address. I will probably be in Warsaw shortly. If circumstances allow it, we could arrange to meet in Warsaw, and I would then show you the place. If it is not possible for you, then when I am in Warsaw, I will ascertain the precise place where it happened and will write to you.

I await your answer.

Respectfully,

Henryk Romanowski

Last Will and Testament of Calel Perechodnik

I, CALEL PERECHODNIK, the son of Ussher and née Sara Góralska, born on September 8, 1916, in full possession of mental and physical faculties, am writing down the following will and testament. As a result of the order of German authorities, I and my entire family, as well as all the Jews of Poland, have been sentenced to death. At the present time this sentence has been almost completely carried out, and there remain only a few Jews who are hiding from the Germans, having little chance to survive the war. From my entire family, only I and my mother have survived. Eventually, it may turn out that my older brother, Pesach, lives, if he was able to save himself from the pogrom on Jews in the eastern occupied territories. I do not have any personal property, but at the present time I am the legal heir of property left by my father, Ussher, as well as that of my wife, Chana of the family Nusfeld. As for the property left by my father, Ussher Perechodnik, that includes:

a. Villa in Otwock on Kościelna Street, 10, referred to in mortgage by the title Zareba lit. "A"

b. A lot situated in Otwock at Andriollego Street, referred to in mortgage by the title Szerespol

c. A lot situated in Otwock at Wierzbowa Street, referred to in mortgage by the title Wawrzyniec Glinianki

All that which will legally belong to me at the time of my death, and which I can assign according to the letter of Polish law, I bequeath in the event of my death to Władysław Błażewski, a master of law, an officer of the Regional Mutual Cooperative in Otwock, residing presently in Warsaw on Chłopicka Street, 14, as well as to Mr. Stefan Maliszewski, an officer of the parish chancellery in Otwock, residing there on Mickiewicz Street, 1, to be equally divided at 50 percent each.

As concerns the property left by my wife, Chana Nusfeld Perechodnik—that is, the villa in Otwock on Sienkiewicz Street, 4, referred to in mortgage by the title Rozalin 130—the entire share assigned to me I bequeath in the event of my death to Miss Maria Błażewska Erdman, living in Warsaw on Chłopicka Street, 14.

I have the impression that 42 percent of the villa as well as the movie house "Oasis" belongs to me as inheritance. The exact percentage will be established by the Polish court after the war. I, however, as the last surviving witness, wish to establish only the succession of the deceased from the family Nusfeld, the co-owners of the movie house "Oasis" as well as the entire villa.

The villa as well as the movie house "Oasis" belonged in equal portions to the families Nusfeld, Wolf, and Motel, brothers Nusfeld as well as Rajzel Frydman and Chana Perechodnik, the Nusfeld sisters.

In September 1939, Motel Nusfeld, a bachelor, fell at the front. On November 11, Wolf Nusfeld, who left behind him a son, Jezajasz, and a wife, Mindla, born Wajnsztok, was shot at Śródborow. In June 1942, Jezajasz Nusfeld, the heir to one-third of the entire property, died of an illness in Warsaw. Because he died without siblings, half the property after him was assigned to his mother, Mindla, and half to the leading member of the father's side, according to article 746 of the civil code. Thus, the property belonged legally to the sisters Nusfeld, around 84 percent of the entire villa.

On August 9, 1942, the husband of Rajzel Nusfeld, Moses Frydman, was killed by Ukrainians in Otwock. Rajzel and her two small children, as well as my wife, Chana, and my daughter, Athalie, were on that same day deported on a freight car to Treblinka, where they found death at the hands of the German torturers. It is necessary to assume that the children died first, as well as conjecture that my wife Chana, as the younger one, lived longer than her older sister, Rajzel Frydman. With reference to article 720 as well as 722 of the civil code, my wife, Chana, was prior to her death the legal co-owner of the property Rozalin in the amount of 84 percent. I, therefore, as her husband remaining alive, have a legal right according to article 223 of the civil code to 21 percent, or eventually to 42 percent if they do not find closer relatives of Chana (Nusfeld) Perechodnik up to fourth degree of inclusion. The entire portion wholly and legally mine I assign to Maria Błażewska Erdman, as testimony of my gratitude for her willingness to save my daughter, Athalia.

If Władysław Błażewski and Stefan Maliszewski come into legal possession of the villa on 10 Kościelna Street in Otwock, I would ask them that the apartment no. 2, consisting of one room as well as verandah on the first floor in the new house, be leased at no cost for her lifetime to Miss Dąbrowska, a master of pharmacy, owner of a villa in Otwock, at 7 Warszawska Street; while the apartment consisting of kitchen, one room, and a verandah on the first floor in the corner house be leased for her lifetime to Miss Magdalena Babis, residing in Warsaw at 104 Poznańska Street.

Please note that all these legacies are proof of my gratitude for the efforts to save my life as well as the lives of my parents at the time of anti-Semitic pogroms. I would ask Magister Władysław Błażewski to see to the publishing of my memoirs that are in his possession. Naturally, this is only a moral obligation since it may turn out that they are not suitable for publication.

As to the order of deaths of my family members, my sister, Rachel, perished in August 1942, her husband, Jakub Frajnd, in January 1943. My father died on September 15, 1943, in Warsaw, leaving me as well as his wife, Sara, and possibly an older brother, still alive. I ask the Polish court to make possible the execution of this will according to both the spirit of my wishes as well as the law involved. I am not a lawyer by profession, and so I cannot write a will that would be entirely in order, and I cannot in the present circumstances ask for help from the outside. This is handwritten, and the authenticity of my signature may be verified in the ministry files as well as with the help of witnesses. I wish the abovementioned persons that in the event of my death they feel peace of mind to enjoy 100 percent the property they morally deserve.

Written in Warsaw, on October 23, 1943

Afterword (from the Polish Edition)

by Paweł Szapiro

CALEL PERECHODNIK began to write his "confession" on May 7, 1943, completing it in 105 days.[253] The events presented, the resulting emotions and reflections, all these took place immediately before and even during the writing. To classify its genre, the text combines in itself the elements of a memoir, a chronicle, and a diary.

We know from the last pages that Perechodnik, influenced not so much by prophetic intuition as by a sober evaluation of the situation, intended to give the manuscript for safekeeping to his Polish friends. The text survived the period of occupation in the hands of the Magister, Władysław Błażewski. Right after the war it was handed over to the brother, Pesach Perechodnik. Shortly thereafter, a typewritten copy of these notes—along with permission to publish, as was the last wish of the author—was delivered to the Central Jewish Historical Commission in Poland. Today it is located at the natural successor of the commission, the Jewish Historical Institute. The original manuscript, as far as is known, was deposited in the Yad Vashem Archives in Jerusalem.

For almost half a century, Perechodnik's remembrances lay on a shelf in the archives, covered by an ever-thickening layer of dust. The text was not altogether unknown. It was read by historians. Selected segments were published several times, first in Israel and then in Poland. But there was no consideration to publish it in its entirety until now. What is more, in the thousands of works dealing with the Holocaust, no one cited even one single sentence from this unique record.

Certainly not even a casual reader of this work needs to be convinced that what we have here is one of the most exceptional eyewitness testimonies of the Holocaust. No equally exhaustive chronicle of a provincial ghetto exists. (Writing about the fate of Polish Jewry in 1939–1943, Perechodnik also creates a chapter in the history of Poland.) The manner of juxtaposing certain entries with events taking place gives the work an exceptional tenor. I know of no testimony that speaks to the reader with greater strength that the Holocaust was not only the Warsaw ghetto, the April uprising, Mordechai Anielewicz, and the imprecise number of 3 million murdered. A memoir of a policeman from the ghetto, it is one of the few existing ones (no other has so far been published) and one so little given to self-censure.[254] To date we have not had an opportunity to come into contact with an authentic written confession of a man who, while being unquestionably a victim of the Holocaust, also took part to such a significant degree in its implementation and spoke about it so openly. . . .

In the underground archives of the Warsaw ghetto, the so-called Archivum Ringelbluma,[255] is a note by an unknown author, written on the reverse side of a special armband for workers in the Infectious Diseases Hospital, Czyste, on duty at *Umschlagplatz*—the place from which the Jews of Warsaw were deported to the death camp Treblinka. This armband—made of white cardboard and measuring 260 by 95 millimeters, displayed a red Star of David, a black overprint "Seuchen-Krankenhaus +Czyste,+" and a round, red seal of the hospital—protected the wearer on the spot from being deported to Treblinka. In keeping with the regulations at the time of the big deportations, only that one person was protected; no one else, not even the closest members of the family. And so it was in the case of the anonymous wearer of the armband. For he wrote on it with a blue pencil:

> September 9, 1942, 6 P.M.—wife and sister
> September 10, 1942—parents

We know that the author of these few words was an eyewitness to the deportations of his near ones. He should have realized, although he might not have believed it, what the purpose of the deportation was: Treblinka, the train platform, gas chamber, and crematorium. We shall never know what this man knew, thought, and suffered when he saw his wife, sister, mother, and father entering the cattle cars, what impulse guided him when he took out the pencil from his pocket and removed the armband from his left arm. . . . We can only imagine what he thought and felt for the rest of his life.

Perechodnik's text helps us understand. I assume that because of the special knowledge that he carried with him, the text remained so long on the shelf.

Many portions of Perechodnik's remembrances may not be acceptable—even to an outsider. Not because of the cruelty in the events portrayed (the literature of the Holocaust has inured us to scenes of murder and violence). Rather, because we are more prepared to believe the victim than the collaborator in the crime.

Confessions, or, more strictly speaking, depositions, we reserve for the court, possibly for the confessional, but never for literature, particularly if it is a literature dealing in facts. When the figure of an actual tormentor rather than a literary character is immortalized, when this is achieved with his own words, it humiliates us, insults our faith in a moral order in the world, and forces us to doubt elementary justice. The inclination of the perpetrator to render a public confession, particularly if done in the pages of a book, we read as a display of shamelessness, a lack of scruples, a deficient conscience, rather than as proof of an authentic penitence.

There have been (and still may be) considerations that argue against the publication of Perechodnik's text. For many Jews it is a very painful—an understatement, to be sure—violation of the accepted sanctity of the victims. There is no point in denying that the author's recollections, not only when he writes about himself but also when he writes about others like him, besmirch the memory of the majority of Jewish martyrs. Perechodnik undermines the meaning of the Holocaust, according to which every victim placed on that altar of history (in order to be accepted) must be clean and innocent. For many Poles, however, the author's opinions may bring forth a fierce opposition because of his accusations about the character of the witnesses to the Holocaust.

During the war, a relatively large number of people—not just the inhabitants of the ghetto—kept diaries and wrote down their reminiscences. Although the chief motive for these texts was usually the portrayal of individual experience, on nearly every page of every memoir of the Holocaust we find the same thought—the awareness of the *responsibility* incumbent on every witness to the Holocaust. The source for this awareness—not necessarily a conscious one—is the feeling of responsibility for the fate of the world. Without testimony to the truth, without an account of acts that warrant accusations, elementary justice would be impossible, and the fate of humankind could turn to an evil direction. It was often a need so filled with unselfishness that the authors did not seek to sign the texts with their own names.

Paper, pen or pencil, afforded one a chance to write oneself into world history, a conversion of an anonymous annihilation into an unjust, cruel, undeserved, but in some form, human in character and dimension, death. Not extermination, gassing, or burning—just death. Thus, writing provided some meaning for the life of an individual human being.

Every motivation for the writing had to be accompanied by an unshakable belief in the destruction of the Hitlerian order. A conviction of an eventual victory by and consolidation of the Third Reich would have undermined the likelihood of any action that could be judged by future generations. With deep faith in the restoration of freedom, with a sense of active memorializing and its value for posterity, these motivations testify to the intense and well-conceived efforts that Jewish writers undertook so that their writings would last until liberation.

The manuscripts were transmitted beyond the borders of the closed-off neighborhood or at least hidden in an area of the ghetto. Sometimes they were taken on the last journey to a concentration camp. Then they were lost. From 1944 on those who operated the crematorium in Birkenau began to preserve the documents found with those who were murdered. They hid them most conveniently in the most accessible and secure packaging—namely, in the empty cans of Zyklon B—and buried these afterward. One of the stokers, a certain Zelman Leventhal, hiding in the ground a found memoir, wrote: We are hiding everything that is interesting, useful, words, letters. . . . We shall leave everything to historians and researchers. . . . That is why he who would find this packet of material will consider it his responsibility to hide it so that it would survive a long time. Also so that this work will not be done in vain. And even more so that the world in the future. . . ."[256]

An inhabitant of the Lwów ghetto, an Oświęcim prisoner, Michał Borwicz, analyzing the texts written by people condemned to extermination in ghettos, camps, and prisons, observed the increasing activity in writing as a gratification in and of itself. The act of writing contradicted the conditions for existence imposed on the occupant: Namely, it achieved an existence for oneself, not one willed by others. It was peculiar to the situation, which afforded few opportunities for self-realization, and at the same time provided a therapeutic measure—an anaesthetic—for a person standing in the presence of the inevitable Holocaust.[257]

Taking into consideration the circumstances that arose, and the motives that inclined the author to reach for his pen, we may assume that *Perechodnik's text comprises the truth*. We can trust the author. This judgment should not, however, induce us to give him complete, uncritical trust.

I do not assert that Perechodnik speaks the *whole* truth or that he speaks *only* the truth. It seems that he is silent, or speaks somewhat less, about matters of which he surely knows and wishes to hide. He is mistaken sometimes as to facts, reconstructs at times events that did not take place, and passes often rash and unjust judgments. The situation is not always as the author asserts or thinks it was.

Nonetheless, first, we have a right to note that, if not in everything, then in most of the judgments, he writes with a full conviction as to their truthfulness. Perechodnik does not lie, does not invent—except what is easy to decipher because it is not camouflaged, the occasionally adapted literary fiction. In general—and this is remarkable—he does not make mistakes in the description of events in which he did not personally participate. He is, at most, badly or inaccurately informed. He is a good observer and an attentive listener, so mistakes happen rarely.

Second, Perechodnik remembers everything excellently. Living without the perspective of his own future, he still wants to go on living. But he knows that even if he should escape physically from this wartime cataclysm, he will always be a victim of the Holocaust. And those condemned have an obsessive skill in remembering all their experiences, impressions, and knowledge of what happened. Moreover, if his act of contrition is to gain him a redemption from guilt, his confession must be complete.

And third, even the untruthful information that he renders belongs to the entire span of wartime reality, mirroring, without falsehood and later retouching, his awareness and the thoughts of other Jews living at the same time and place.

The chief place for this action is Otwock. According to the Polish prewar encyclopedia:[258] "The town has 10,877 inhabitants, a gymnasium, a row of sanatoriums and hospitals, a meteorological station, a summer theater and considerable business. . . . Otwock is situated in the midst of pine forests, on loose sandy soil, and thanks to its closeness to the capital it was a frequently used summer resort, a climatological station and a health center for diseases of the chest. It is visited yearly by about 12,000 people."

In a pertinent entry in the *Encyclopedia Judaica*,[259] we find that Otwock was established as a popular health resort among Jews of middle incomes; that in 1908, 2,346 Jews constituted practically 21 percent of the local population (in 1921 the figure was 5,408); and that in 1924, in the local Jewish loan bank, among its 357 members were 162 artisans, 156 merchants, and 39 representatives of other occupations. In addition, in the prewar period the number of Jews in Otwock rose steadily to reach around 14,000 on the eve of the war; in comparable numbers it meant that they constituted at least 75 percent of the general population.

With the start of the war, the Jewish population of Otwock was deprived of practically all the sources of its former existence. The town was not an industrial center; it was not a trade center for the neighboring areas. For the majority of the inhabitants, the basis of its existence was its curative character. Throngs of sick and convalescent came to town before the war (Perechodnik's father, among others, lived from the rental of rooms and apartments). A significant portion of the permanent inhabitants of Otwock was also drawn from those ill with tuberculosis.

The war caused many of the visitors there for the cure to leave Otwock. Only the permanent inhabitants remained, as well as people denied any opportunity to return to their homes. The Jewish inhabitants of the town, deprived of the rural hinterland after losing their former sources of subsistence, were in a particularly difficult situation.

A successive worsening came with the establishment of the ghetto, the second in terms of size in the Warsaw district. The consequences of this were a deepening of destitution and a successive decline of the already modest possibilities for livelihood. The former owners of tenements were deprived of all of their real estate.[260] Numerous artisans lost their workshops and a significant part of their clientele. However, those Poles who wished could move about freely in the ghetto.

But this outline of events in Jewish Otwock was not only the history of Jews but also a Polish history because it was the Special Commission for Fixing Boundaries of the Jewish Residential and Health Resort Neighborhoods that occupied itself with these restrictions. The commission was composed of the representative of Kripo [Kriminalpolizei, or Criminal Police], the already familiar Hauptscharführer Schlicht; the vice mayor of the town, Wacław Czarnecki; and two representatives of the local population, Dr. Tomasz Papczak and Dymitr Nesterenko. The division of the town into Polish and Jewish neighborhoods, aside from the inhuman character of such an undertaking, was not at all easy to bring about.

All suffered, although the Jews clearly suffered the most. But Poles suffered losses, too. There were Polish properties in the area of the ghetto to be administered by the *Judenrat*, as well as ten businesses belonging to Poles, that the Germans hurried to liquidate at the end of 1940.

To this town administration flowed a wave of petitions from the Polish population requesting exemptions from certain parts of the future ghetto and petitions from Jews requesting the enlargement of the territory allotted to them. The whole affair was definitively cut off with the decree of Kreishauptmann Ruprecht on October 29, 1940, forbidding the examination of such petitions.

The preceding description belongs perhaps to another survey of Polish-Jewish relations during World War II. It reminds us, however, that the only known way for avoiding the resentments connected with this topic is to perceive the mutual relations of both communities, which, although to a different degree, had to surrender to force and were threatened with extermination.*

All the events presented in this volume took place in the central part of Poland, in an area established by the occupier as a single administrative district—that is, the Warsaw district. At the start of the last ten days of July 1942, more than six hundred thousand Jews lived in forty-three ghettos created on this territory. Three months following that date, the Warsaw district had only six Jewish places of habitation. In the spring of the following year, there weren't any.[261]

Perechodnik writes about himself, about his family, about other Jews and Germans, about everyone with whom he has come into contact, and about whose fate, either as an individual or as part of the collective lot, he heard. As we read, it is not possible to withstand the sensation that all the mentioned figures are introduced for only one reason: They are all victims, perpetrators, observers, witnesses, or architects of the Holocaust. I do not judge this to be a literary treatment or even a conscious thought. The place in time and space from which the author observed the world proved that all, without exception, became "participants" in the Holocaust.

The picture of life in the ghetto presented here departs clearly—to its advantage—from what we know of the daily occurrences in the Warsaw and, especially, the Łódź ghettos. We know that the reality was worse. It is necessary then to ask if the horror of later events, or if the personal status of the author, altered that vision. Perechodnik, if only by reason of his occupation, belonged to the ghetto elite. He was well-to-do. He lived unexpectedly well in the ghetto. At the same time, the situation of the provincial closed-off quarters, weakly guarded, with easier contacts with

---

*Szapiro states that the Polish population was threatened with extermination to the degree that the Jews were. The Polish losses were enormous, but Szapiro's statement has to be challenged. Not every Polish man, woman, and child was to be hunted down and killed!

the Polish world, was better than that of ghettos in the bigger towns. Of course, this was not the case for the very poor.

Perechodnik the policeman also had to introduce his friends from the Order Service. It is worth noting that the number of those willing to serve in the police was generally greater than the number of places available. Volunteers were found because there was no employment. For many the police was a chance to live; it protected against deportation to labor camps.

What is significant is the way Perechodnik writes about the police. To begin with, he expresses only two opinions before the period of the mass extermination *Aktion*: "The Jewish police, although it has absolute authority, takes into account the people at large. After all, nobody wants to be hanged after the war." We are not informed what the daily police duties were in the Otwock complement. Did it oversee the borders of the ghetto? Did it supervise work on sanitation delegated to it by Germans? Furthermore, we obtain other information as if by accident, in spite of the author's will. The context of this information is always as if it's part of some other problem. When Perechodnik describes the conditions in the ghetto, he remembers "everyone must. . . . pay taxes to the Judenrat or to the police." An anonymous hero of the book, a Jew of Otwock, wishing to avoid being sent out to work, says, "I won't go because I can afford to give one thousand złoty to the police." When there is talk about a roundup for forced labor, we find out that "it was fortunate that the Jewish police did the choosing and sent out the poorest. Some are satisfied that they were ransomed."

Surely Perechodnik, if he wished, could have written more. "The Jewish gangster police made use of every situation in order to line its own pockets. . . . Jewish police. . . also distinguished itself by terrible corruption and demoralization." This is only a fragment of what the chronicler of the ghetto had to say about the Warsaw police. We can assume that the Otwock police was not very different from its counterpart in the capital.[262] We may safely assume that Perechodnik lived not only off his service pay and prewar wealth.

In the summer of 1942 an event occurred in Otwock that was spectacular in its cruelty, exceptional even in the conditions of occupation. The Polish underground newspaper described this occurrence: "The commandant of the criminal police, Schlicht, personally conducted the execution of three Jews from whom he had formerly taken bribes for freeing them from Treblinka. The condemned had to dig a pit, around which the gentleman Schlicht danced an Indian dance and shot at the victims with his pistol. The Blue Police maintained a cordon around the game of this gentleman commandant, while the director of the Arbeitsamt, Dürr, his wife, as well as the police interpreter Kuca, made up a gallery of spectators roaring with laughter."[263]

We have come across the names of Schlicht, Dietz, and Kuca several times in the pages of this memoir, but the incident is not mentioned. Why? The Jewish inhabitants of Otwock, in particular the policemen, at least because of their steady contacts with the Blue Police, could not have avoided knowing about it. We need not deduce from this any farfetched conclusions. We may be satisfied with the knowledge that the author of the memoir, customarily so detailed in his description of German crimes, this time says nothing. Evidently there were reasons for this.

A special category of persons—heroes of his recollections, not mentioned by name—are outstanding figures of Jewish political life. Perechodnik summons to the pages of his memoir leaders of religious, socialist, and Zionist parties in order to present a despairing account of the harmfulness—assuredly, according to him—of slogans promulgated by them before the war. He analyzes all the mistakes they committed, presents his own vision of what they should not have done and what they should have done. In his suffering he forgets that it is not possible to turn back the clock. He does not observe, for instance, that Jewish society was deprived of leaders and authorities—many left the country in September 1939—and lost a significant number of its able defenders. We may admit the possibility in other places as well that his opinions and values are mistaken.

In judgments directed at his brethren—and not only in those opinions—the memorialist is more than severe. He is downright unjust. Actually, he does not speak badly of a few leaders and even speaks well in three or four specific cases. These are (or rather were) people who managed to actively oppose the Germans. This is of essential value to the author, a subject of admiration and of unconscious envy. That is why the insurgents of the Warsaw ghetto were singled out positively as a whole group. Perechodnik also expresses a conviction that the Jews who perished deserved the fate prepared for them—he equally so. Magnanimously—in his opinion—he frees from the burden of responsibility only women and children.

We are amazed at how little space Perechodnik devotes to those who perpetrated the Holocaust. We may have the impression that up to a certain point he did not know the occupier. It was probably the same way for the rest. For a long time, the Germans enforced their rule over Jews through the administration of the Judenrat and their own police. So it happened that the provincial communities, confined in ghettos that the Germans were not allowed to enter, knew the Germans better from their official orders for discrimination, more often by hearing of re-pressions and anti-Jewish crimes, than from any direct contact. This does not change the fact that sooner or later the majority of Jews, liter-ally on their own skin, learned what contacts with a man in a German uniform meant.

Unmistakably, although only after a time—it could not be otherwise—the author deciphers the aim of the Germans and their methods for ex-termination. Practically before the eyes of the reader, in a manner quite unique in literature, the consciousness of the Holocaust is transformed into an absolute certainty. We see how from a certain moment Pere-chodnik perceives and understands the sources of psychological reac-tion, the use of false rumors, deceitful promises, and assurances. He realizes—as one of a few Jews of his time—that without all these socio-technical measures, it would have been impossible to round up a mass of humanity several million strong, load them in cattle cars, and trans-port them to extermination centers.

Perechodnik does not seem to realize that by writing about the stages of his own fate, he unwittingly exposes one of the most unique and terri-fying features of the machinery of the Holocaust: the fact that if the ma-chinery was to function efficiently, the victims *would have to* become cogs in it. As Raul Hilberg asserted elsewhere, the collaboration of the torturers and the victims created a "fate." It is necessary to ask ourselves at this point an important question: What happens when the victims agree to cooperate, and at what moment does this occur? Perechodnik answers this with one statement: "Seeing that the war was not coming to an end and in order to be free from the roundup for labor camps, I en-tered the ranks of the Ghetto Polizei." Freedom from roundups, about which the author reminds us, did not at the same time bring about free-dom from taking place in them; it was only an exchange of roles, from the one rounded up to one who did the rounding up.

How does Perechodnik present and appraise Poles? We know that this is a portrait—similar to the one of Jewish society—painted with exclu-sively dark colors. What is true is that there are a few heroes in the scenes depicted in the memoir who help the author and other Jews. Perechodnik knows that without them this memoir would not exist. Let us add that they help for various reasons and in various circumstances. But it is in general an indifferent and aloof anti-Semitic majority that is the source of a constant threat. It is those who—rarely from ideological incentives, more often for reasons of ordinary greed—take part in persecutions organized by the occupier.

Perechodnik directs many accusations at the *entire* Polish society of that period: anti-Semitism tout court, the participation of the Blue Police, as well as the population at large, in acts of extermination, in the robbing of Jews of their property, and in the blackmailing of those in hiding, otherwise known as extortion.

Is this picture Perechodnik presents overdrawn? Could he know the entire, complicated, multidimensional truth? Did not feelings of injustice warp his outlook? Did Jews—if we speak of the possibility of knowing the world of occupation—not find themselves in the position of slaves in Plato's cave? Did they not construct a whole picture only from what was known to them, only from what was of interest to them, only from isolated episodes?

Let us try to listen to (possibly equally subjective and less representative) voices from the other side—namely, from those to whom these accusations are directed.

The monthly *Barykada* [Barricade], the press organ of the ONR-Szaniec [Rampart], commented on the changing attitude of Poles resulting from acts of extermination:

> While under the influence of fellowship, individuals are beginning to guide themselves by compassion, and not cold circumspection. . . . There are also those who see in Jews fellow brothers who are being murdered by Germans. Under the momentary influence of such feelings, we are willing to share with the Jews the rights of the landlord of the Polish soil and Polish state. We are ready to let them return to the political and economic life of Poland. But that we must not do! We can condemn the Germans for their bestial methods, but we cannot forget that the Jewry was and always will be a destructive element in our national organism. The liquidation of Jews on Polish lands has great meaning for our future development, for it liberates us from a parasite of many millions.[264]

The organ of the Catholic organization Front Odrodzenia Polski [Front of Poland's Rebirth] carried the following commentary: "On the other hand, there is still the burning question of the demoralization and brutalization that the slaughter of the Jews introduces among us. Not only the *szaulisi, Volksdeutsche,* or Ukrainians are being used in monstrous executions. In many places (Kolno, Stawiski, Szumow, Deblin), the local population voluntarily took part in the massacres. . . . God does justly what He does, but people who on their own free will become the instruments of His punishment, it is better if they had not been born."[265]

In the footnotes the reader has come across voices of the Polish underground press on incidents of Jews being robbed of their possessions. I shall only highlight the fact that there was a serious difference of opinion within the independence camp about this phenomenon. Even as the writer of the AK newspaper asserted, "The moral level of the Polish masses is indeed horrifying. . . . The massive occurrences of plunder of Jewish possessions testify most eloquently to the advance of depraved behavior,"[266] the organ of the organization Miecz i Plug [Sword and Plough] opined, "Jews in large numbers are not a desired factor among us. That's why it is permitted to occupy places of industry and trade; that is why a school of getting along without Jews should be put to scientific use."[267]

And a fragment from an article published in the organ of the General Command AK commented, "On the second page of the *Biuletyn Informacyjny* [Information Bulletin] we publish a condemnation by the Administration for Civil Struggle of blackmailings practiced in connection with Jews who live outside of the ghetto. It is necessary to stress that, even though in the capital and in the country the frequency of denunciations has in general *diminished,* at the same time there have developed simultaneously groups of professional blackmailers, who use bribery as a daily occupation."[268]

It is possible to say that the Poles of that period, put by history to a Satanic test, did not necessarily come out of it guilt free. It was not possible for society to defend Jews against German persecution, and the underground government could not—although it tried—protect them against those citizens who acted together with the German executioners.

Editorial changes in the original text were aimed at achieving certain slight abbreviations, eliminations of repetitions, and corrections in the spirit of contemporary usage. Fragments in which there was a clear expression of artistic intent were treated with all possible solicitude, most scrupulously in those parts that may help in discovering the author's world outlook. There was a new division of sections. A title was provided; it has—as a quote from Perechodnik's text—an authentic character. We reveal consciously the author's question in the title—if Perechodnik had not asked it himself, he probably would not have taken pen in hand.

I wish to thank Dr. Teresa Prekerowa and Dr. Ruth Sakowska as well as Professor Jerzy Szapiro for valuable consultations and for the opportunity to discuss the themes that are the content of this book.

Notes (from the Polish Edition)

1. Treblinka II ("B"), the center for mass extermination, operated from July 23, 1942, to November 1943. The number of those murdered in Treblinka is estimated at around 750,000. These were mostly Jews from the Warsaw ghetto, other ghettos in occupied Poland, and Germany, Austria, Czechoslovakia, Greece, and other countries. The first information on Treblinka reached Warsaw in the first ten days of August 1942. The name of the camp appeared in different versions: Treblinka, Tremblinka, Treblinki. Because Perechodnik uses these names interchangeably, they have been retained in their original form in the interest of preserving the characteristic expressions of the period.

2. It is difficult to decide the reason for the date 1925, although the concluding date is true enough. Starting in the mid-1930s, propaganda and anti-Semitic activities in Poland became more extreme under the influence of German fascism and embraced wider circles of society. Slogans for economic boycott, for the removal of Jews from social and cultural activities, and for the bringing about of racist legislation were ever more commonly proclaimed. There were demands for mass emigration of Jews. From June 1935 on, there was a wave of anti-Jewish excesses, resulting in pogroms (as, for example, in Przytyk, Mińsk Mazowiecki, and Lwów).

3. The Society of Jewish Youth Trumpeldor in Poland, the youth branch of the New Zionist Organization, so-called Zionists revisionists, led by Włodzimierz Żabotyński, who wanted to create a Jewish state through a political and armed struggle. Members of Bejtar received military training, and they wore uniforms on the occasion of group and national ceremonies.

4. The decision to study abroad was naturally caused by the domestic situation (*numerus clausus*), whereas the choice of subject matter (agronomy) was in a sense typical of the author's environment. Among those in the middle class who held Zionist views, there were inclinations to change from the traditional occupational structure (trade, handicrafts, and to a lesser extent, learned professions) to a more productive career, particularly agriculture, referred to in Jewish publications as "productivization." Productivization was the area of interest to such foundations as that of Baron Hirsch and the Society for Aiding Agriculture (Toporol), which organized agricultural courses. There were also agricultural cooperatives (kibbutzim) that prepared Jewish youths for practical work in agriculture. The skills acquired were to be used, in the indeterminate future, in settlements in Palestine.

5. There were repeated uses of force under the influence of anti-Semitic propaganda and calls for the removal of Jewish youths from Polish schools. Such incidents, organized as a rule by elements of Endecja [National Democrats], made use of knives, sticks, brass knuckles, razors, and tear gas and often ended with injuries to schoolboys or older Jewish students.

6. "Very good grade. Congratulations from the Examining Commission" (French).

7. Emanuel Ringelblum was of this opinion. See *Stosunki polsko-żydowskie w okresie drugiej wojny światowej* [Polish-Jewish relations during World War II] (Warsaw, 1988, p. 38): "Anti-Semitism blossomed, even in sectors where it was

necessary to avoid any emphasis of ethnic differences, namely, in the military area. Jews were not admitted to officer grades, even if they had the best abilities." One may opine, nevertheless, that discrimination against Jews in the army did not have an "official" character but was done on the "private" initiative of anti-Semites in uniform.

8. A Polish-language newspaper distributed by the occupation forces in Warsaw, beginning in October 1939. Circulation of the *Nowy Kurier Warszawski* [New Warsaw Courier] reached two hundred thousand copies. In spite of the boycott of the "reptilian press," as it was called by the underground, the newspaper was bought and read mainly because of the extreme hunger for information: columns for locating missing persons, jobs wanted, classifieds, advertisements, and obituaries. There was also a general need for paper for packing and for toilet paper.

9. Some of the nationalistic slogans were actually implemented—or strengthened the implementation—by the state administrative powers of the Second Polish Republic. In 1936 there was a proposal in the Sejm to completely bar ritual animal slaughter. [It was in fact a limitation on the quantity that could be ritually slaughtered.] In 1937, the Ministry of Religious Beliefs and Public Enlightenment made it possible for the rectors of higher educational institutions to promulgate so-called ghetto benches. In that same year the government placed before the Parliament a project for applying *numerus clausus* to the bar. The Perechodnik text carries an allusion to the words of Premier Felicjan Sławoj-Składkowski, spoken in 1936 in the Sejm: "My government considers that no one may be abused in Poland. . . . Economic warfare, all right, but no injury."

10. A portion of the costs of supporting the armed forces and the expenses for its development were voluntarily covered by domestic defense loans as well as the Fund for National Defense and the Fund for Naval Defense.

11. There were about 120,000 Jews in the ranks of the Polish army during the September campaign. More than 30,000 Jewish officers and soldiers fell, and about 60,000 were taken prisoner. [There were approximately 800 Jewish officers among the 26,000 officers and enlisted men of the Polish armed forces killed by the Russians at Katyń and other still-unidentified places. See Simon Schochet, "An Attempt to Identify the Polish-Jewish Officers Who Were Prisoners in Katyń," in *Working Papers in Holocaust Studies II* (New York: Holocaust Studies Program, Yeshiva University, March 1989).]

12. On September 6, around midnight, the chief of propaganda of the staff of the commander in chief, Colonel Roman Umiastowski, without clearing it with anyone, hysterically broadcast a radio message calling on all men to evacuate to the eastern shore of the Vistula. This appeal was obeyed by tens of thousands of people.

13. A substantial decline of anti-Semitic expressions in the period immediately preceding and in the course of the September campaign was also noted by Ringelblum, *Stosunki,* pp. 38–42.

14. Information on the behavior of the Jewish population in the area of Soviet occupation was known to the Polish population thanks to, among others, the underground press. The version of these occurrences—which Perechodnik at this point expresses polemically—became one of the central elements in anti-

Semitic propaganda. It probably exerted an influence on the form of mutual relations during the war. See also J. T. Gross and I. Grudzinska-Gross, *W czterydziestym nas matko na Sibir zesłali* [In the forties, Mother, they deported us to Siberia] (Warsaw, 1989), pp. 28–33.

15. Such possibilities existed up to October 23, 1941, when a rule forbidding emigration went into effect. It is known that the Italian Insurance Society [*Riunione Adriatica di Sicurita*], active in Warsaw from the early 1930s, helped a number of Jews in 1940 to depart for Palestine. Those Jews who left Poland were mainly citizens of North and South America (the United States was not yet in a state of war with Germany).

16. In mid-December 1939, the occupation authorities imposed on Jews the obligation of reporting their entire property, a step prior to confiscation.

17. Ringelblum also wrote about the widespread custom among Jews of wearing high boots (*Stosunki*, p. 213): "I heard an interesting interpretation of the fashion for boots with high tops. They are impressed with the strength and the bearing of the others [Germans]. Some Jews wish to stand out from the rest and to impress them."

18. Actually it was Faberowicz, the author of popular prewar thrillers. Both men were arrested for illegal possession of arms. Nachalnik, at the moment of arrest, is supposed to have shouted: "Don't think you can spill Jewish blood without being punished. The end will come for you, too." See *Sefer Yizkor, Otwock-Karczew* (Jerusalem: Yad Vashem, 1968) (Hebrew and Yiddish), p. 909.

19. The version cited by Perechodnik, except for unimportant details, comports with the actual course of events. See Michał Grynberg, *Żydzi w rejencji ciechanowskiej* [Jews in the region of Ciechanow] (Warsaw, 1984), pp. 93–95.

20. During World War II, citizens of European countries under German occupation who were of German origins declared themselves as belonging to the German nation, that is, as *Volksdeutsche*, as distinguished from the *Reichsdeutsche,* who were citizens of the Third Reich.

21. The interpretation of events undertaken by Perechodnik is evidently misleading but interesting as a record of Jewish awareness in the initial period of war. Another diarist, Chaim Kaplan, noted: "It is possible that the bad relationship with Jews is not dictated from above, but that individual soldiers, who acquired their hatred of Jews at home, are acting on their own, and those injured are afraid to complain to authorities out of fear of terrible consequences."

22. The Goldberg synagogue in Otwock (Warszawska Street) was burnt in 1939 ("Report of Stanisław Nisenszal," *Arch. ZIH* [Żydowski Instytut Historyczny, or Jewish Historical Institute], prot. 301/4064; hereafter cited as "Nisenszal"). Ringelblum (*Stosunki*, p. 154), noted under the date September 16, 1940, "In Otwock they have started to demolish the synagogue because they need bricks for a German building. Judenrat is ready to buy bricks in order to save the building." The referenced synagogue, meaning the Wajnberg (on the corner of Reymont and Żeromski), was demolished in 1941.

23. Ringelblum remembered analogous incidents in the Warsaw ghetto (*Stosunki*, pp. 89, 90).

24. As in "Nisenszal": "The relationship of German authorities to the Jewish population was at first a liberal one."

25. Ringelblum (*Stosunki,* pp. 46–47) noted, "Because Jews did not yet wear a special emblem, it was difficult for German catchers to distinguish Jews from non-Jews. Anti-Semitic riffraff came to help and obediently pointed out to the Germans who was a Jew."

26. Ringelblum was of the same opinion (*Stosunki,* pp. 64–66): "One of the most important economic matters—as it concerns Polish-Jewish relations—is the matter of Jewish possessions and goods given to Poles for safekeeping. . . . The war demoralized people who were decent and honest all their lives, and now without any scruples they appropriated for themselves Jewish property. . . . In the majority of cases, almost 95 percent, they did not return either possessions or goods, excusing themselves that this was done by the Germans through theft, etc."

27. The Gendarmerie des Reiches was a formation of the German Order Police in the Generalgouvernement (Ordnungspolizei-Orpo), discharging its duties in the provincial centers. On the district level the police was led by the *Kommandeur der Ordnungspolizei* (from whence came the roving *Ortskommandant*). The *Kommandeur der Gendarmerie* was directly subject to him. Members of this formation were commonly referred to as gendarmes (not to be confused with the Feldgendarmerie, which was a formation of the Wehrmacht).

28. Alchimowicz tried—probably at the instigation of the older Perechodnik— to obtain the position as administrator of real estate belonging to the latter.

29. Established by a decree of Hans Frank on November 28, 1939, as an organ of the occupying power in areas of Jewish concentration, later in closed-off districts, the *Judenrat* [Jewish Councils] occupied themselves with such aspects of life as forced labor and general employment, food supply, health services, police, and administration of prisons. The makeup of the *Judenrat* usually consisted of influential members of the Jewish community, who were compelled to serve. The *Judenrat,* formally independent, were in fact always there to carry out German decrees. They played a significant role in implementing German acts of extermination. They were referred to generally as Communes.

30. In the area of Lublin there were several dozen forced labor camps for Jews from the district of Lublin, Warsaw, and Radom. See T. Berenstein, *Obozy pracy przymusowej dla Żydów w dystrykcie lubelskim* [Forced labor camps for Jews in the district of Lublin] *Bul. ZIH,* no. 24 (1957).

31. Perechodnik is very reticent in describing this event. Ringelblum (*Stosunki,* pp. 148, 150) noted: "In Otwock during the past week they seized Jews for forced labor camps. They shot six Jews and wounded eighteen who had run away from some villas. One was shot in a wardrobe, through a wall. . . . They say that the murder in Otwock resulted from the intervention by the Judenrat, which could not manage with the Jews who were assigned to forced labor camps but did not want to go there. They brought in the SS in order that they should suppress the revolt against the Judenrat."

32. The underground press circulated information about the forced labor camps, as, for example, in the *Biuletyn Informacyjny* [Informational Bulletin] January 9, 1941: "The Jewish labor camp is not different from Oświęcim. People are not at all prepared to work in the fields in the winter, are without proper clothing, starved, driven from farms and villages, and are quartered in unheated barns and workshops to work on fortifications. They are sadistically mistreated. There is a high death rate."

33. Labor Offices were established in the fall of 1939. They regulated the conditions of work for the population in the Generalgouvernement. At first they occupied themselves with registration of the unemployed; shortly thereafter their main task was the recruiting of volunteers to go to the Reich, which soon was changed into an organized impressment. The only information we have about the activities of the Otwock Arbeitsamt (toward the Jews) is in the *Gazeta Żydowska* [Jewish Gazetteer], no. 51 (June 27, 1941): "From the order of the Labor Office in Warsaw, Otwock Branch, of May 28, 1941, the Jewish population of Otwock is informed of the following: All men ages twelve to sixty, inhabitants of Otwock as well as those recently arrived, are charged to register themselves in the below-mentioned outposts of the Jewish Council. At registration it is necessary to present a valid coupon for registration for compulsory labor, as well as an identity card. Those who register will receive a confirmation of registration. At the expiration of registration, there will be a check made by authorities; men who did not register will be declared as those avoiding work and subject to imprisonment for ten years. . . . All who register will pay to the Jewish Council for a new identity card 50 gr. Those who are under the care of the Welfare Board do not have to pay."

34. Perechodnik is either mistaken or has not remembered the name. The director of the Otwock Arbeitsamt was Hugo Dietz. Known for the cruelties he committed during the roundups in Otwock and its environs, and earlier in Podlasiu, he was shot on April 12, 1943, by the soldiers of the Kedywu KG of the People's Army. [Most probably this refers to the Home Army.] An inhabitant of the Otwock ghetto, Guta Katz, remembered that Dietz had the habit of entering the synagogue on Saturday, dragging out the Jews who were praying there, and forcing them to work digging ditches and cleaning out the villas of German officials, etc. (*Sefer*, p. 878).

35. Perechodnik, very likely absorbed in reporting on his own life, does not mention an important event that took place in September 1940. Ringelblum (*Stosunki*, p. 147) wrote, "In Otwock they seized Jews for labor camps, the majority ran away, and more than ten paid with their lives." More details are provided by Ludwik Landau, *Kronika lat wojny i okupacji* [Chronicle of Wartime Occupation] (Warsaw, 1962), p. 684: "We now have information about the course of 'events in Otwock.' They arranged to call up five hundred men for work. About thirty showed up. Then they prepared a raid. They found around two thousand in homes, and they brought them to the assembly point. Those who were trying to hide were killed on the spot. As a result, seventeen men were shot that day." Perechodnik's silence about this matter is very surprising.

36. The occupation authorities had already taken steps in September 1940 to organize the closed neighborhood in Otwock. Ringelblum (*Stosunki*) wrote that two ghettos were established there: one around the institution for the mentally ill called Zofiówka (that is, the health resort ghetto), the second one in town (so-called residential area). In fact, as the *Gazeta Żydowska* [Jewish Gazetteer], no. 51 (June 27, 1941), informed us, the Otwock ghetto was divided into three sections: "The Little Town," or Shtetl, the neighborhood called "Central," and the neighborhood referred to as a "Health Resort." "From the Central ghetto to the Health Resort ghetto and return, one would go down the middle of Reymont Street, that is, from Żeromski Street to the corner of Samorządowa. From the Central ghetto to the Little Town, one could go freely by the train track. All of the

ghettos were fenced in partly with wooden planks or with wires from the main thoroughfares. . . . Aryans could move about freely throughout the existence of the ghettos, having the entire area open to them" (*Nisenszal*).

37. Judenrat der Stadt Otwock [Jewish Council of the Town of Otwock], created in the fall of 1940, was located on Warszawska Street, 5. Its first chairman was the proprietor of the pension Palladium, Izaak Lesman. As Guta Katz wrote, the most eminent people in town were members of it, but they did not last too long, not being able to satisfy the expectations of the Germans (*Sefer*, p. 874). Among these were Solnicki, former president of the Commune, and Efroim Rikner (the proprietor of the locksmith workshop).

38. Jüdischer Ordnungsdienst [Jewish Order Service], commonly referred to as the Jewish police—Perechodnik consistently uses the name Ghetto Polizei—was called into being on the instructions of the Gestapo generally before the establishment of a closed district. Its task was to watch against escapes from the ghetto, direct street traffic, enforce compulsory labor, and prevent the spread of epidemics. It was formally, although not factually, subordinate to the so-called Blue Police on the territory of the General-gouvernement. During the period of the deportation of Jews to death camps, it was the chief executor of policies of extermination. The police in the Otwock ghetto numbered at first thirty-one functionaries, later around one hundred. Its commandant was Bernard Kronenberg, his deputy was Efroim Rikner, and the director of the labor section was Norbert Ehrlich ("Nisenszal").

39. "Nisenszal" told us: "Smuggling of foodstuffs into the ghetto was easy to accomplish, especially in nighttime. Normally one could buy anything. Jewish artisans continued their handicrafts and sold their products to the people in the Otwock region. Store owners opened their shops in the ghetto. Others lived from the sale of goods and from their own stocks. There were collections of contributions from the wealthy for the poor. The immigrants to the ghetto organized mess halls, orphanages, which were partly financed by the local population, and particularly by a man prominent in the Warsaw area, the co-owner of the brush-making workshop, Wajsberg. Shows were organized; there were lotteries for seized goods and theatrical offerings, with the funds earmarked especially for orphanages and contributions to beggars."

40. "Everything that I own I had with me" (Latin). Perechodnik lampoons the statement of Cicero (*Paradoxa*, 1,1,8): *Omnia mea mecum porto* (I carry all my property with me).

41. Many of the packages sent from a foreign country into the ghetto, until June 22, 1941, came from the Soviet Union. Many of the hundreds of thousands of Jews who found themselves in the Soviet Union in the years 1939–1940 sent packages to their relatives and friends. These packages were a subject of much discussion, of general yearning, and even of envy among the inhabitants of the ghetto.

42. Food allotments for the inhabitants of Otwock were represented by the following figures, according to the "Report of the Jewish Council of the Town of Otwock," from February 10 to May 31, 1941 (*Arch. ZIH:* cited hereafter as "Report"):

	Aryans	Jews
Bread for the week	1,050 g	700 g
Sugar for the month	400 g	200 g
Flour for the month	400 g	none
Meat for the week	200 g	none
Candies for the month	100 g	none
Coffee for the month	125 g	none
Eggs for two weeks	1	none
Marmalade	Uncertain quantity	none
Macaroni for children	Uncertain quantity	none

The chairman of the *Judenrat* in August 1941 stated that "there are daily cases of deaths by starvation."

43. There was a typhus epidemic in Otwock in the fall of 1941. "Memorial of the Jewish Council of the town of Otwock to the Jewish Self-Help Society," *Arch. ZIH*, ZSS 184 (hereafter cited as "Memorial"), stated: "The situation of the Jewish inhabitants of Otwock is now catastrophic. Because of the outbreak of spotted typhoid fever, the Jewish neighborhoods of Otwock are completely closed off. The Jewish Council is forced to conduct mass disinfections and delousing as well as to maintain in the isolation building a considerable number of people in the vicinity of those who are ill. We are commanded by the authorities of the district to expand the isolation building and to prepare it for the temporary housing for several hundred people; this also applies to the Resorts, which—in spite of recent work—have shown themselves to be inadequate and which we now have to expand."

44. In the Otwock area there were six communal kitchens in operation by mid-1941. These were located at Joselewicz Street, 28; Polna Street, 17; Pałacowa Street, 4; Słowacki Street, 18; Górna Street (House of the Child), 22; Staszic Street (Asylum TOZ), 39. In the course of a four-month period they distributed one hundred thousand meals. See "Report."

45. There were four institutions that occupied themselves with the care of children: House of the Child at Górna Street; the Shelter TOZ named after G. Kaminska at Staszic Street, 39; the Educational-Therapeutic Institute Centos on Gliniecka Street, 1; as well as the Shelter for Children Centos, at Gliniecka Street, 5. See "Report."

46. Of the close to fourteen thousand Jewish inhabitants of Otwock, those who applied for social services during the period of the report numbered 3,925. Those who received help in the form of meals, allotments of dry products, and help with clothing, finances, medicine, housing, and the law numbered 3,369 people. (See "Report.") The situation worsened dramatically. In the following quarter, "people's kitchens are delinquent in dispensing five thousand dinners daily; the number of dinners dispensed is only fifteen hundred to sixteen hundred. Significant difficulties are also experienced by the activities of Social Welfare. The number of those under its care is about fifty-five hundred people." See "Memorial."

47. "Nisenszal" was of a contrary opinion. "The Judenrat is obligated to supply daily a definite quota of Jews to various German units stationed in the Otwock area. These laborers were very badly treated, beaten, and spat on."

48. Lazar M. Kaganowich, a Russian political figure from Stalin's most intimate circle, during World War II was a member of the Committee of National Defense and a member of the Council of War for several fronts.

49. Samuel Rosenman, an American political figure before and during World War II, was an adviser to President Franklin D. Roosevelt.

50. The division of administration within the Generalgouvernement was of two levels—districts and urban and rural townships. At the head of the townships was a *Stadthauptmann;* those in the rural area were headed by a *Kreishauptmann.* In spite of introducing its own administration, the Generalgouvernement let remain in place Polish self-governing institutions at the local level—towns and communes, led by mayors and heads of villages.

51. It is difficult to verify whether Gadomski, the mayor of Otwock during wartime, actually undertook such initiatives. He enjoyed the bad opinion held of him by the Jewish community perhaps because he signed—together with the *Kreishauptmann* of the Warsaw district, Dr. Ruprecht—all anti-Jewish directives. The underground paper in the Warsaw ghetto, *Wiadomości* [The News], no. 2 (November 22–December 4, 1942), carried the following information: "In the days that followed, three thousand Jews who were in hiding were shot. This was done by the gendarmerie from Rembertow . . . *inspired* by the mayor of Otwock, Gadomski." One has to realize that such an initiative had no influence on the conduct of the Germans.

From other sources it is also known that the Germans wanted to strengthen the impression that the Poles provided assistance in acts of extermination. *Małopolski Biuletyn Informacyjny* [Information Bulletin for Little Poland], no. 6 (50) (February 7, 1943), announced: "The shady work of German propaganda takes root, however weakly, here and there. That is what happened in Słomniki, where some individuals on the initiative of the subprefect conducted a drive in order to express thanks for the liquidation of . . . Jews(!) These funds were remitted to the army. It was otherwise in Miechow, where irresponsible circles turned their attention to the *Kreishauptmann* with a memorial asking whether the town was completely rid of Jews." Another underground newspaper, *Do Celu* [On Target], no. 3 (January 20, 1943), informed of similar initiatives—closer to Otwock—namely, in the district of Karczew.

52. Perechodnik is particularly laconic in this portion of his memoir on what was happening at the same time in Otwock. *Gazeta Żydowska* [Jewish Gazetteer], no. 63 (July 27, 1941), in an article titled "Otwock," stated: "The Jewish community in our town is living of late under the impact of great changes, which took place in the area of the local Jewish Council. On an order from the authorities, the then president of the Jewish Council was recalled from the position he occupied, and at the same time the entire Jewish Council, consisting of 24 councillors, was dissolved. The newly nominated president energetically undertook to reconstitute a new slate of councillors, who are to represent all the factions of the Jewish community in the three neighborhoods (the Little Town, Central, and Health Resort). Conferences held for several days with repre-

sentatives of different groups brought about satisfactory results. From it was constituted a representation of twelve citizens, who will make up the new Jewish Council. In connection with the above, a briefing took place at the inner court-yard of all the functionaries of the Jewish district police, where a representative of the German authorities for the town of Otwock presented the newly nomi-nated president and appealed to all the Jewish policemen, about one hundred in number, to remember their responsibilities and to closely fulfill the instructions of the commandant of the Jewish police and of the Jewish Council. Both of these authorities were to be respected by the functionaries of the district police. Following the presentation by the newly nominated president, the members of the new Jewish Council, the representative of the German authorities for Otwock, together with the commandant of the Jewish police and the new presi-dent attended a conference." The new leader of the Judenrat was Szymon Górewicz. Ringelblum wrote on this matter (*Stosunki,* p. 284): "May 6–11, 1941, in Otwock, when they could not find a sufficient number of workers, they took to labor camps one hundred employees of the Jewish community."

53. On November 4, 1941, more than ten thousand Jews perished at the hands of the Wehrmacht and Lithuanian fascists in Słonim.

54. From the fall of 1941, the territories of the occupied Soviet Union—in the new boundaries created by war—were also administered by a civilian administration.

55. Treblinka I ("A"), a punitive labor camp for Poles and Jews, was activated in the fall of 1941. It confined people who committed minor infractions against oc-cupation rules: illegal trade, inadequate quotas, etc.

56. These fifteen Jews were deported to Kosów Lacki and were used to help construct the extermination center Treblinka II. After the completion they were probably—some of the first ones—murdered in the gas chambers. News about the fate of the deported Otwock people was made available by a teenager who escaped while on a work detail. See *Sefer,* p. 882.

57. An inhabitant of Otwock, Moszek Braff, declared after the war to the Communal Court of the Central Historical Committee of Polish Jews: "Even prior to the deportations, the Judenrat, with the help of the Jewish Police, arranged for roundups for the camps. They assigned a general quota, and individual non-commissioned officers divided up quotas that were to be achieved by individual policemen" (Communal Court, "The Trial of the Policeman Herzig," *Arch. ZIH, CKZP*).

58. *Gazeta Żydowska* [Jewish Gazetteer], no. 46 (April 19, 1942), in an article entitled "Two Seders," noted about the course of the Passover holidays in Otwock: "An unheard-of attraction for the inhabitants of our neighborhood was the solemnly observed seder in the newly organized Orphans' Home in a spe-cially reconditioned hall. In the presence of several dozen invited citizens of our town, a traditional evening seder was joined. An oration, beautiful for its content and form, pronounced by the local rabbi, the chief organizer of the Orphans' Home, created a strong impression on all present, promising to come with ex-penses to the aid of the newly established institution. After the reading of the Haggadah every child received one egg, one matzo, and a mixture of potatoes and eggs gathered for this purpose by the Youth Committee. The happy mood among the children created an impression on the invited guests. In the prison

on Górna Street, the Patronage for Prisoners arranged a seder for all the prisoners. Poor prisoners were given items of clothing as gifts. Before the holidays there was a general cleanup in the entire prison building."

59. Passover, the greatest and most significant of Jewish holidays, lasts eight days. During the entire holiday one may eat only unleavened bread, or matzo. In 1942 (5702 on the Jewish calendar) the Passover holiday fell on April 2–9.

60. On March 6, 1942, the first transport (one thousand six hundred Jews) was sent out from the Lublin ghetto to the Belzec extermination camp. In the seven days that followed, the number of those transported grew by at least several thousand. These deportations were accompanied by murders committed as well against those found at home.

61. Actually, Majdan Tatarski, south of Lublin. In order to prevent hiding by Lublin Jews in shelters prepared in the area of the ghetto, German authorities transferred to Majdan Tatarski around four thousand people.

62. In March 1942, during the first deportation of Lublin Jews, the Germans murdered children and personnel of the local orphanage numbering around 320 people, liquidated Jewish hospitals, and killed the sick on the spot.

63. "Now all are content" (French).

64. Dr. Ruprecht was the *Kreishauptmann* of the Warsaw district (Warschau Land) where Otwock was located.

65. In 1942, German authorities decided to distribute on the territory of the Generalgouvernement its own proof of identity, the so-called cards of identification. Up to that time they availed themselves of Polish proofs of identity. The introduction of the *Kennkarte* was announced in a decree by Hans Frank in October 1939, but the pertinent directives for implementing it appeared over two years. All non-German inhabitants of the Generalgouvernement were compelled to have a *Kennkarte*. The introduction of the *Kennkarte* provided an opportunity for many Jews in hiding to secure "Aryan papers."

66. "It is not being considered" (German).

67. Perechodnik could not have realized this already in July 1942. He acquired knowledge of it a couple of months later, when he was in Piekiełko. Besides, he wrote about that himself. The clear lack of continuity of the thought he started with shows that Perechodnik made editorial changes in his manuscript.

68. Heinrich Himmler, *Reichsführer SS,* head of the German Police, and one of the chief instigators of the extermination of Jews, visited the Warsaw ghetto on January 9, 1943. On July 22, 1942, he traveled only through Warsaw.

69. The Warsaw ghetto numbered at that time 370,000 inhabitants.

70. This remark was suggested to Perechodnik by a subsequent event, namely, the ghetto uprising, during which time he wrote his impressions.

71. Adam Czerniaków was an engineer and a social and political leader. From November 1939, he was president of the Jewish Council in Warsaw. On July 23, 1942, on the second day of the great deportation of Warsaw Jews to Treblinka, he committed suicide.

72. These were German workshops utilizing a Jewish labor force. Jews working in such workshops were immediately protected from deportation.

73. The contents of this conversation may be considered in the category of "poetic license." They do, however, contain a good many facts. Czerniaków him-

self told of the events of July 22. "At 10 o'clock, there appeared Sturmbannführer Höfle and companions. . . . They informed us that, with few exceptions, Jews, regardless of sex or age, will be deported to the east. Today, by 4:00 in the afternoon, we must furnish six thousand people. And so it will be required (at minimum) daily" (M. Fuks, ed., *Adama Czerniakowa dziennik getta Warszawskiego* [Adam Czerniaków's Warsaw ghetto diary] [Warsaw, 1983], p. 302). Perechodnik, when he was writing his memoir, must have had contacts with Jews hiding in the Warsaw area. He could not have had such exact information earlier.

74. Czerniaków took his own life on July 23, 1942. Before dying, he left a letter for his wife: "They demand from me that I should kill with my own hands the children of my people. There is nothing left for me to do except to die." He also left a note to the board of the Judenrat: "Worthoff and his companions came to me and demanded that I prepare a transport of children for tomorrow. This fills my bitter cup to the brim; I cannot send defenseless children to their death. I decided to remove myself. Do not consider this an act of cowardice; rather, look at it as an escape. I am helpless, my heart breaks from sadness and pity, and I cannot bear this any longer. My act will reveal the truth to others and maybe will lead to a proper course of action. It seems to me I am leaving you a heavy burden to inherit." This stand and his death were, and are, appreciated differently. The underground groups in the Warsaw ghetto were critical of him, seeing in the suicide proof of weakness. See Fuks, *Adama Czerniakowa* and Roman Zimand, *W nocy of 12 do 5 rano nie spałem* [I did not sleep from 12 to 5 in the morning], a public reading of the diary of Adam Czerniaków, Paris, 1979.

75. This phrase had a somewhat different meaning then than it does today. Ringelblum (*Stosunki*, pp. 241, 283) remarked, "'The wardrobe plays' is the most popular epithet favored by the Jewish community. 'If it will be thrown into the wardrobe, it will play.'" . . . "'A playing wardrobe' was the name given the most prominent of bribe takers." There is no doubt that Perechodnik writes about the hopes of the Jewish policemen for profits during the *Aktion*.

76. Janusz Korczak, actually Henryk Goldschmidt—writer, physician, educator, and director of the House of Orphans in the Warsaw ghetto—went voluntarily with his charges to the *Umschlagplatz* on August 6, 1942. He gave up the possibility of saving himself outside of the ghetto. Whether he knew what would await him on this journey will always remain an unresolved question.

77. This is an allusion to Janusz Korczak's novel *Mośki, Jośki, and Srule*, published in 1910.

78. A Polish-language German publication for the Jewish population in the Generalgouvernement, *Gazeta Żydowska* [Jewish Gazetteer] appeared from July 23, 1940, to August 30, 1942, two or three times weekly.

79. The German authorities conducted acts of disinformation among the Jews precisely at that time. See *Gazeta Żydowska* [Jewish Gazetteer], no. 42 (April 10, 1942): "The leader of the Jewish Council of the town of Otwock announces that if individuals intend to conduct in 1942 all kinds of enterprises, they need to apply to the Jewish Council (Room No. 7) in order to deposit applications and register fees for the license taxes. Sanctions in the form of fines and immediate sealing up of the business will be applied toward individuals who do not fulfill the above, in accordance with the rules of the municipal administration of the town

of Otwock. In connection with the proclamation there was held in the neighbor-hoods a Month of the Child, a series of enterprises that had as their aim the strengthening of the responsible Welfare Office for Children. Likewise, the Jewish Council announced an order that the responsible departments will col-lect for this purpose additional taxes, that, for example, all taxes on the postal forms will be increased by 50 percent, and that during the exchange of ration and lighting cards, there will also be a surcharge for the Month of the Child." At the same time, the Judenrat—on the instruction of German authorities—con-ducted a distribution of seeds for home gardens. (*Sefer*, p. 885).

80. The area bordering on the streets Stawka, Niska, and Zamenhof, together with the railway siding leading to the Gdańsk Station. At the time of deporta-tions, this area, together with the neighboring hospital building at Stawka, 6, was the assembly point for Jews, of whom three hundred thousand were transported from there and murdered at Treblinka. The term *Umschlagplatz* is used by Perechodnik to connote every place where Jews were assembled to be loaded into cattle cars.

81. This description of the big *Aktion* of deportations from Warsaw comports for the most part with the actual events. Perechodnik probably knew this from Jews who survived and possibly also from the Polish underground press. He may have acquired knowledge of it after the liquidation of the Jewish quarter in Otwock, very likely during the period he was in hiding in Warsaw. Thus, the en-tire fragment is an anachronism. The Jews of Otwock—although they knew about the *Aktion* and followed its course—did not know precisely of the events in the ghetto of the capital.

82. Telephone contact, used even for long distance calls, was the essential breach in the isolation of the Warsaw ghetto and other ghettos. From other rem-iniscences it is known that telephone contacts during the *Aktion* aimed at liqui-dation enabled many people to find shelter in the Polish neighborhood.

83. Lüppschau.

84. "Otwock is not being considered" (German).

85. Sarah Najwer, an inhabitant of the ghetto in Falenica, in a report of August 1942 wrote: "In front of the house I come across several figures with bags on their backs. They came to their acquaintances. Perhaps they will get something or will buy because, after all, 'you will not be able to take everything anyway'" (*Arch. ZIH*, prot. 4496).

86. "There is danger in delay" (Latin; Livy, *Ab urbe condita*, 38, 25, 13).

87. Under this designation is hidden an official of the Regional Agricultural-Commercial Cooperative, Władysław Błażewski. Perechodnik considers that his memoir may fall into improper hands. He thus maintains his record in such a way that in case of an unforeseen accident it cannot be used as evidence against others. When he writes about people dear to him, whose safety depends on him, he uses initials or only first names. Names of people who are indifferent to him or who have injured him, he mentions without any scruples. This principle that he applies remains unchanged. The rule for coding the names certainly does not include Jews against whom no evidence is necessary.

88. Thanks to the acts of the Municipal Council in Otwock (Number 1067), it is possible to reconstruct the circumstances in which Perechodnik and Błażewski

probably met each other. The latter worked during wartime as a storehouse superintendent in the Regional Agricultural-Commercial Cooperative in Otwock. The storehouse was located in the movie house Oasis, the property of Perechodnik's wife. In November 1940, Perechodnik approached Błażewski with the proposition of becoming the administrator of this property. The approval of the mayor was required for such an agreement. Błażewski made a proper application but did not receive a positive decision.

89. The *Aktion* for the liquidation of the Warsaw ghetto began on July 22, 1942, and lasted until September 21 of that year. In the course of two months the Germans transported to the Treblinka extermination center around three hundred thousand Jews. Between August 19 and 24, there was a pause in the deportations from the capital. At that time exterminations teams liquidated the smaller ghettos in the Warsaw district. The confusion and disorientation set in motion by the suspension of the deportations from Warsaw caused numerous cases of transfers of Jews between city and province. Among others, Izabela Czajka-Stachowicz came from Warsaw to the ghetto of Otwock the day before that was liquidated. See I. Czajka-Stachowicz, *Ocalił mnie kowal* [A blacksmith saved my life] (Warsaw, 1956). Some of the personnel of the sanatorium Zofiówka escaped to Warsaw.

90. *Sondekommando der Sicherheitspolizei-Umsiedlung,* also called *Judenvernichtungskommando*—extermination police team, which took over control of the inhabitants of the Warsaw ghetto when the Germans put into effect the big deportation in July 1942. It was composed of members of the Warsaw Gestapo (subordinate to the head of the office of Sipo and SD, Ludwig Hahn) and the section of Lublin staff of *Einsatz Reinhardt* (the code name for the extermination of Jews in the Generalgouvernement), under the leadership of Hermann Höfle. Hauptsturmführer Karl Brandt, a Gestapo functionary, was an employee of the office IV B—Jewish affairs, one of the commanders of the *Sonderkommando der Sipo-Umsiedlung,* and one of the chief agents to implement the liquidation of the Warsaw ghetto. [There was no unit bearing the name *Judenvernichtungskommando*—such a title would have revealed the secret plans of the Germans. Hermann Höfle was not the leader of *Einsatz Reinhard.* This post was held for the duration by SS Brigadführer Odilo Globocnik. Höfle was only a *Sturmbannführer,* or major. As for Karl Brandt, he was only an *Untersturmführer,* or second lieutenant. Office (*Amt*) IV B was the "total" Gestapo unit responsible for the investigation of opposition to the established government. Within the Gestapo the office that dealt with Jewish affairs was IV B 4. To be called "one of the commanders of the *Sonderkommando*" is a contradiction in terms. Karl Brandt was too outranked in Warsaw to merit the distinction of being one of the chief agents in the liquidation of the Warsaw ghetto. From correspondence with Michael Hershon.]

91. Until the start of acts of extermination, the authority over the Jewish population was in the hands of civil authorities. Later it was exclusively in the hands of police organs. Perechodnik naturally did not know this.

92. Efroim Rikner.

93. The place in question was Kosów Lacki.

94. An inhabitant of the ghetto in Falenica, Sara Najwer, wrote in her report, "This morning they are deporting people from Otwock. . . . In spite of the terror

of the situation one can still find those who believe naively that maybe they will be the fortunate ones who will remain in place" (*Arch. ZIH*, prot. 4496).

95. The sister of the Magister (Władysław Błażewski), Maria Erdman, lived on Chłopicki Street, 14.

96. The Polish police (Polnische Polizei) was established on the basis of an order of the occupying authorities in the fall of 1939. The commonly used name was Policja Granatowa, or Blue Police, so-called after the color of their uniforms; it is necessary to stress that Polish society did not apply to it the name "Polish police." This was a way of distancing itself from the fact of the unit's existence and its service to the occupying power. Perechodnik makes use consistently of the names "Polish police," "Polish policeman." The Polish police consisted mainly of the functionaries of the prewar national police as well as volunteers. Although it had its own command (Kommando der polnischen Polizei), it was in fact dependent on the German Order Police (Ordnungspolizei). It was used basically for assignments of a secondary importance from the point of view of the occupying authorities, more in the nature of keeping order than doing political work. Nonetheless, it carried out orders that had to do with policies of extermination directed against both Polish and Jewish communities. The Otwock police station was located at Sienkiewicz Street, 3.

97. Dr. Miller, who was the director of the sanatorium, and some others escaped. Drs. Levin and Maślanko committed suicide. Part of the medical personnel escaped in an ambulance to Warsaw; some of the orderlies, in preparing themselves for the escape, tinted their hair. See *Sefer,* pp. 828–829.

98. Second Lieutenant of the Polish police Bronisław Marchlewicz.

99. Guta Katz, hiding in the attic of the house on Warsaw Street, 3, asserted that around six in the morning she heard the singing of Germans marching to the ghetto and, shortly afterward, the first shots. See *Sefer,* p. 886.

100. At Warsaw Street.

101. Attorney Norbert Ehrlich survived the war. After liberation he lived in Warsaw.

102. Sara Najwer, an inhabitant in the Falenica ghetto, thus described the occurrences of the following day in her birthplace: "They were all sitting, crammed together in the square. There is no water, and it is not permitted to bring any. All around the *szaulisi* are sitting and guarding so that no one may escape. Because it is a boring occupation, they amuse themselves. They pick on someone from this crammed crowd and shoot at this living target. Will he hit or not?" (*Arch. ZIH*, prot. 4496).

103. "A Polish woman or a Jewish one?" (German).

104. *Bist du ein Polizist, du Hund, oder Umleigung?* (Are you a policeman, you dog, or is it death?) (German).

105. A member of the Judenrat.

106. *Du bleibst* (You remain) (German).

107. "Are you a man?" (Yiddish).

108. *Wir danken Herr Leutnant* (We thank the lieutenant) (German).

109. *Zofiówka* was a hospital for the mentally ill. *Nowy Dzień* [New Day], no. 351 (August 27, 1942), noted that "during the time when the Jews of Otwock were murdered, the inmates of the Jewish sanatorium for tuberculosis *Zofiówka*, the medical personnel of the sanatorium displayed a courageous spirit deserving of

remembrance. The doctors helped those who were ill to go out to the improvised square of execution, supporting them and encouraging them. When almost all of them were shot and a handful put into cattle cars, all the doctors took their own lives by taking cyanide." During this liquidation of the hospital, Adela Tuwim, the mother of the poet Julian Tuwim, and the well-known actor Michał Znicz perished. [In his poem, *"Matka"* (Mother), Tuwim, who buried his mother's remains in the Łódź cemetery after the war, wrote of her corpse being thrown out of a window onto "the holy pavement of Otwock."]

110. This episode was also described by Orenstein. See *Sefer,* p. 822.

111. Before the war, Willendorf fulfilled the functions of secretary of the Trade Union of Gastronomical Workers, then under the influence of Communists. In the ghetto, even though he was a policeman, he enjoyed a good reputation. See *Sefer,* p. 828.

112. Juliusz Słowacki, *Lilla Weneda.* Perechodnik probably has in mind a fragment from the Prologue.

113. Actually, Central Association for Protection of Orphans and Abandoned Children, a Jewish charitable association maintaining places for care of children such as kitchens, day care centers, and orphanages. The center *Centos* in Otwock was located on Gliniecka Street, 4. Its director was Dr. Szmuszkiewicz.

114. The Maccabees, a priestly family from the second century B.C., ruled in Judea from 140 B.C. In 167 B.C. the Maccabees Judah, Jonathan, and Simon stirred up a revolt against Seleucid rule that attempted to introduce a cult of pagan gods. They were able to liberate a greater part of the territory of Judea and declare its independence.

115. The Warsaw underground newspaper *Wiadomości* [The News], no. 2 (February 1942), stated, "Last August 19, seven thousand Jews were deported from Otwock to Treblinka. During the loading of Jews into cattle cars, one of the SS officers made a speech in which he assured those being deported that they would be sent via Warsaw to the east."

116. Transports from areas around Warsaw were first directed to Warsaw, and from there via two routes—the shorter one, through Wołomin, Tłuszcz, Łochów, Małkinia; or the longer one, through Siedlce, Sokołów, Podlaski, Kosów Lacki—they made their way to Treblinka.

117. The standard speech of the officers at Treblinka. Perechodnik probably learned it from one of the escapees from the camp.

118. "All Jews are bathing and journeying to the east" (German).

119. This sentence is a somewhat altered quote from Adam Mickiewicz, *Crimean Sonatas.*

120. Perechodnik probably owes information about the flights of Soviet planes over Treblinka to an escapee from the camp, Jakob Rabinowicz, who came to the Warsaw ghetto in the third week of September 1942. It is not clear how this information about the airplanes reached Perechodnik.

121. A German expression denoting slanderous propaganda alleging cruelties. It comes from the period of World War I and was used by the Germans to describe English propaganda on the subject of German atrocities allegedly committed in the area of occupied France.

122. "God full of mercy" (Hebrew). These are the first words of the mourning prayer, which is recited over the graves of the departed right after the funeral, on

the anniversary of the death, and at every solemn occasion when the departed are remembered.

123. "My beloved wife, Anno, you will be avenged! My daughter, Athalie, you will be avenged. The ashes of 3 million men, women, and children, you will all be avenged" (French).

124. Guta Katz wrote in her reminiscences, *"Die pustkeit in getto straszet"* (The emptiness in the ghetto is frightening) (Yiddish).

125. The Polish underground paper *Nowy Dzień* [New Day], no. 351 (August 27, 1942), stated: "Already during the hideous butchery, and for two days afterward, bands of Otwock rabble pillaged the abandoned Jewish homes. Poles also took part in the roundup of those who ran away from the slaughter. Among those who took part in the pillaging there was no lack of the so-called *intelligencja*. A German gendarme shot two people, a father and a daughter, returning for the third time with loot from the area of the ghetto. The robbing of Jewish possessions by Poles, their disgraceful participation in the degenerate German actions, must shock the deep conscience of every enlightened Pole, agitate the heart, and call forth a blush of shame."

126. *Nomina stultorum scribuntur ubique locorum* (The names of fools are written everywhere) (Latin).

127. Before liquidation, the ghetto in Falenica, established September 15, 1940, contained around five thousand people.

128. *Nowy Dzień* [New Day], no. 351 (August 27, 1942), stated: "The Jews of Falenica, Świder, Jósefów, Międzylesiu, Radość, Miedzeszyn and Rembertow were subjected to the same fate as were Jews of Otwock. Everywhere there were many massacres and sadistic cruelties practiced against those who were murdered. In Falenica, in an institution for the mute, they killed the children, crushing them with their boots into the sand. In a private clinic for children, a Jewish doctor forestalled the torturers by giving his charges swiftly acting poison and committing suicide himself.

129. Najwer.

130. Perechodnik has very exact information about the Falenica *Aktion*. Daughter of the owner of the sawmill, Sara Najwer, thus described the occurrence: "Hard upon the loading of the cattle cars, Mr. H. arrived with some Germans. They went up to my daddy, stood to the side, and told him to choose quickly from among the assembled several thousand one hundred men, because they don't have time. I was numb with sorrow. If there is a hell, then Father went through it here on earth, during those ten minutes, when he had to decide someone's life or death" (*Arch. ZIH*, prot. 4496).

131. "Treblinki, where there is a place for every Jew" (Yiddish).

132. The ghetto in Mińsk Mazowiecki was established in 1940 and liquidated during August 21–22, 1942. Before liquidation it numbered around five thousand people—local Jews and those expelled from Kalisz, Pabianice, and Kałuszyn.

133. In none of the collected reports in *ZIH* from the inhabitants of Mińsk is there any mention of a "good German." I am inclined to presume that the opinion of the inhabitants of Otwock established one of these legends with which Jews in the entire Generalgouvernement deluded themselves, denied as they were of every hope.

134. The Jewish police in Otwock had its own jail. *Gazeta Żydowska* [Jewish Gazetteer], no. 34 (March 20, 1942), announced with satisfaction: "Through the

efforts of the citizens of the Jewish neighborhood a Patronage for the Prisoners was established with the Jewish Council. Until now all those who were arrested were kept in a house for detention prepared for that purpose. From the moment that the number of arrested Jews grew, a need arose to establish a prison. The abovementioned Patronage took on itself that responsibility. In a short time, thanks to the activity and energy of the members of the Patronage, a separate prison was established for men and for women. The prison also has an isolation area in the event of the outbreak of disease among the prisoners. The Patronage also exerts efforts in order to ease the life of the prisoners, supplying them with books. Among the prisoners a committee was established to care for the hygiene and order in prison."

135. Dr. Juliusz Pomper—in contrast to other Otwock doctors who ran away from the town the day before or on the day of the *Aktion*—remained in place. Because he knew the commandant of the gendarmerie, Schlicht, he considered himself safe. Schlicht robbed Pomper and afterward sent him to the camp in Karczew. See *Sefer*, p. 382.

136. *Rassenschande* (disgracing of race) (German).

137. In 1942, a work camp was established in Rembertow. About four hundred Jews worked there for the firm of Smitt and Junk.

138. It is similar, although with less detail, to the report of this episode by Moszek Braff in the reminiscences preserved in *Arch. ZIH.*

139. "The traitor does not sleep" (Yiddish).

140. There is an obelisk now on that spot with the inscription "The place of 5,000 Jewish victims, who on 19 VIII 1942 perished at the hands of the Hitlerite genocidal murderers. Honor to their memory!"

141. Part of a ritual garb, a white cloth with black stripes.

142. *Alles Geld, Geld mussen sie abgeben oder wirst du erschossen* (Money, all the money, you have to surrender it, or you'll be shot) (German).

143. *Erschossen* (to be shot) (German).

144. "Our God" (German).

145. *Wirst du erschossen* (you'll be shot) (German).

146. The monthly of the Catholic organization Front Odrodzenia Polski [Front of Polish Rebirth], *Prawda* [The Truth], reported in October 1942: "Jews from Wołomin, Otwock, or other communities near Warsaw, hiding in the woods like wild animals for several weeks, afflicted with hunger and cold, driven to the brink of despair, are reporting themselves to police posts 'for shooting.' Some such cases have been confirmed. One whole group presented itself to one police post: 'Kill us. We prefer death to such a life.'

"The gendarmes did not have enough ammunition. One of them took a bike and went for ammunition. The condemned waited. He returned. They shot them."

147. Kronenberg himself led his father to the *Umschlagplatz*. See *Sefer*, p. 828.

148. Probably this was the aforementioned court officer Stefan Alchimowicz, living at Sienkiewicz Street, 4.

149. Perechodnik, although he only uses an initial, provides enough additional information to establish without any difficulty that this is Stanisław Maliszewski, an inhabitant of Otwock.

150. The ghetto in Parczew numbered around six thousand people. The Germans assembled in it local people as well as those from Kraków and Lublin.

On August 19, 1942, they deported to Treblinka around four thousand three hundred people. The next transport, of about two thousand five hundred people, was sent to Treblinka at the end of August. In September 1942, they transferred to Międzyc Polaski a portion of the inhabitants. The remainder were shot at the start of October.

151. As follows from a later account in the memoir, the third person was Michał Frajbergier.

152. Tefillin (phylacteries), two small leather boxes with strap thongs, contain rolled parchments with four citations from the Bible (Deut. 6:4–9, and 11:13–21; Exod. 13:1–10, 11–16) and are fastened to the forehead and left forearm by Jews during weekday prayers.

153. Sara Najwer, in her report on the liquidation of the Falenica ghetto, wrote, "Sometimes a quite different pleasure occurs: Someone asks to be killed. But he must really ask, and the granting of it is a great act of kindness. But what pleasure is it to kill someone who craves it?" (*Arch. ZIH,* prot. 4496).

154. The ghetto in Kołbiel included around one thousand people and was liquidated on September 27, 1942.

155. This sentence is a garbled fusion of two verses from Part II of Adam Mickiewicz's "Dziady" (Forefathers' Eve):

Verse 111
Whose earthly bliss had no alloy,
Ne'er shall taste of heavenly joy.

Verse 326
Who never felt for humankind,
Human help can never aid.

[George R. Noyes, ed., *Poems by Adam Mickiewicz* (New York: Polish Institute of Arts and Sciences, 1944), p. 104.]

156. September 1, 1942 (5702 on the Jewish calendar).

157. The Wilanów camp, established in April 1942, was liquidated at the start of December of that year. It contained around four hundred Jews.

158. "Everything is in order" (French).

159. In the first phase of occupation Jews were not arrested en masse, tortured in the buildings of the Gestapo and prisons for political suspects, sent to concentration camps, and, under any pretext or without a pretext, murdered as were large groups of the Polish *intelligencja.* As a consequence, this strategy by the occupying power gave rise to the opinion—held commonly in the Jewish area—that Jews were chiefly threatened by terror and economic oppression and Poles, by oppression and political terror. Certainly in the period on which Perechodnik reports, such an opinion was not only false but also plainly an aberration.

160. Perechodnik may have in mind a concrete organization, namely, Armja Krajowa (AK). It is more likely, however—not being able to orient himself in the practical matters of the Polish underground—that he is treating the independence movement as a single unified organization.

161. The central organ of the chief command of Armja Krajowa, a weekly informational program, distributed nationwide.

162. Such communiqués only appeared in mid-1943, when the campaign to liquidate *szmalcowniki* started. This was undoubtedly a late initiative but quite necessary because of the large number of Jews in hiding. The first blackmailer shot in Warsaw as a result of a sentence by the Special Court was Bogusław Pilnik, sentenced to death in July and killed in August 1943.

163. It is difficult to establish where Perechodnik got the information about the armed help from the Polish Workers Party for the underground in the Warsaw ghetto. A source of information could have been the underground press.

164. In March 1943, a communiqué from the Kierownictwo Walki Cywilnej (KWC) [Leadership of the Civil Struggle] appeared in the underground press: "Nonetheless, there have been individuals lost to all honor and conscience, recruited from the criminal world, who have created for themselves a new source of vicious profit by blackmailing Poles hiding Jews and Jews themselves. KWC warns that this kind of blackmail is recorded and will be punished to the fullest extent of the law, if possible presently and in any case in the future."

165. The last phase of liquidation of the ghetto began on Sunday, September 6. That day the Germans began to hand out "numbers for life." These were yellow registration cards, with handwritten numbers, provided with a seal (employer's or Sicherheitsdienst's) and a signature. These had to be worn pinned to the chest. They were granted to only thirty-five thousand Jews. These were the officials of the Judenrat, policemen, workers in sanitary corps, and those employed in workshops.

166. Jakub Lejkin, lawyer, chief of the Jewish police after the attempt on the life of Szeryński, directed the *Aktion* for deportations; he was shot by a fighter of the Żydowska Organizacja Bojowa (ŻOB) [Jewish Fighting Organization] in October 1942.

167. Perechodnik has in mind the order of the plenipotentiary for the deportations in the matter of registration of ghetto inhabitants at the intersection of Smocza, Gęsia, Zamenhof, and Szczęśliwa Streets and Parysowski Square. This order appeared in the form of an announcement of the Judenrat on September 5, 1942.

168. As a result of selection among the inhabitants of the ghetto, conducted from September 5 to 12, about fifty thousand were sent to Treblinka.

169. Perechodnik repeats himself here.

170. Ringelblum (*Stosunki*, p. 30) made a similar observation: "If last summer wagons loaded with snatched Jewish men, women, and children had moved through the streets of the city, would there have been on the other side of the wall the laughter of an unbridled rabble, or would there have been a dull indifference toward the greatest tragedy of all times? There is another question: Was it not possible in some way to give expression of some feeling toward the slaughter of an entire people? Why—we ask—did the Dutch, the Belgians, and the French put on the armbands with the Star of David the moment they were established for Jews, and in Poland, when millions of Polish citizens of Jewish origin fell at the hands of the executioner under the sign of the swastika, this has not been documented?" Without negating the validity of this opinion, I wish to point out that Ringelblum did not distinguish, for example, between the conditions of occupation in Poland and in Western Europe or the fact that Poland had the largest concentration of Jews in Europe. (To compare: In Poland there were over 3 mil-

lion Jews, who constituted 10 percent of the whole population, whereas in France the Jews made up 0.8 percent and in Belgium, 1.2 percent.)

171. Perechodnik's information does not find confirmation in available sources. French Jews, with the help of French police, were assembled in collection camps and, beginning in March 1942, were transported to death camps on the territory of the Generalgouvernement. Their number is estimated at around sixty thousand.

172. Emanuel Ringelblum, *Kronika getta Warszawskiego* [Chronicle of the Warsaw ghetto] (Warsaw, 1983), p. 416, made a similar remark: "Jews from Western Europe do not know what Treblinka is. They assume that it is a work settlement and ask in train how far is *der industrieler Betrieb* (the industrial works)."

173. "Place of settlement" (Hebrew).

174. *Agencja Prasowa* [Press Agency], no. 25 (53) (April 1, 1941), reported: "The familiar announcement about the voluntary enlistment for camp guards aroused panic in Jewish circles and, among others, a question as to what kinds of barracks these are that the organized guards must watch. This problem was explained by the *Deutsche Ostwache* [Watch of the East]. The Germans intend to proceed with the improvement for regulating the flow of the Vistula and, as characteristic of their new spirit, wish to undertake this project on a great scale. They are building dikes, raising the level of the Vistula, building protective ramparts, regulating the flow, all to be started simultaneously. With that in mind, the occupying authorities are enlisting twenty-five thousand Jews, locating them in thirty camps located along the length of the Vistula."

175. The *Aktion* in Kołbiel began on Tuesday, September 27, 1942.

176. From September 22 to October 5, the Nazis deported to Treblinka, or killed in place, around forty thousand Jews from Częstochowa.

177. The ghetto in Legionów, established in 1940, contained around three thousand people. *Biuletyn Informacyjny* [Information Bulletin], edition "P," no. 49 (October 16, 1942), stated: "On Saturday, October 3, the Legionów ghetto was liquidated with the help of dozens of the Blue Police, brought from another place and not known in the area of Legionów. Approximately, two thousand one hundred Jews were deported, around nine hundred in the direction of Radzymin, where they were subsequently loaded into cattle cars and transported via Warsaw. The remaining one thousand two hundred Jews scattered in the surrounding woods. In the two days that followed, there was a roundup in the region, and the captured Jews were beaten. The attitude of a certain portion of the Poles was abominable; there were instances of Jews being seized and handed over to the Germans. The Germans, as a reward for those who denounced the Jews, left them the clothes of those who were killed, as Jews had to undress before being shot. A goodly number of Poles from outlying villages threw themselves on the belongings left by the Jews. At first, the Germans and the Blue Police barred access, and a dozen or so Poles were shot. Later, probably after robbery of the more precious items by the German and Blue Police, there was no opposition to the pillaging by the population. The Blue Police did most of the stealing. The commandant of the Legionów post seized all the furnishings of a doctor. During Sunday, they buried in the area of the ghetto several dozen Jews—according to other reports, around two hundred. The Jewish police, which was allowed to remain in the place, did the burying." Isaiah Trunk, *Judenrat*

(New York, 1977), p. 514, asserted that a portion of the Jews who escaped during this *Aktion* managed to get to the ghetto at Nowy Dwór. The local Jewish police-men arrested them and placed them in the local prison in order to hand them over to the Germans.

178. *Prawda* [The Truth] (July 1942) reported: "In one of the localities, situated in the territory of the Generalgouvernement, the Germans killed, in their familiar way, all the Jews. A handful of the condemned was able to run away and hide in the surrounding national forest. They stayed there like nomads for a while, hiding like wild animals, foraging out at night to the neighboring villages to beg for pota-toes and bread. Several *Polish* village youths found the hiding place of the es-capees. First they robbed them completely, and then they handed them over to the gendarmes. The German police surrounded the forest and shot all the Jews. Thus behaved Polish youths, sons of landlords, officials, and deportees."

179. Juliusz Słowacki, "Hymn on the Sunset over the Sea," third verse:

Petulant as an infant when his mother
Leaves him alone, I see the sky grow red.
Its last beams rise from water as I smother
The tear I almost shed.
Though dawn will bring fresh daylight as before,
Master, my heart is sore.

[*Five Centuries of Polish Poetry*, Jerzy Pietrkiewicz with Burns Singer, eds. (London: Oxford University Press, 1960, pp. 72–73.]

180. *Biuletyn Informacyjny* [Information Bulletin], edition "P," no. 53 (No-vember 20, 1942): "In Legionów and the surrounding area the Germans, every few days, shoot from several to several dozen Jews who ran away before the liq-uidation of the ghetto and are now being seized. Recently, near Zerania on the Vistula, they shot three groups, numbering thirty, forty, and seventy Jews."

181. Hela's actual name was Magdalena Babis. She died in the 1980s.

182. Wacław's last name was Banasiuk. He died in the 1980s.

183. This ghetto in the locality Sobienie Jeziory, established in September 1941, numbered around nine thousand five hundred Jews. It was liquidated on October 12, 1942.

184. *Głos Warszawy* [Voice of Warsaw], no. 22 (114) (March 14, 1944), reported, "There are many known instances when people (even so-called honorable ones) took from well-to-do Jews who anticipated their deaths substantial sums of money for which they undertook the upbringing of the Jewish children—but they took the money and handed the children over to the Gestapo." In the Otwock book of remembrance, Guta Katz wrote that she hid a child the day before the *Aktion* with a neighborhood peasant. Three days after the *Aktion* she went to claim the child. Then she found out that the peasant, on the day of the *Aktion*, convinced that the mother was deported, led the child back to the ghetto" (*Sefer*, p. 890).

185. A neighborhood in Otwock.

186. Stanisław Nisenszal, a policeman of the Otwock ghetto, survived the war.

187. Perechodnik is mistaken or is speaking of another occurrence. The Jewish camp in Rembertow was liquidated in May or June 1943.

188. Benjamin Orenstein, a prisoner of the Karczew camp, in his own reminis-cences wrote: "A few days later, Welwl Kolokowicz assembled all the inhabitants

of the camp and said, 'Brothers, the situation is tragic. Whoever has a chance must run away. Nothing good awaits us here. In any case, I am running away. I would have to be completely devoid of national consciousness if I left you to your own fate without warning you" (*Sefer,* p. 382).

189. Izaak Klajnman, an escapee from the Będzin ghetto, wrote: "When I just stood at the shore, young men arrived, and somehow recognizing that I was a Jew, three of the scamps fell on me. They pulled down my pants and began to shout: 'Jew, Jew, Jew.' Then they seized me, twisted my arms to the back, and began to deliberate whether to drown me or hand me over to the German police" (W. Bartoszewski and Z. Lewinowna, *Ten jest z ojczyzny mojej* [He is from my homeland] [Kraków, 1969], p. 758).

190. The enterprise conducting the work of regulating rivers on the territory of the entire Generalgouvernement.

191. It seems that these sentiments were quite typical. Ringelblum (*Kronika,* p. 480) noted at the end of January 1943, "The period of the ghetto seems to the Warsaw Jew, now closed up within the narrow walls of his *shop,* to have been a paradise. And the period before the creation of the ghetto—simply idyllic."

192. "Lie down to be killed" (German).

193. The last words of a dying Jew are supposed to be a fragment from the prayer the Shema: "Hear, O Israel. The Lord is our God. The Lord is One."

194. The Jewish commandant of Zofiówka wrote: "Because of an unfenced area of the hospital, we had the opportunity to move about freely, with some deciding to stay here and others who wanted to go to Otwock. Among those who came here from the camp in Tarchomina were Calek Perechodnik and his brother-in-law Freund. Perechodnik stayed with us three days, and later, on the day that we were sent to the camp in Karczew, he went into hiding" ("Nisenszal").

195. This order was handed out on October 28, 1942, when the extermination of the concentration of Jews in the Warsaw ghetto was finished. It was undoubtedly an effort to pull Jews out of their hiding places.

196. Ringelblum (*Stosunki,* p. 421) expounded more fully on this subject: "In the opinion of many knowledgeable people, about 10 percent of Jews were allowed to remain in Warsaw not for reasons of economy but for exclusively political ones. . . . If they had removed all the Jews from Warsaw and the Generalgouvernement, they would have deprived themselves of a Jewish issue. It would have been more difficult then to burden Jews with the blame for all difficulties and failures. . . . There is something else. . . . That is the world public opinion."

197. In order to receive the *Kennkarte,* the following were necessary: application for a lapsed one, birth certificate, identity card, or, possibly, written declaration of witnesses, the so-called depositions that would replace lost documents. Four area Bureaus for Public Evidence occupied themselves with the distribution of the *Kennkarte.* On receipt, they took a print of the applicant's middle finger of both hands, which was affixed to the document.

198. This was the house on Pańska Street, 104. It no longer stands.

199. "A favorable environment" (French).

200. Perechodnik is describing the so-called January defense. The concluding stages for the liquidation of the Warsaw ghetto were to come at the end of the second and third weeks of January 1943. The Germans intended to deport to Treblinka about 20 percent of the inhabitants. Early in the morning on January

18, German divisions began the *Aktion*. The invading police divisions were confronted, for the first time in the history of closed-off neighborhoods, with an organized armed opposition. During four days more than one thousand Jews died on the spot, and six thousand—less than the Germans had planned—were deported. On January 22, the *Aktion* was discontinued. The events in the ghetto were known to the contemporary society, among others, thanks to the underground press. In this context it is remarkable that Perechodnik does not mention the taking up of arms by Jews. This omission may be considered a measure of the isolation in which he found himself.

201. Perechodnik has in mind here membership in the resistance movement.

202. In the fall of 1939, a group of noncommissioned officers and officers of the Polish army created a Jewish underground organization, Świt [Dawn]. In 1942, Świt was reformed into the Żydowski Związek Walki [Jewish Struggle Alliance]; following that it took on the name of Żydowski Związek Wojskowy [Jewish Army Alliance]. At the start of 1943, the alliance numbered around four hundred members, probably better armed than the ŻOB. It worked closely with Polish army organizations: Polska Ludowa Akcja Niepodległościowa [Polish People's Action for Independence] and Organizacja Wojskowa Korpus Bezpieczeństwa [Organization of the Armed Corps for Security].

203. Perechodnik probably has in mind one of two parties: Żydowska-Socjalisteczno-Demokratyczna Partja Robotnicza [Jewish Socialist-Democratic Workers' Party] (Poalej Syjon-Lewica) or Żydowska Socjalisteczna Partja Robotnicza Jewish Socialist Workers' Party] (Poalej Syjon-Prawica). Both parties entered into the Coordinating Commission, from which emerged the ŻOB.

204. Before the war Josef Szeryński (Szenkman) had been an inspector for the National Police. He was condemned to death by the decree of the Jewish Fighting Organization for the zeal he displayed in carrying out the *Aktion* to liquidate Jews. An unsuccessful attempt on Szeryński took place on August 25, 1942. Szeryński recovered from his wounds, but in January 1943, after the initial struggles between ŻOB and the Germans, he committed suicide.

205. The work camp in the Lublin area was designated at first for Soviet prisoners and beginning in 1943, for Jews. All the prisoners of that camp were shot in November 1943.

206. The work camp for Jews organized in 1942 in the Lublin area in the place where the Germans had previously liquidated Poles, Russians, and Ukrainians, who were shot or deported to Majdanek. All the prisoners of that camp were shot in November 1943, within the framework of the so-called *Aktion Erntefest* (Harvest Home).

207. Perechodnik doubtlessly knew from the underground press about the course of events in the Warsaw ghetto. Information about the shooting of the members of the Judenrat he probably drew from *Agencja Prasowa* [Press Agency], no. 19 (161) (May 12, 1943).

208. The author's mistake. This is a fragment from a poem by Adam Asnyk, *"Dla Młodych"* [To the Young].

But do not trample out the fires of old,
Though yours appear a more aspiring flame,
For still, not wholly are the embers cold,

And on them, as on you, its ancient hold
Love doth maintain.

[M. M. Coleman, ed., *Wayside Willow* (Trenton, N.J.: White Eagle, 1945), p. 37.]

209. Jan Kochanowski, "Lament XI." Actually, "Whom his own good nature preserved from evil" (Jan Kochanowski, *Wybor Poezji* [Poetry Selections] [Łódź: Książka, 1946], p. 128).

210. "Who knows this?" (French).

211. "Let every man look out for himself" (French).

212. During liquidation of the camp, prisoners—numbering about one hundred inmates—were shot. Only one was able to run away.

213. During the night of May 12–May 13, 1943, around 11:30, there was a powerful Soviet air raid on Warsaw, the second since the preceding year. As a result, there was interference with rail traffic and even with the movement of trolley cars in the area of the city. According to an official communiqué put forth by the Germans, 149 people died, 11 were missing, and 233 people suffered serious or light injuries.

214. May 4, 1943, the surrender of the Italian-German forces in Tunis ended military activities in northern Africa.

215. Discussion of events in 1942.

216. Discussion of events in 1943.

217. This is the only fragment that proves that Perechodnik probably heard about the so-called January defense.

218. Perechodnik is mistaken. April 25, 1943, fell on a Sunday.

219. From Adam Mickiewicz, "The Storm," *Sonety krymskie* [Crimean sonatas]:

One man has swooned, one wrings his hands, one sinks
Upon his friends, embracing them. Some say
A prayer to death that it may pass them by.
One traveller sits apart and sadly thinks:
"Happy the man who faints or who can pray
Or has a friend to whom to say goodbye."

[George R. Noyes, trans., *Poems by Adam Mickiewicz* (New York: Polish Institute of Arts and Sciences, 1944), pp. 154–155.]

220. German train watchman.

221. "Resourceful lad" (French).

222. During the night of April 28–29, according to an understanding with the People's Guard, about forty soldiers of the ŻOB and civilians exited the sewers through a manhole at the corner of Ogrodowa and Żelazna Streets. The rest of the night and the following day and night they spent on the top floor of an abandoned house at Ogrodowa, 29. On April 30, in daylight and in full view of the passersby, they left the building and were transported by a truck beyond Warsaw.

223. The underground paper *Dziś i Jutro* [Today and Tomorrow], no. 51 (June 25, 1943), commented on the activities of the *szmalcowniki*: "Such characters really took a great liking to such an extremely easy and well-paying occupation. They walk the streets, seek in the crowds a Semitic type and then begins the real

expert business. 'My dear sir, allow me. Please step to the gate. And what, kind sir, are you doing in the Aryan neighborhood? Ah, do you have proof? Aha! Such papers? Apparently you are a villager from Garwolina? And it seems, sir, you are not Jewish? Not a Bedouin? It is not pleasant for you to go to the ghetto, you yid? You're lost, you mangy yid! Didn't you want to go for some fresh air to Trawniki? I am not a plainclothesman—I tell you this ahead of time—for Jews I feel an inborn distaste. What, you have a little money? Ah, that's something else. This business will cost you five hundred and change. Good-bye, Mr. Witkowszczak. Will you lead this gentleman to the other gate?' It is beyond belief how large a number of young and old are occupied with this kind of trade—but it is particularly for the young. A large group of people takes part in such a hunt, divided into rear and forward guard. The forward guard is mostly made of crowds of street urchins."

224. The discussion is obviously about *Nowy Kurier Warszawski* [New Warsaw Courier].

225. The most solemn of the three regular daily prayers is the morning prayer, the *Shmone Esrei* (Eighteen Benedictions). It is also referred to as the *Amidah* (Prayer recited while standing), which may not be interrupted.

226. Jan Kochanowski, "The Charm of the Polish Village":

O village blest with quietness,
What tongue thy glories shall confess?
The comforts and rewards that fall
From hand of thine what voice recall?

Here uprightly mankind may lead
The round of life, unsmirched by greed,
Here piously each strain endure,
And forward look to profit sure.

[M. M. Coleman, ed., *The Polish Land* (Trenton, N.J.: White Eagle, 1943), pp. 87–88.]

227. Actually, Pantelleria, an Italian island in the Mediterranean that was an important Italian air and naval base during the war. Bombed frequently by Allied planes starting in May 1943, it was taken on August 11, 1943, by U.S. forces.

228. Leon Blum was a French political leader, writer, and journalist of Jewish extraction.

229. These sentences are Perechodnik's commentary on the continuing German propaganda (offered as an explanation of events), according to which all Jews seek to dominate the world.

230. Ogólno-Żydowski Zwiazek Robotniczy Bund w Polsce [National-Jewish Union of Workers Bund in Poland], a Jewish socialist party founded in 1897 as part of the international worker's movement. The Bund strongly emphasized the fact that the homeland of Polish Jews was Poland.

231. Actually, Agudas Isroel [Society of Israel]. This chief orthodox and conservative party had a significant influence among the older generation of the middle and lower classes. The fundamental task it set for itself was the defense of

religious rights as well as economic interests of Jews in the countries where they resided. Emigration to Palestine was a secondary issue, to which Orthodox Jews attached more importance only in the 1930s.

232. Some Zionist political workers, assisted by the Palestinian office in Geneva, made use of permits to leave for Palestine. Adam Czerniaków assumed a very critical attitude on this matter in his diary: "H[artglas] and K[oerner] declare that they received certificates to Palestine. K, a hypocritical prude, considered it even necessary to accompany it with a commentary. H was quiet. . . . They offered me a certificate to Palestine—I refused to be placed on the list" (Fuks, *Adama Czerniakowa*, pp. 71, 85).

233. This is an altered version of Psalm 56:12, "In God do I trust, I will not be afraid; What can man do unto me?"

234. This is a fragment of a Psalm from the period of the Babylonian exile (Ps. 37:1–9). For the Babylonian Jews, the only place in the world where they could offer sacrifices to Yahweh was at the holy altar in Jerusalem.

235. During the war, the council was a social welfare organization exclusively for the Polish population in the Generalgouvernement. Founded in February 1940, it combined all the social organizations, and its activities had to do with distributing food, clothing, and financial help to the most needy.

236. Operations to eliminate the effects of circumcision were performed by, among others, Drs. Feliks Kanabus and Andrzej Trojanowski. Each one of them performed no less than five hundred such operations. These were done at the children's clinic Zdrowie [Health], on Słowacki Street, sometimes in the outpatient department of the hospital on Kopernik Street, more rarely in private homes. Patients were sent by their friends, most frequently by doctors. In general these were colleagues-doctors, their fathers, and sons.

237. Vittel.

238. Already during the uprising in the Warsaw ghetto, a center for legal Jewish emigration was established at Hotel Polski. The registration of applicants—in anticipation of later exchange for German nationals—was conducted on the basis of foreign passports or so-called certificates of proof of citizenship. These documents were drawn up by the consulates of countries in both Americas or by the British authorities in Palestine. Jewish Gestapo agents sold to the applicants documents of dead persons, which provided an opportunity for departure of illegals. Twice, in November 1943 and in March of the following year, there was an exchange of internees transported earlier to the camp at Vittel. Later authorities of South American governments refused to receive internees, questioning with vague conditions the value of the documents. Jews with passports of South American countries were sent to Oświęcim. On July 13, 1943, all those who were gathered in Hotel Polski were sent to the Pawiak prison, where most of them were shot. Altogether, four to five thousand people passed through Hotel Polski, of whom about 10 percent survived the war.

239. The French health resort Vittel, situated near Nancy, was turned into an internment camp at the start of the war. People sojourned here who were transported from all over occupied Europe, including about 350 Jews who were brought on five transports from Hotel Polski. [For an account of the handful of people who were saved from Vittel, see Leni Yahl, *The Holocaust: The Fate of European Jewry* (Oxford: Oxford University Press, 1990), pp. 618–621. See also

Abraham Shulman, *The Case of Hotel Polski: An Account of One of the Most Enigmatic Episodes of World War II* (New York: Holocaust Library, 1982). Paweł Szapiro's recent book on the Polish underground press cited comments on Hotel Polski, *Wojna żydowsko-niemiecka: Polska prasa konspiracyjna 1943–1944 o powstaniu w getcie Warszawy* [Jewish-German War: Polish Underground Press 1943–1944 on the Warsaw Ghetto Revolt] (London: Aneks, 1992), pp. 294–295. Cf. Zbigniew Stańczyk, "Lista Ladosia" [The Rolls of Ładoś], *Przegląd Polski* [*Polish Review*], August 25, 1994, pp. 1, 15. For an interesting recent account of the "Palestine exchange lists" and how a small number of Jews were saved from death transports, see Netty C. Gross, "Last Address Unknown," *Jerusalem Post,* January 21, 1995, pp. 10–12.]

240. Not a Gestapo man but a Gestapo agent, and a Jew, Leon Skosowski, known in the ghetto and beyond as Lolek S., was sentenced to death by the Special Court. He was shot in the fall of 1943 in the Warsaw Inn on Nowogrodzka Street. There is no doubt that he believed in the success of the undertaking that he organized. Proof of this is that the second transport that left Hotel Polski for Vittel included his wife, Cecilia, and three of their children: Izydor, Lucyna, and Jadwiga.

241. Adam Żurawin, a Jew and Gestapo agent, was the co-organizer of the so-called Cases of Hotel Polski. Like Skosowski, he believed in the success of the undertaking he organized. He went out to Vittel with the second transport together with his wife, Leah, and a child of several months. He was able to escape from a transport to Oświęcim and probably lives at this time in the United States.

242. Those interned at Vittel lived in luxurious surroundings. They were in hotel apartments, had an opportunity to move around to the local parks, received ample food and abundant packages from the Red Cross, and had an unlimited right of correspondence.

243. Perechodnik undoubtedly means Starachowice.

244. The air and sea landing on Sicily took place from July 10 to August 17, 1943.

245. The visit of the old Perechodnik followed on July 21. A week earlier, the inhabitants of Hotel Polski were transported to the Pawiak prison and shortly afterward, shot. The underground press announced this fact only at the end of the month. Deprived of contact with the outside world, the tenants of Miss Hela's could live even longer in ignorance of this.

246. Following the landing of the Allies on Sicily came the overthrow of Mussolini by the Great Fascist Council. The head of the new government was Marshal Pietro Badoglio.

247. Perechodnik makes use here of a popular Jewish saying: "You let the featherbed fall so that you can pick up a feather."

248. Perechodnik's brother presently lives in Israel.

249. Allied forces landed in Italy on August 3, 1943. That day there were signs on the walls in Warsaw: "Mussolini today, Hitler tomorrow."

250. "Run!" (German).

251. These are the beginning words of the Kaddish, the prayer for the dead.

252. Perechodnik is quoting a version of a song popular in the ghetto: "Zol Zayn." His translation is slightly garbled.

253. Perechodnik continued to write his memoir. The text, inserted in a tin can, was buried in a cellar during the Warsaw uprising in 1944. It is probably irretrievably lost.

254. Some fragments of the Perechodnik memoir and those of two other policemen, Jan Mawulta (Stanisław Gombinski) and Samuel Puterman, were published by Michał Grynberg in *Pamiętniki getta warszawskiego* [Memoirs of the Warsaw ghetto] (Warsaw, 1988). A portion of the Perechodnik text was published earlier in Israel in *Sefer*. The Archives of the Jewish Historical Institute in Poland contain a few—much less extensive in comparison—reports of former policemen, among them that of the functionary in Otwock, Stanisław Nisenszal. Information about the police may be found in the materials of the Municipal Commission, part of the Central Historical Commission of Polish Jews; probably also in the Archives MSW and certainly in the archives of Yad Vashem in Jerusalem. [Among a number of books in a variety of languages on ghetto policemen is Stanisław Adler, *The Warsaw Ghetto: 1940–1943* (Jerusalem: Yad Vashem, 1982).]

255. Archive Ringelblum, *Warsaw Ghetto, July 1942–January 1943* (Warsaw: Ruta Sakowska, 1980), pp. 120–121.

256. *Szukajcie w Popiołach. Papiery znalezione w oswiecimiu* [Search in the ashes for papers found in Oświęcim], translated from Yiddish by Szymon Datner Łódź GKBZH, cited by Jerzy Jedlicki, "Dzieje doświadczone i dzieje zaświadczone" [History of affliction and history of testimony], in *Dzieło literackie jako zródło historyczne* [Literary Works as Sources for History] (Warsaw, 1978).

257. Michał Borwicz, *Kazimierza Moczarskiego "Rozmowy z katem"* [Kazimierz Moczarski's "Conversations with a Torturer"], in *Zeszyty historyczne* [Historical notebooks], no. 59 (Paris: Zeszyty Historyczne, 1980).

258. *The Great Illustrated General Encyclopedia*, vols. 11–12.

259. *Encyclopedia Judaica*, vol. 12.

260. On authority of the order by the *Kreishauptmann* on November 4, 1940, 391 Jewish homes in Otwock were transferred to the Bureau of Jewish Real Estate in the Aryan Section of Otwock. The income from the rent was collected by the Municipal Office; the administrator of the building, commonly a Pole, received as a reward 6 percent of the gross income.

261. See Tamara Brustin-Berenstein, *Deportacja i żagłada skupisk żydowskich w dystrykcie warszawskim* [Deportation and extermination of Jewish masses in the Warsaw district], *Bull. ZIH*, n. 13 (1952).

262. Ringelblum, *Kronika*, p. 471.

263. *Agencja Prasowa* [Press Agency] (August 7, 1943).

264. "Sprawa bardzo ważna" [A very important matter], *Barykada* [Barricade], no. 3 (March 1943).

265. "Proroctwa sie wypełniają" [Prophecies Fulfilled], *Prawda* [Truth] (May 1942).

266. "Wartości moralne—fundamentem przyszłości" [Moral values—foundations for the future], *Agencja Prasowa* [Press Agency], no. 43 (134) (October 28, 1942).

267. "Co wolno—czego nie wolno" [What is permitted—what is not permitted], *Komunikat Informacyjny i Głos Polski* [Polish voice and the communiqué for information], cited in *Pobudka* (Reveille), no. 206 (June 9, 1942).

268. "Hieny" [The Hyennas], *Biuletyn Informacyjny* [Information Bulletin], March 18, 1943.

About the Book and Editor

In this moving memoir, a young Polish Jew chronicles his life under the Nazis. In the vain hope of protecting himself and his family, Calel Perechodnik made the wrenching decision to become a ghetto policeman in a small town near Warsaw. The true tragedy of his choice becomes clear when during the *Aktion* he must witness his own wife and child forced to board a train to the Treblinka extermination camp.

Filled with loathing for the Germans, the Poles, his Jewish brethren, and himself, Perechodnik fled the ghetto to shelter with a Polish woman in Warsaw. In the course of 105 terror-filled days in hiding, he poured out his poignant story. Written while Nazi boots pounded the streets of the neighborhood and while his tortured memory was painfully fresh, this memoir has a rare immediacy and raw power.

Shortly before his death in 1944, he entrusted the precious diary to a Polish friend. The document was eventually deposited in the Yad Vashem Archives in Jerusalem. Left nearly forgotten for half a century, it was finally published in Poland in 1993. We owe a great debt to historian Frank Fox for bringing us this sensitive translation, which reminds us anew of the power and truth of historical memory.

Frank Fox was professor of East European history at West Chester University. As owner of one of the largest private collections of Polish poster art, Fox has had a number of poster exhibits and has written extensively on the subject. He has traveled to Poland many times in recent years to interview and write about artists involved in a project to promote Polish-Jewish understanding. He is currently at work on a manuscript dealing with aerial photography and the Katyń massacre.